DIABETIC
DIET COOKBOOK
FOR BEGINNERS

1500 DAYS QUICK, EASY & TASTY RECIPES FOR DIABETES, PREDIABETES AND TYPE 2 DIABETES NEWLY DIAGNOSED | 28-DAY MEAL PLAN FOR BALANCED MEALS AND HEALTHY LIVING INCLUDED

By Amanda Ray

© COPYRIGHT 2023 BY AMANDA RAY – ALL RIGHTS RESERVED.

THE CONTENT CONTAINED WITHIN THIS BOOK MAY NOT BE REPRODUCED, DUPLICATED OR TRANSMITTED WITHOUT DIRECT WRITTEN PERMISSION FROM THE AUTHOR OR THE PUBLISHER.

UNDER NO CIRCUMSTANCES WILL ANY BLAME OR LEGAL RESPONSIBILITY BE HELD AGAINST THE PUBLISHER, OR AUTHOR, FOR ANY DAMAGES, REPARATION, OR MONETARY LOSS DUE TO THE INFORMATION CONTAINED WITHIN THIS BOOK. EITHER DIRECTLY OR INDIRECTLY.

LEGAL NOTICE:
THIS BOOK IS COPYRIGHT PROTECTED. THIS BOOK IS ONLY FOR PERSONAL USE. YOU CANNOT AMEND, DISTRIBUTE, SELL, USE, QUOTE OR PARAPHRASE ANY PART, OR THE CONTENT WITHIN THIS BOOK, WITHOUT THE CONSENT OF THE AUTHOR OR PUBLISHER.

DISCLAIMER NOTICE:
PLEASE NOTE THE INFORMATION CONTAINED WITHIN THIS DOCUMENT IS FOR EDUCATIONAL AND ENTERTAINMENT PURPOSES ONLY. ALL EFFORT HAS BEEN EXECUTED TO PRESENT ACCURATE, UP TO DATE, AND RELIABLE, COMPLETE INFORMATION. NO WARRANTIES OF ANY KIND ARE DECLARED OR IMPLIED. READERS ACKNOWLEDGE THAT THE AUTHOR IS NOT ENGAGING IN THE RENDERING OF LEGAL, FINANCIAL, MEDICAL OR PROFESSIONAL ADVICE. THE CONTENT WITHIN THIS BOOK HAS BEEN DERIVED FROM VARIOUS SOURCES. PLEASE CONSULT A LICENSED PROFESSIONAL BEFORE ATTEMPTING ANY TECHNIQUES OUTLINED IN THIS BOOK.

BY READING THIS DOCUMENT, THE READER AGREES THAT UNDER NO CIRCUMSTANCES IS THE AUTHOR RESPONSIBLE FOR ANY LOSSES, DIRECT OR INDIRECT, WHICH ARE INCURRED AS A RESULT OF THE USE OF INFORMATION CONTAINED WITHIN THIS DOCUMENT, INCLUDING, BUT NOT LIMITED TO, ERRORS, OMISSIONS, OR INACCURACIES.

A Special Request

Hello and thank you for purchasing the book!

Your brief amazon review could help me.

You know, this is very easy to do, go to the **ORDERS** section of your Amazon account and click on the **"Write a review for the product" button.**
It will automatically take you to the review section.

or

Scan the QR-CODE **NOW** !
It will take you to my Amazon author page!

BONUS FREE EBOOK!!

Hello and thank you for purchasing the book!
I have prepared a **NICE SURPRISE FOR YOU**.
Scroll to the end and scan the QR CODE to download your free eBook!!

TABLE OF CONTENTS

INTRODUCTION 8

CHAPTER 1: 10
INTRODUCTION TO DIABETES 10
What is Diabetes? 10
How to Prevent and Control It 10
Formation of Diabetes 11

CHAPTER 2: 12
UNDERSTANDING NUTRIENTS 12
Carbohydrates, Protein, Fat, Fiber, Sodium 13
Main Carbohydrates and Nutritional Values 14
Glycemic Index 15

CHAPTER 3: DIABETES-FRIENDLY DIETARY SUGGESTIONS 15
Best Diets When You Have Diabetes 15
The Best Supplements to Use in Case of Diabetes .. 19
Exercise and Diabetes 21
Tips for Counting Carbs 22
Stocking a Diabetes-Friendly Kitchen 24
Putting the Guidelines into Practice: Building a Complete Meal 26

CHAPTER 4: BREAKFAST RECIPES 29
1. Breakfast Cheese Bread Cups 29
2. Breakfast Cod Nuggets 29
3. Vegetable Egg Pancake 29
4. Oriental Omelet 30
5. Pumpkin Pie French toast 30
6. Crispy Breakfast Avocado Fries 30
7. Cheese and Egg Breakfast Sandwich 30
8. Baked Mini Quiche 31
9. Peanut Butter and Banana Breakfast Sandwich 31
10. Eggs and Cocotte on Toast 31
11. Crunchy Fried French toast Sticks 32
12. Pumpkin Oatmeal with Raisins 32
13. Mushroom and Black Bean Burrito 33
14. Yogurt Raspberry Cake 33
15. Spinach and Tomato Egg Cup 33
16. Egg Muffins with Bell Pepper 34
17. Egg-in-a-Hole 34
18. Egg and Cheese Pockets 34
19. Huevos Rancheros 35
20. Jalapeño Potato Hash 35
21. Shrimp Rice Frittata 36
22. Vegetable Frittata 36
23. Ginger Blackberry Bliss Smoothie Bowl ... 36
24. Heart-Healthy Yogurt Parfaits 37
25. Toads in Holes 37
26. Canadian bacon and Egg Muffin Cups 37
27. Sausage and Pepper Breakfast Burrito 37
28. Pumpkin Walnut Smoothie Bowl 38
29. Melon sandwich 38
30. Buttermilk lentil 38
31. Stracciatella Omelet 39
32. Plum muffins 39
33. Easy Buckwheat Crêpes 40
34. Shakshuka 40
35. Eggplant Breakfast Sandwich 41
36. Perfect Egg Scramble with Simple Salad .. 41
37. Blueberry-Chia Smoothie 42

CHAPTER 5: VEGETABLE RECIPES 42
38. Spinach, Artichoke, and Goat Cheese Bake. 42
39. Roasted Broccoli with Sesame Seeds 43
40. Corn on the Cob with Herb Butter 43
41. Rainbow Vegetable Fritters 43
42. Roasted Veggies with Yogurt-Tahini Sauce . 44
43. Avocado-Tofu Scramble with Roasted Potatoes 44
44. Easy Sweet Potato Hash Browns 45
45. Skinny Pumpkin Chips 45
46. Cheese Stuffed Roasted Peppers 45
47. Sweet Potato Chips with Greek Yogurt Dip 46
48. Greek-Style Roasted Tomatoes with Feta.... 46
49. Sweet Corn Fritters with Avocado 46
50. Greek-Style Vegetable Bake 47
51. Pureed Peas 47
52. Tomato Toasts 47
53. Collard Greens 48
54. Keto "hummus" 48
55. Sweet Potato Fritters 48
56. Red Cabbage Mix 49
57. Beets Dijon 49
58. Cilantro Lime Chicken Salad 49
59. Fennel and Trout Parcels 49
60. Slow "Roasted" Tomatoes 50
61. Brussels Sprout Hash and Eggs 50
62. Parsley-Lemon Salmon 50
63. Greek Tuna Salad.. 51
64. Glazed Carrots and Cauliflower................. 51
65. Broth-Braised Cabbage 51
66. Feta Brussels sprouts and Scrambled Eggs .. 51
67. Baked Feta with Delicious Vegetables 52
68. Cauliflower Avocado Mash with Chicken Breast 52
69. Tomato-Herb Omelet 53

CHAPTER 6: MEAT RECIPES 53

70. Cheesy Stuffed Chicken 53
71. Beefy Pie.. 53
72. Mediterranean Feta Chicken 54
73. Greek Turkey Burgers 54
74. Roasted Leg Lamb 55
75. Lamb Chops Curry 55
76. Pork Cutlets in Cucumber Sauce 55
77. Grilled Lamb Chops 56
78. Beef Moroccan Kebabs.................................. 56
79. Lamb Kebabs 57
80. Pork Medallion in Lemon Caper Sauce 57
81. Roasted Pork with Currant Sauce................ 57
82. Roasted Steak and Tomato Salad 58
83. Beef-Vegetable Ragout................................... 58
84. Greek Flat Iron Steaks 59
85. Pork Chops with Grape Sauce 59
86. Roasted Pork and Apples 60
87. Irish Pork Roast 60
88. Sesame Pork with Mustard Sauce 60
89. Steak with Mushroom Sauce 61
90. Steak with Tomato and Herbs 61
91. Barbecue Beef Brisket 61
92. Beef and Asparagus 62
93. Braised Lamb with Vegetables..................... 62
94. Rosemary Lamb 63
95. Mediterranean Lamb Meatballs 63
96. Cranberry Pork Roast.................................... 63
97. Crock Pork Tenderloin 63
98. Conventional Beef Pot Roast........................ 64
99. Applesauce Meatloaf 64
100. Ham in Cider 64
101. Roasted Pork Loin 65
102. Grilled Greek Chicken 65
103. Guacamole Chicken Salad 65
104. Greek Chicken Salad 66
105. Shredded Turkey Breast 66
106. Chicken Saute 66
107. Duck Patties 67
108. Grilled Marinated Chicken 67

CHAPTER 7: FISH AND SEAFOOD 68

109. Shrimp and Artichoke Skillet 68
110. Sardines with Zoodles 68
111. Chimichurri Grilled Shrimp 68
112. Salmon and Cucumber Panzanella 69
113. Blackened Tilapia Tacos 69
114. Parmesan Shrimp with Curry Sauce 69
115. Pistachio Salmon with Shallot Sauce 70
116. Sicilian Zoodle and Sardine Spaghetti........ 70
117. Shrimp and Daikon Noodle Panang........... 71
118. Sour Cream Salmon Steaks........................... 71
119. Coconut Mussel Curry 71
120. Crab Patties 72
121. Seared Scallops with Chorizo 72
122. Creamy Herbed Salmon 72
123. Mussels and Coconut Milk Curry 73
124. Alaska Cod with Butter Garlic Sauce........... 73
125. Seared Tuna with Niçoise Salad................... 74
126. Lemony Paprika Shrimp 74
127. Tiger Shrimp with Chimichurri 75
128. Grilled Salmon with Greek Green Salad 75
129. Tuna Carbonara.. 76
130. Flavors Cioppino.. 76
131. Mediterranean Fish Fillets 76
132. Delicious Shrimp Alfredo.............................. 77
133. Tomato Olive Fish Fillets 77
134. Halibut Tacos with Cabbage Slaw 77
135. Pistachio Nut Salmon with Shallot Sauce..... 78
136. Coconut Crab Cakes 78
137. Tuna Cakes.. 79
138. Chili-Lime Tuna Salad 79
139. Lemony Sea Bass Fillet.................................. 79
140. Curried Fish with Super Greens 80
141. Garlic-Lemon Mahi Mahi 80
142. Scallops in Creamy Garlic Sauce.................. 81
143. Israeli Salmon Salad 81

CHAPTER 8: SNACKS AND APPETIZERS RECIPES 82

144. Cauliflower Poppers 82
145. Roasted Radishes with Brown Butter Sauce 82
146. Sweet Onion Dip 82
147. Keto Trail Mix 83
148. Cold Cuts and Cheese Pinwheels 83
149. Zucchini Balls with Capers and Bacon 83
150. Plantains with Tapioca Pearls....................... 84
151. Sweet Orange and Lemon Barley Risotto 84
152. Homemade Applesauce 85
153. Homemade Beet Hummus............................ 85
154. Coconut Pudding with Tropical Fruit........... 85
155. Tofu with Salted Caramel Pearls.................. 86
156. Homemade Hummus.................................... 86
157. Parmesan and Pork Rind Green Beans 87
158. Berry Jam with Chia Seeds............................ 87
159. Nectarines with Dried Cloves 87

CHAPTER 9: SALADS AND SOUPS RECIPES 88

160. Roasted Portobello Salad 88
161. Drop Egg Soup 88
162. Shredded Chicken Salad................................ 88
163. Cherry Tomato Salad..................................... 89

164. Asian Cucumber Salad 89
165. Sunflower Seeds and Arugula Garden Salad 89
166. Tabbouleh- Arabian Salad 90
167. Cauliflower and Onion Salad 90
168. Corn Tortillas and Spinach Salad............ 91
169. Orange-Avocado Salad 91
170. Israeli Salmon Salad 91
171. Simple Lemon Farro and Steamed Broccoli 92
172. Cauliflower and Spinach Salad 92
173. Slow Cooker Chicken Posole 92
174. Slow Cooker Lentil and Ham Soup 93
175. Beef Barley Vegetable Soup 93
176. Slow Cooker Corn Chowder 94
177. Potlikker Soup 94
178. Burgoo 94
179. She-Crab Soup 95
180. Spicy Chicken Stew 95
181. Down South Corn Soup 96
182. Carrot Soup 96
183. Four-Bean Field Stew 97
184. Pork Mushroom Stew 97

CHAPTER 10: VEGETARIAN RECIPES 98
185. Lentil Snack with Tomato Salsa 98
186. Stuffed Eggplant 98
187. Lentil Salad with Nuts and Feta 98
188. Vegetarian Chipotle Chili 99
189. Smoky Carrot and Black Bean Stew 99
190. Hummus and Salad Pita Flats 100
191. Avocados with Walnut-Herb 100
192. Beans with Mustard Sauce and Spicy Cucumbers 100
193. Mashed Butternut Squash 100
194. Cilantro Lime Quinoa 101
195. Oven-Roasted Veggies 101
196. Garlic Sautéed Spinach 101
197. Creamed Spinach 102
198. Beet Salad with Basil Dressing 102

CHAPTER 11:   VEGAN RECIPES 103
199. Tomato, Avocado, and Cucumber Salad 103
200. Cauliflower "Potato" Salad 103
201. Loaded Cauliflower Mashed "Potatoes" 103
202. Keto Bread 103
203. Vegan Stuffed Mushrooms 104
204. Perfect Cucumber Salsa 104
205. Soia Yogurt and Avocado Dip 104
206. Keto Macadamia Hummus 104
207. Eggplant Chips 104
208. Creamy Mushrooms with Garlic and Thyme 105
209. Veggie Fajitas 105
210. Air Fryer Soft Pretzels 105

CHAPTER 12:   DESSERTS RECIPES 106
211. Chocolate Raspberry Parfait 106
212. Mango Cashew Cake 107
213. Keto Waffles 107
214. Coconut Brown Rice Cake 108
215. Peanut Butter and Berry Oatmeal 108
216. Paleo Almond Banana Pancakes 108
217. Cherry, Chocolate, and Almond Shake 109
218. Greek Yogurt Sundae 109
219. Almond Berry Smoothie 109
220. Gluten-Free Carrot and Oat Pancakes 109
221. Peaches and Cream Oatmeal Smoothie 110
222. Kiwi-apple Smoothies 110
223. Raspberry Frozen Yogurt 110
224. Figs with Honey and Yogurt 111
225. Rice Dumplings in Coconut Sauce 111
226. Tropical Yogurt Kiwi Bowl 111

CHAPTER 13:   BONUS RECIPES 112
227. Pork Loin, Carrot, and Gold Tomato Roast 112
228. Spicy Grilled Portlets 112
229. Bacon and Feta Skewers 112
230. Avocado and Prosciutto Deviled Eggs 112
231. Sloppy Joes 113
232. Steak Sandwich 113
233. Shrimp and Pork Rind Stuffed Zucchini 113
234. Easy and Perfect Meatballs 113
235. Roasted Cauliflower with Prosciutto, Capers, and Almonds 114

CHAPTER 14: 28-DAY MEAL PLAN 116

APPENDIX 1: CONVERSION TABLES OF THE VARIOUS UNITS OF MEASUREMENT 117

APPENDIX 2: SHOPPING LIST 118

APPENDIX 3: THE DIRTY DOZEN AND THE CLEAN FIFTEEN 119

CONCLUSION 120

INTRODUCTION

Diabetes is a disease that interferes with the production of insulin by your body. Insulin aids your body's utilization of glucose for energy Without enough insulin, the excess glucose builds up in your blood instead of being absorbed by cells. The more excess glucose there is in your blood, the higher the amount of sugar in the urine. This causes large swings between high and low blood-sugar levels and can cause problems with neuropathy and kidney disease, as well as increased risks for heart disease and stroke over time.

One of the most prevalent diseases in the world is diabetes. It is estimated that 172 million people worldwide have diabetes, and nearly 85% of them live in less developed regions. With rates more than tripling since 1980, diabetes has recently become an epidemic.Prediabetes is also on the rise with nearly 30% of people over 40 with prediabetes and 86 million Americans with prediabetes. Pre-diabetics are at very high risk for developing type 2 diabetes within 5 years if they do not change their eating habits and lifestyle to prevent or reverse these dangerous blood sugar levels.

Many factors affect the development of diabetes, including what we eat, how active we live, and how much weight we gain. Genetics and age also play a role. If someone is pre-diabetic or has type 2 diabetes, then they may not be able to reverse these health problems through lifestyle changes alone. . It is crucial for those who have prediabetes to get tested for diabetes so that it can be treated at an early stage.

You may already have diabetes if your blood glucose levels are consistently above normal or 140 mg/dL while your doctor monitors your blood glucose levels over a period of time without improving them with treatment.

The diet for diabetics is based on many facts. . It is simple to comprehend and has a significant result. The diabetic diet limits the amount of sugar intake. Sugar: causes high blood glucose levels which leads to type 2 diabetes.

Why is a particular diet required for diabetics?

When blood glucose levels are excessively high, insulin may become dysfunctional and prevent the body from storing and using glucose as an energy source in the cells. Through blood testing, the amount of glucose in a blood sample can be analyzed to determine the blood glucose level.

Glucose comes from carbohydrate foods, which are usually digested and broken down to glucose so that they can be absorbed into the bloodstream. Carbohydrates are found in grains, starchy vegetables, sweets, fruits, and others. The digestion process of carbohydrates involves lots of chemical reactions that produce glucose inside the gastrointestinal tract. So, high levels of carbohydrate intake will increase the production of insulin that is needed to convert this glucose into an energy source.

But if the pancreas is not able to produce enough insulin, then some of this glucose will build up in the blood. If it increases above normal levels, then your body will become very sensitive to it. More glucose is produced, so insulin is needed, which can result in more production of glucose metabolites that cause hyperglycemia. Having high blood glucose levels can cause many medical problems such as blindness, kidney failure, and damage to nerves and other organs.

So, diabetics need to pay attention because maintaining proper control of glucose levels is essential and that's why they need to follow a special diet plan and regular exercise activities to avoid complications associated with diabetes.

These recipes herein will make you enjoy the taste of your diabetes-friendly foods and will make you feel happy and positive about your diet. The recipes will also teach you how to go to a healthy eating lifestyle, by weaning yourself from the usual sugary and fatty food that we usually love eating.

CHAPTER 1: INTRODUCTION TO DIABETES

What is Diabetes?

Type 2 Diabetes type 2 ("adult-onset diabetes") is the most common type of diabetes in a person older than 25. Some people with the condition have a genetic predisposition, which means they are more likely to be diagnosed with diabetes while others may be predisposed but only develop symptoms later in life.

It's not clear why some people develop insulin resistance, but it could be due to genetics or excess weight. Obesity is a major risk factor for type 2 diabetes and many people are diagnosed with the condition after they've lost a significant amount of weight. In fact, overweight diabetics are usually diagnosed at a younger age than non-obese diabetics, according to the National Institutes of Health (NIH).

You'll be encouraged to lose any excess weight and exercise regularly to help manage your blood glucose levels. If you take insulin injections, you may need to make some adjustments to your treatment to match your changing insulin needs.

How to Prevent and Control It

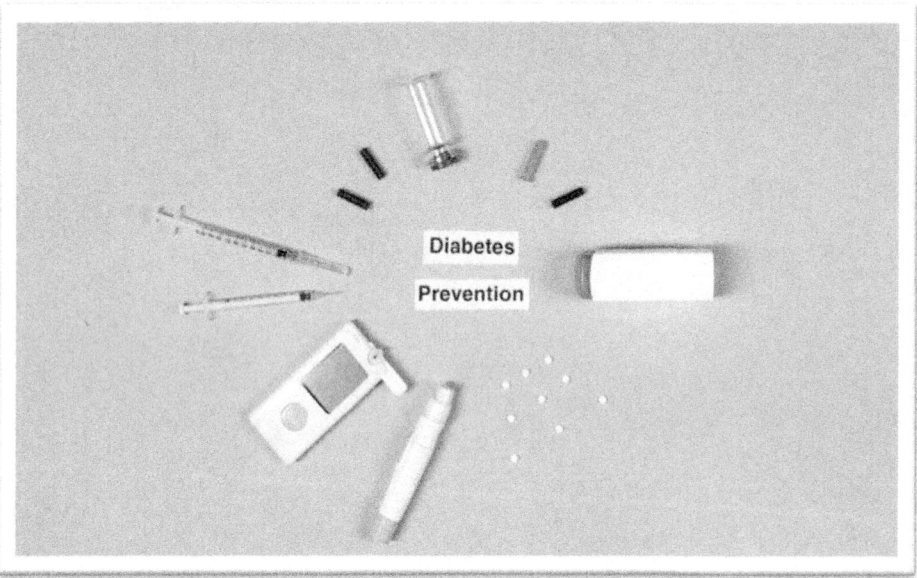

Type-2 Diabetes is a disorder that occurs when body cells don't use insulin effectively, causing excessive blood glucose levels. It's usually associated with obesity and abdominal fat accumulation, but people of all sizes can develop it.

It's not a single disease as there are a number of different types and causes of type 2 diabetes. People can also develop type-2 diabetes after being diagnosed with another form or level of the disease at some point in the past. Given this complexity in the diagnosis process, prevention is one of the best ways to avoid type 2 diabetes — especially among those most at risk for it (in adults).

Preventing type 2 diabetes can be done by adopting a healthy lifestyle, including exercise, eating healthy foods, and producing less body fat. The right nutrition plan will help you lose weight, gain muscle, and control blood sugar levels. If you put these measures into practice but fail to take medications as prescribed, your efforts will likely fail.

In its early stages (if diagnosed early), type 2 diabetes is caused by an inadequate or inefficient diet and/or lifestyle habits, including smoking, poor sleep habits, and physical inactivity. As it progresses, other factors that affect blood sugar levels become more of a factor in causing the disease than the original cause of it.

In order to make lifestyle changes, you must first be aware of the different types of type 2 diabetes and how it develops. Knowing what kind of diabetes you have and taking the right action can help control your blood sugar levels.

Formation of Diabetes

The beta cells in our pancreas secrete insulin and secrete it regularly. These cells have to do this because they need to keep the blood sugar levels in our body within a healthy range. It's the job of these cells to stop the glucose from flowing into our bloodstream too quickly. When your body isn't using enough insulin, either because you're fasting or eating a high-fat, high-sugar diet that causes an imbalanced amount of carbohydrates, your blood sugar levels rise too fast and become too high for these cells to handle efficiently.

When this happens, there is not enough insulin being produced by these beta cells in your pancreas, so you develop type 2 diabetes. This is what the fat cells have essentially done to the beta cells. The fat cells have essentially eaten up the beta cells, making them not work properly.

When this happens, you can develop insulin resistance, which is an early sign of type 2 diabetes. The body's insulin receptors will become resistant to normal amounts of insulin and are treated with larger doses of insulin in an attempt to raise blood sugar levels back into a healthy range. Other mechanisms are activated by the body in an attempt to compensate for the lack of insulin that cannot keep the blood glucose levels within healthy ranges anymore. These compensatory mechanisms may cause side effects that could lead to long-term complications and other serious health problems if left untreated or unmanaged over a prolonged period of time. These complications could include the development of heart disease, stroke, kidney disease, blindness, amputations, and much more.

There are two main types of diabetes: Type-1 and Type-2. Type-1 diabetes is an autoimmune disease characterized by a complete lack of insulin production and function by the pancreas. In this form, the beta cells in our pancreas have completely died from an autoimmune process initiated by our own immune system and not from outside forces such as viruses or bacteria. Then your body is no longer able to "detect" that it needs to produce insulin, and thus it will continue to try to keep up with its own production all on its own. This is the most common form that occurs in children.

Insulin is not at all produced by the body. There are no beta-cells in the pancreas, and thus no insulin is secreted into our bloodstream. The body continues to try to keep up with its own production of insulin all on its own as well, but it can't because the beta cells have been destroyed by the immune system, which is attacking it from within. Type 1 diabetes can be diagnosed in childhood or adolescents and is a very rare form of diabetes that occurs in only around 5% of those diagnosed with type 2 diabetes.

Type 2 diabetes is not an autoimmune disease. The age when one starts to develop type 2 diabetes varies depending on genetics, lifestyle choices, and other factors.

There is a link between the number of fat cells one has and type 2 diabetes. When the immune system kills off these beta cells, it begins to recognize and attack these fat cells themselves as well, which leads to an increase in fat cells. This can happen both as a result of beta-cell death or when there is an increase in the number of fat cells. There is an increase in body weight that can lead to obesity, which in turn leads to the development of type 2 diabetes if not managed properly.

In many cases, where obesity is present, type 2 diabetes can develop even if all of your other risk factors for developing it are absent. Fat: cells are very important because they contribute to insulin resistance. These fat cells are capable of driving the body's ability to use insulin, which is one of the primary issues in type 2 diabetes. The result is that the body does not get enough insulin, which leads to a decline in overall health, poor health, and cognitive decline over time.

Type 1 diabetes results from the autoimmune process that destroys the beta cells in our pancreas. This happens when there is an immune attack on these beta cells from within our own bodies. One of the main causes of this is a deficiency in vitamin D. Vitamin D is an essential micronutrient that is required for proper immune system function.

Consequently, deficiency in vitamin D can lead to high blood levels of calcium which can lead to or worsen type 1 diabetes if not treated properly. Vitamin D plays a major role in regulating the immune system and maintaining healthy living systems all throughout our bodies. Anything that operates within the body must have optimum levels of vitamin D in it.

Vitamin D is not just limited to our skin and digestive system. In fact, it plays a role in regulating many other major systems of our bodies, such as having a healthy immune system, helping us absorb calcium for strong bones, regulating digestion, maintaining the

CHAPTER 2: UNDERSTANDING NUTRIENTS

People with type-2 diabetes have a poor ability to metabolize carbohydrates and use insulin properly. This means that they have high levels of glucose in the blood, which can damage their vital organs and cause other problems.

What's more, people with type-2 diabetes often experience a diminished feeling of fullness following meals. They may also eat a lot of carbohydrates or fat because they think they need lots of calories to feel satisfied; however, excess food intake only exacerbates glucose levels and the risk for obesity-related illnesses.

As a result, a healthy eating plan for type 2 diabetes should include moderate amounts of carbohydrates and fat, low amounts of protein and fiber, and regular physical activity.

What is the best way to get enough energy to meet your body's needs while also managing your diabetes? And how can you manage your glucose levels without taking medication?

The answer may lie in nutrients. Each macronutrient — carbohydrates, protein, and fat — contains calories. How many calories depend on the amount of each macronutrient you eat relative to recommended intakes?

Moreover, each macronutrient affects your blood glucose differently. In general, low-glycemic-index carbohydrates (such as whole grains, beans, and some fruits and vegetables) help control blood glucose levels. On the other hand, high-glycemic-index carbohydrates (such as sugary drinks or white potatoes) can spike blood glucose. Protein: helps maintain healthy body weight and enhances muscle growth. Fat: also maintains healthy body functions such as absorbing fat-soluble vitamins and protecting internal organs.

Vitamins, minerals, and phytochemicals are nutrients that your body needs in small amounts to work properly but that you cannot make or store. Some of these nutrients help your body use macronutrients for energy. For instance, vitamins D and E are involved in hormone production that helps you get more energy from food and boost your immune system. Calcium is necessary for strong bones, muscle contraction, nerve conduction, and blood vessel integrity. Folate is a kind of B vitamin that helps convert foods into energy and may also help the body deal with stress.

Nutrients you can get from the food you eat are called essential nutrients. Other nutrients that don't need to be gotten from your diet but rather break down over time (such as minerals) are called non-essential nutrients.

Carbohydrates, Protein, Fat, Fiber, Sodium

The American Diabetes Association has a set of guidelines for people with diabetes to follow in order to maintain a healthy balance of the body's hormones. These guidelines outline what nutrients and foods to eat to manage type 2 diabetes, but it can be hard for people with type 2 diabetes themselves to know which nutrients are important when managing their condition. I have put together this helpful guide that will explain what each nutrient does and how they affect blood sugar levels.

Sugar

Sugar: is a carbohydrate. Carbohydrates are the body's main source of fuel. They are broken down into glucose for the body to use in a relatively short amount of time. Sugar: is an important source of carbohydrates as long as you don't eat too much at once and make your blood sugar levels spike. The average person should consume no more than 50 grams of sugar per day, and it's important to keep your blood-sugar levels under control if you want to avoid symptoms that can complicate the management of your diabetes, such as increased thirst and hunger, or even weight gain or loss.

Fat

Fat: is a nutrient that is found in a variety of foods. It can be difficult to calculate how much fat you should consume daily because it's difficult to know how much fat is in each food. Managers of diabetes must avoid trans fats at all costs as they can increase the risk of heart disease and other complications if eaten in large quantities. Instead, choose unsaturated fats like nuts, fish, and oils. Also, avoid saturated fats if you want to avoid complications like heart disease or obesity.

Protein

A lot of the confusion surrounding managing type 2 diabetes comes from not knowing exactly what protein does for the body and metabolism. Proteins are used in energy production and in immune system activity. Protein: needs are extremely high while people are recovering from surgery or any other condition that causes a patient to lose a lot of muscle mass. It's important to eat a protein-rich diet because it will help keep your immune system healthy, help you recover from these conditions, and keep your body at peak performance levels.

Carbs

Carbs are essential for the body to function properly, as they provide fuel for the body and carbohydrates include starch, which is used for energy production. Carbohydrates can cause blood sugar spikes when eaten with foods that produce insulin quickly, such as fruit or milk products. Eating carbohydrates in moderation is a key part of managing type 2 diabetes. Your body needs to process carbs in order to get energy from them, so it's important to choose complex carbohydrates that take longer for the body to break down like whole grains and whole-grain products instead of simple carbs like sugar.

Fiber

Diabetics should focus on getting a variety of fibers in their diet because it can help control their blood-sugar levels and keep them regular. The type of fiber you consume might not always matter, but it's easier for the body to process if you consume soluble fiber that dissolves in water, as well as insoluble fiber that doesn't dissolve in water. Both are equally beneficial, but it's important to consume healthy fiber because it can keep blood sugar levels stable and is found in many different foods like whole grains, beans, and greens. It would be best to try getting at least 25 grams of fiber daily.

Vitamins and Minerals

Diabetics need to maintain a good balance of vitamins and minerals in their diet as well as enough protein. Vitamins A and E have been shown to help with cell regeneration, which is important for keeping the body's immune system healthy. Minerals like magnesium and calcium help regulate nerve impulses and muscle function, so they're also important for diabetes management. Vitamins C, K, and D are also important for regulating blood pressure and immune system activity.

Main Carbohydrates and Nutritional Values

If you are on a type-2 diabetic diet, it's important to know that carbs can affect your blood sugar levels. Carbohydrates from regular food include bread, rice, potatoes, and pasta. There are four major types of carbohydrates — simple carbs like table sugar (sucrose), complex carbs like starch (starch is made up of sugars that contain chains of glucose molecules forming long polymers), fiber, and polysaccharides such as cellulose and pectin (made in plant cell walls). Different types of carbs can affect your blood sugar levels in different ways, but the most important thing is to know the difference between main and complex carbs. Main carbohydrates are obvious because they are found in foods that you would normally eat. Complex carbo are often referred to as fiber and can be found in whole-grain sources as well as other food like fruit, vegetables, legumes, and nuts.

Whole Grain vs. Refined Grains

When choosing whole grains, it's important to make sure that the entire grain is still present in the product; otherwise, it can't be considered a whole grain product. The bran, germ, and endosperm are the three components of whole grains.

Whole grain will have at least two out of these three parts. White and wheat bread, for example, are made from flour that has only the endosperm. When the bran and germ are removed, you lose many of the nutrients that are present in whole grains.

If you're unsure if a product is made of whole or refined grains, look at the ingredient list. If it has whole grain at the beginning of the list (like whole-wheat bread), then it's probably a whole-grain product. Otherwise, you will have to do some research to see if it's unrefined or not. You can also use this resource to see if a product is made of refined grains or unrefined grains.

How Carbohydrates Affect Blood Sugar

Main carbs are digested slowly, which is why they don't raise blood sugar levels as quickly. Main carbs include foods like milk, fruit, vegetables, and pasta. The body digests these types of carbohydrates most slowly and contains less glucose than the refined carbohydrates (which refers to the sugar that's left over after the main carbs have been digested). If you're eating a lot of main carbs, your blood sugar levels will stay stable. On the other hand, when you eat more refined carbohydrates (like white bread), your blood sugar levels can spike dramatically.

It's important to know that every person is different in their response to complex carbs because they digest them differently as well. Their bodies digest them at a different rate, and their blood glucose levels might increase or stay stable. For example, some people will develop more insulin resistance than others. This means that the body is less sensitive to the insulin it produces, and therefore your blood sugar levels will increase by eating complex carbs.

Glycemic Index

Glycemic Index is a measure of the speed at which a food raises blood sugar. The glycemic index estimates how your blood sugar will change after eating one portion of a particular food, helping you determine how low or high-glycemic foods are for you. It's important to know the glycemic index of any foods that may be part of your meal plan to help ensure that you're including or excluding safe choices. A rating between 0 and 100 is assigned by comparing the food's glucose response with that of pure glucose solution. Foods with a low glycemic index are often rich in fiber and are useful for blood sugar balance, or for minimizing the rise after meals.

The glycemic index of most foods is not known, so the GI is calculated by using glucose as the reference food and assigning arbitrary values of 100 to glucose and 0 to starches that have no effect on blood sugar levels (for example, white rice). Foods with a GI of less than 10 are low-glycemic foods; foods with a GI of more than 70 are high-glycemic foods. For example, carrots have a GI of 72 and pasta has an index of 78.

If the glycemic index is used in combination with the glycemic load, which accounts for the typical serving size and the amount of carbohydrates in each serving, it can be used as a tool to predict insulin demand and to compare the blood-sugar levels following meals containing different food types.

CHAPTER 3: DIABETES-FRIENDLY DIETARY SUGGESTIONS

Best Diets When You Have Diabetes

- **Paleo**

The Paleo diet is a nutrition plan, which has been around for over 6,000 years and it's based on eating foods that were available to hunter-gatherers during the Paleolithic era. It's not a fad diet as people often think; it was originally developed to prevent disease and improve health, not restrict certain foods.

The Paleo diet is also called the Caveman Diet because of how closely it focuses on what our ancestors would have eaten. In essence, this means eating meat (grass-fed or wild) and fresh vegetables in addition to fruit. There are no restrictions when following this way of life and many people experience a variety of benefits from doing so.

This diet is all about eating as if they were still living in the Paleolithic Era. It's pretty much any kind of fresh meat, eggs, fish, nuts, seeds, fruits and vegetables, and even little bits of cheese.

Benefits of the paleo diet:

1. Eating lean, organic meats can help limit your risk of cancer and diabetes.
2. The Paleo diet contains ample fiber, a nutrient lacking in many conventional diets that has been linked to lower cholesterol levels and a reduced risk for heart disease.
3. If you have issues with digestive health, such as irritable bowel syndrome or Crohn's disease, the Paleo way can be very effective at reducing symptoms by eliminating foods that may be hard to digest.
4. The Paleo diet is low-glycemic and has been shown to help control blood sugar levels and promote weight loss.
5. Research shows that the Paleo diet can improve blood sugar levels, body composition, and memory in older adults with mild cognitive impairment or Alzheimer's disease. Although the research is still in its early stages, the Paleo diet may be useful for preventing or slowing these conditions in those who already have them.
6. The Paleo diet has been linked to a reduced risk of heart disease because it excludes processed foods, like sugary cereals, white flour, processed meats, and deep-fried foods.
7. The ingredients that make up the Paleo diet are all foods that have been eaten by humans for thousands of years, meaning they are more nutrient-dense and less inflammatory than foods like cereal grains and dairy products.
8. Eating Paleo can help those with allergies to wheat and other commonly-allergic foods like egg, peanuts, soy products, and corn because it avoids these ingredients in favor of alternatives, such as almond flour, coconut flour, and gelatin.
9. Research has found that eating a high-fiber diet can reduce your risk for certain types of cancer. Studies show that fiber can help decrease levels of insulin in colon cells which may slow down the growth rate of tumors.
10. The Paleo diet may help those who are experiencing or have experienced mood and behavioral disorders like anorexia and depression because it can improve your brain health at many levels.
11. The Paleo diet could improve your cardiovascular health and help you maintain a healthier weight. Studies show this type of diet can prevent atherosclerosis, reduce blood pressure, improve insulin sensitivity, and lower inflammation as part of a healthy lifestyle change.
12. Eating Paleo has been shown to reduce the risk of osteoporosis, and some research shows that your risk may be reduced even further when combined with regular exercise.

- **Low Carb**

The low-carb diet is a low-carb, high-fat eating pattern that shares many similarities with other types of popular diets. It typically involves cutting out most carbs and sugars from your diet, but still eating some carbohydrates via vegetables and nuts. This can help promote weight loss for people who need to lose a small amount of weight or keep it off (e.g., people with Type 2 diabetes).

Benefits of Low-Carb Diet

According to research, low-carb eating can increase:

1. Genes that allow you to burn fat;
2. Fiber: in food and fiber supplements;
3. Increased satiety (a sense of fullness);
4. Reduced levels of triglycerides and LDL cholesterol, which are both known to increase the risk of heart disease;
5. Decreased insulin levels, which protect your heart and decrease your risk of diabetes;
6. Increased levels of HDL cholesterol (the "good" kind), which decreases the chances of developing cardiovascular problems;
7. Increased production of prostaglandins and nitric oxide, hormones that protect against inflammation in your body and prevent clotting in your blood vessels.

- Mediterranean

The Mediterranean diet is a way of eating which includes ingredients from the traditional cuisines of Greece, Italy, France, and Spain. It emphasizes vegetables, fruits, whole grains, olive oil, and herbs and spices. The diet has been associated with increased longevity in the region and in particular with a lower risk of atherosclerosis.

Grey zones exist between the Mediterranean diet as traditionally conceived and its idealized form — although it is usually not problematic to eat food outside this zone without compromising on overall health benefits. A recent review by the European Society of Cardiology has proposed an update of the Mediterranean diet as a way of improving cardiovascular health. Several components, such as fish and seafood, fruit and vegetables, whole-grain carbohydrates, and monounsaturated fats have been recommended in addition to the traditional ones. The advice on saturated fat remains unchanged.

The Mediterranean diet is linked to a lower risk of obesity and diabetes but is not recommended for people with allergic disorders or CVD [cardiovascular disease]. It has also been suggested that some medications may interact adversely with foods included in this type of diet. Hence, the current evidence is insufficient to guide specific dietary recommendations for people with CVD.

It is important to note that Mediterranean diet components are generally inexpensive, which may play a role in its acceptance by the public and its inclusion in different educational programs. Adequate control of dietary energy and saturated fat intake has been suggested as possible nutrition targets for individuals with reduced cardiovascular function. As a lifestyle approach that combines several dietary patterns, the Mediterranean diet may be considered healthy if it is consistently followed, which many people find difficult.

Research studies have shown that there is no direct causal relationship between following the Mediterranean diet and the risk of cardiovascular disease. This is the opposite opinion of that held by many other researchers and studies. On the contrary, it has been found through various researches that eating this type of diet can reduce risks for heart disease.
When you eat your meals on a regular schedule, you won't give yourself time to binge on unhealthy foods and have an extra calorie-filled snack attack in between. This diet plan can help kick off new habits that can change your whole life outlook, like moving toward a healthier diet or starting a movement toward getting fit. You'll learn how to fill yourself up without being heavy or feeling stuffed.

Since this diet is low in sugar and high in fresh fruits and vegetables, it's an excellent way to help diabetic patients manage their blood sugar levels. This diet is also great for preventing cancer since it keeps the blood vessels healthy and helps control blood pressure. You can as well reduce your risk of developing dementia by eating the right foods when following this diet plan.

There's no reason to be bored with a healthy diet filled with whole grains like whole-wheat bread or brown rice, lots of fruits and vegetables, nuts for protein, beans for fiber, and fish for omega-3 fatty acids. If you're tired of the Standard American Diet, try this plan to kick off a healthier lifestyle.

Benefits of the Mediterranean Diet

A Mediterranean diet has been praised for providing a wide range of health benefits ranging from reduced risk of cancer to improved heart health. Medical experts and diet professionals have studied this type of diet. Here are some benefits of a Mediterranean diet that is backed by science:

1. Increases Life Span and Promotes Heart Health

The Mediterranean diet is widely known to have a positive effect on the health of your heart. According to a landmark study, 7,000 people were selected to follow a strict Mediterranean diet that consisted of nuts and olive oil. These people significantly lowered the risk of major cardiovascular events like a stroke or a heart attack. They also had fewer cardiovascular disease risk factors like central obesity.
In food items like fatty fish, olive oil, and nuts, healthy fats are the key factor that contributes to this fact. For instance, "bad" LDL cholesterol is lowered by Omega-3 fats; it also raises the "good" HDL cholesterol levels, improves insulin resistance, and reduces inflammation. The high levels of antioxidants and fiber from red wine, fruits, and vegetables have a cardio-protective effect as well.
Since you will improve the health of your heart, a Mediterranean diet will also increase your life span.

2. Promotes Metabolism and Healthy Weight

Mediterranean diets focus on food that is whole and real — particularly those that have high fiber content. This makes the diet a great choice for anyone who is looking to improve their overall metabolic health. According to experts, a Mediterranean diet that contains high-fiber content makes you less likely to gain weight by keeping you full and improving glucose and diabetes intolerance.

A Mediterranean diet is far better than a low-fat diet when it comes to weight loss. Additionally, the diet has been linked to reducing the risk of chronic diseases like metabolic syndrome and type-2 diabetes.

3. Improves Mood and Good for Your Memory

For the same reasons why a Mediterranean diet is great for preventing cancer (i.e., it has anti-inflammatory and antioxidant properties), this diet is also great for improving brain health. Research has shown that a Mediterranean diet significantly reduces and/or delays the risk of depression and Alzheimer's disease. A Mediterranean diet consists of vegetables and fruits like melons, apricots, tomatoes, sweet potatoes, kale, spinach, and carrots that have higher carotenoid antioxidants; this has been linked to improving memory and mood.

4. Improves Your Gut Health

A Mediterranean diet consists of vegetables, fruits, and whole grains; this means that this diet is full of antioxidants, minerals, vitamins, and fiber. All these nutrients benefit and improve gut health by feeding the beneficial probiotic bacteria that reside there and also reducing inflammation. A study of primates fed a plant-heavy Mediterranean diet found that the animals had a higher population of good gut bacteria than those fed a meat-based Western diet. The health of your gut is closely related to your mental health, which is another reason why a Mediterranean diet improves mood.

5. Fight against Depression

Anti-inflammatory qualities are found in foods linked with the Mediterranean diet, which can help to decrease depression and improve your mood. One of the scientific research studies shows that the peoples who follow the Mediterranean diet have a 98.6% of lower risk of depression.

6. Reduces Age-Related Muscle and Bone Weakness

Eating a well-balanced diet rich in vitamins and minerals is critical for preventing muscle weakness and bone deterioration. This is especially important as you age. Accident-related injuries such as tripping, falling or slipping while walking can cause serious injury. As you age, this becomes even more of a concern as some simple falls can be fatal. Many accidents occur because of weakening muscle mass and the loss of bone density.

Antioxidants, vitamins C and K, carotenoids, magnesium, potassium, and phytoestrogens are essential minerals and nutrients for optimal musculoskeletal health. Plant-based foods, unsaturated fats, and whole grains help provide you with the necessary balance of nutrients that keep your bones and muscles healthy. Sticking with a Mediterranean diet can improve and reduce the loss of bone mass as you age.

7. Protects Against Type 2 Diabetes

The Mediterranean diet is the most recommended diet by health professionals for those diagnosed with Type 2 diabetes or prediabetes. The Mediterranean diet's combination of healthy foods and regular exercise is one of the key components in helping people manage and even see a remission of symptoms.

When you have type 2 diabetes, your pancreas is either not making enough insulin. Therefore, your cells cannot absorb enough of it, or the insulin is not being used properly, so glucose remains in the body. A build-up of glucose in your body can cause a long list of health complications. For example, the body may turn to use its muscle and fat to get the energy it needs. Blood vessels can also become damaged, which increases the risk of heart attack and stroke.

8. Clear Skin

Healthy skin begins from the inside out. When you are providing your body with wholesome foods, this will radiate through your skin. The antioxidants in extra-virgin olive oil alone are enough to keep your skin looking young and healthy. But the Mediterranean diet includes many fresh fruits and vegetables that are packed with antioxidants. These antioxidants help repair damaged cells in the body and promote healthy cell growth. Eating a variety of healthy fats also keeps the skin elastic and can protect it from premature aging.

- **Alkaline**

Nearly all disease results from acidosis, an excess of acid in your body due to poor diet and lifestyle. The Alkaline Diet shows you how to fight disease by consuming alkaline foods and utilizing the PH Balance Diet. Read more for a list of alkaline foods, what causes acidosis, how to fix it, and why it's essential!

If you are reading this, you probably want to know what an alkaline diet is and how to help reduce your acidity levels and improve your health. An Alkaline Diet is a diet rich in fruits and vegetables, fiber, organic meats, fish, nuts/seeds, herbs, spices, and pure water. It's based upon the foundation of The PH Balance Diet, which is the cornerstone of a healthy lifestyle.

The PH Balance Diet consists of eating whole foods grown close to nature using organic farming techniques whenever possible. It's a diet that consists of high alkaline foods such as green vegetables, sea vegetables, seeds/nuts/fruits, beans/legumes, wild fish, and grass-fed meats.

Eating these foods will naturally increase your alkalinity and help you detoxify. It's crucial to maintain a high alkaline diet because it will prevent chronic disease. The disease can only thrive in an overly acidic body, and by keeping your body healthy, you will be able to live the life you desire!

The PH Balance Diet is a synonym for The Alkaline Diet: How to Detox and Fight Disease Using Alkaline Foods & PH Balance Diet, the first-ever guide on fighting acidosis using foods.

Eating an Alkaline Diet: Detox and Fight Disease Using Alkaline Foods and PH-Balance Diet.
An alkaline diet is a diet rich in fruits and vegetables, fiber, organic meats, fish, nuts/seeds, herbs, spices, and pure water. It's based upon the foundation of The PH Balance Diet, which is the cornerstone of your healthy lifestyle. This diet will keep your body clean and maintain optimal health.

How can alkaline foods help you? When you eat a high acid foods diet, you are, in essence, weakening your body. When eating a high acid food diet, your internal organs cannot detoxify properly, consequently leaving you susceptible to various diseases.

Besides, cancer can thrive in an overly acidic body. Staying alkaline is one of the most important ways you can reduce cancer risk. Cancer is an overgrowth of cells that is caused by unbalanced cellular water.

Although some people may not feel especially hungry on a fast day, most who choose this method of weight loss find that they can still stick to their diet because fat is more satisfying than high-carbohydrate foods. Additionally, intermittent fasting helps people become aware of the habits that lead to overeating, which can ultimately lead to poor food choices. It's important for you to learn how your metabolism works in order to create a plan that you know will work for your body and lifestyle.

The Best Supplements to Use in Case of Diabetes

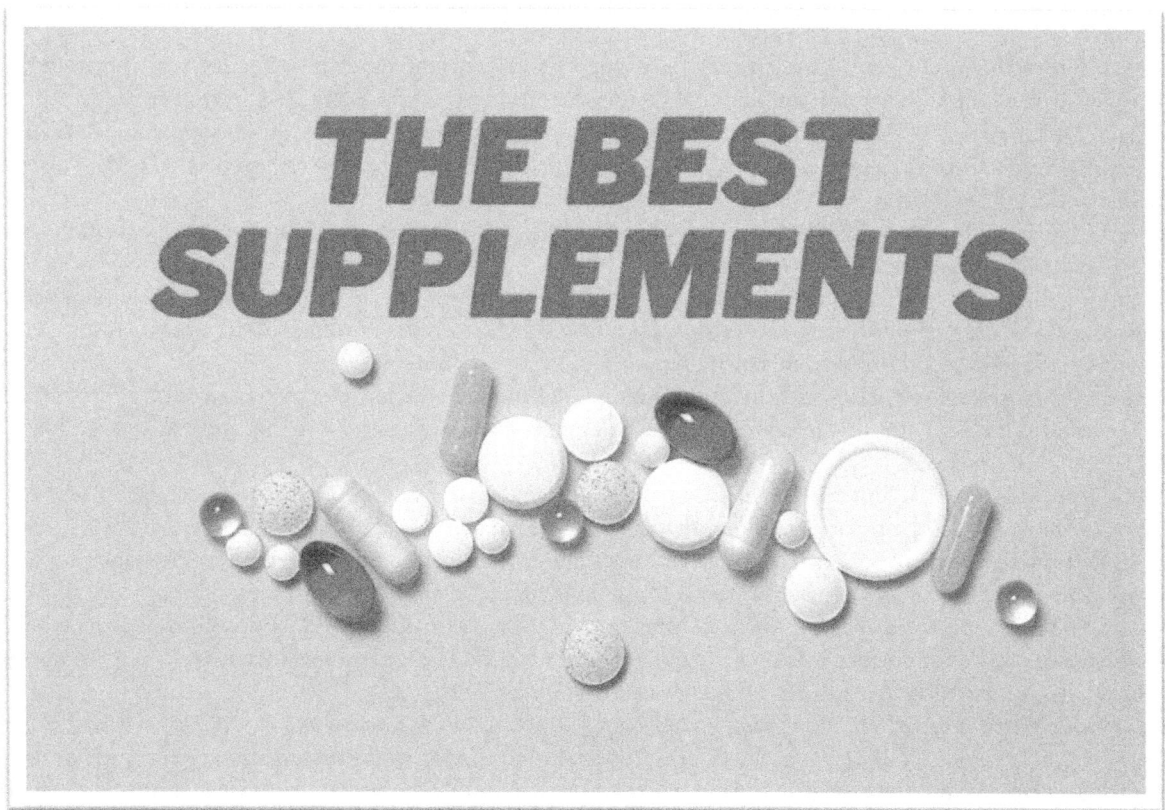

Type-2 or adult-onset diabetes is a metabolic disorder in which the body fails to produce enough insulin to control blood sugar levels. Insulin is needed for glucose, a type of sugar, to enter cells and be used as energy. If not present in the body, glucose can create havoc through an unbalanced diet that leads to weight gain and more serious medical conditions like cardiovascular disease and kidney failure.

An individual with diabetes typically knows they have it when they experience symptoms such as frequent thirst or urination; excessive hunger; extreme fatigue; blurry vision or headaches; numbness in the hands or feet; trouble breathing after exercise, etc. There is a test for diabetes, the fasting plasma glucose test. While it is not a simple test, if the results are above 126 mg/dl in an individual with diabetes, the diagnosis is confirmed.

People with diabetes typically take insulin injections on a daily basis to control blood sugar levels. It is important to monitor blood sugar levels daily and adjust insulin dosage at certain times of the day based on what has been eaten and how much activity has been performed. This becomes more difficult as individual ages because his/her pancreas loses its ability to produce insulin over time.

Supplements that can be taken with meals or just before might enhance the effects of oral medications. These supplements include various herbs and natural ingredients that can help maintain a healthy blood sugar level and control diabetes.

There is no cure for type-2 diabetes, but treatment helps reduce medical risks and promote lifelong good health. Patients may have to take medicines regularly, eat a healthy diet, and exercise regularly. A healthy lifestyle is essential to staying healthy with type-2 diabetes.

A healthy diet and regular physical exercise are essential in maintaining good health regardless of one's age or the risk of developing type-2 diabetes. It helps prevent insulin resistance, metabolic syndrome, and other chronic diseases like high blood pressure, heart disease, and stroke.

It is vital to know that if you have diabetes, it is necessary to monitor your blood sugar levels regularly throughout the day using a blood glucose meter. Your doctor will help you choose the most suitable finger pricking device that can be used to measure your blood sugar levels. Continuous monitoring will aid in controlling your diabetes by evaluating how well your body is responding to treatment or over-medication.

Many supplements can help you manage type 2 diabetes, and we'll cover a few of the most popular:

1. Fish Oil Supplements: Fish oil supplements have been shown in studies to be effective for improving blood sugar control, as well as for reducing inflammation. They also promote weight loss and lower triglycerides.
2. Green Tea Leaf Extract: Green tea leaf extract has been shown to lower blood sugar and improve glucose tolerance in type 2 diabetics. This probably occurs by lowering blood insulin levels. It also improves plasma HDL cholesterol levels, which is good for the heart.
3. Omega-3 Fatty Acids: DHA and EPA are two omega-3 fatty acids that are found in fish oil supplements and can help lower triglycerides and raise HDL cholesterol.
4. Cinnamon: These compounds make cinnamon effective for lowering blood sugar, slowing down glucose absorption, preventing the liver from producing excess glucose, and reducing insulin resistance in the body. This is probably due to its effects on insulin secretion (insulin sensitivity).
5. Gymnema Sylvestre: These extracts from a plant native to India have been shown to lower blood sugar, triglycerides, and cholesterol levels. They also improve glucose tolerance, making it easier for the body to move glucose from the bloodstream into the cells.
6. Alpha-lipoic Acid: ALA is an antioxidant that protects blood vessels from damage by free radicals and helps prevent insulin resistance. It also helps protect the body's cells against oxidative stress, which can damage cells. Research shows that ALA improves glycemic control in type 2 diabetics and makes insulin more effective at lowering blood sugar levels. This may be due to its ability to lower fat levels in the liver and its effects on weight loss.
7. Vanadium: This mineral has been shown to improve glycemic control and reduce insulin levels in type 2 diabetics. Vanadium also improves glucose tolerance, making it easier for the body to move glucose out of the bloodstream into the cells. It is possible that vanadium increases insulin sensitivity.
8. Ginger Root Extract: Research shows that ginger root extract can lower blood sugar and LDL cholesterol levels while increasing HDL (good) cholesterol levels. It also reduces inflammation and protects blood vessels from damage.
9. Vanadyl Sulfate: Studies show that this element can lower blood sugar and triglycerides, as well as improve glucose tolerance in type 2 diabetics. Vanadyl sulfate can also help lower LDL (bad) cholesterol levels in the blood. It may be effective for weight loss as well.
10. Polyunsaturated Fatty Acids: Omega-3 and omega-6 fatty acids are essential elements that the body cannot make, so they must come from food. Omega-3 fatty acids are anti-inflammatory and have been shown to improve blood sugar

control, lower triglycerides, and raise HDL cholesterol levels. Omega-6 fatty acids can also help improve blood sugar control.

11. Soy: Research shows that soy protein can lower blood glucose levels and improve insulin sensitivity. Soy may be most effective at preventing the onset of type 2 diabetes. Soy isoflavones have also been shown to lower cholesterol levels and protect the heart, which makes them beneficial overall.
12. Chromium Picolinate with Alpha Lipoic Acid: This is a supplement that will help release the insulin that your body produces, allowing it to be more efficient in utilizing blood glucose. Also, this supplement can lower the glucose your body produces by converting it into energy instead of storing it as fat. This seems to be the most popular supplement for Type 2 diabetics, as Chromium picolinate is also used to treat diabetes in animals
13. Garlic: This herb can improve the effectiveness of insulin and how it regulates glucose in the bloodstream. Not only that, but it also lowers LDL cholesterol and triglycerides, which are the fats that you want to reduce if you have Type 2 diabetes. Garlic can also reduce blood pressure and prevent blood clots from forming.
14. Vitamin C: A single dose of Vitamin C can reduce blood glucose levels in diabetics by as much as 10% in a short amount of time. Studies have shown that a large intake of vitamin C can keep blood glucose levels low for up to 6 hours. In addition, it also helps strengthen the insulin-producing cells in your pancreas.
15. B12: This vitamin is needed to produce the insulin that your body uses when you consume carbohydrates, so if you don't have enough of it, then you may not be able to effectively use the glucose from your blood. Additionally, B12 keeps insulin receptors open so they are receptive when insulin binds with them
16. Whey Protein: This is a great supplement for Type 1 and Type 2 diabetics as it boosts your immune system to prevent infection caused by bacterial growth in your intestine. Whey protein also has the ability to lower cholesterol, which can also help keep blood glucose levels stable.
17. Vitamin B6: Vitamin B6 is very important for the production of insulin by the pancreas. A lack of vitamin B6 can cause Type 2 diabetes, making it difficult for your body to absorb sugar from food and produce adequate amounts of sugar that can be used by muscles. This is one reason why a good multivitamin should be taken with breakfast.
18. Vitamin A: Vitamin A plays a role in controlling glucose levels by helping to maintain insulin sensitivity by improving the removal of glucose from the bloodstream. Vitamin A deficiency can cause the body's cells to become less sensitive to insulin, making it harder for your body to use sugar for energy and more likely for you to form glucose in your bloodstream.
19. Pantethine: Pantethine is an amino acid that helps slow down the process of glucose absorption into cells, which can help reduce blood sugar spikes. In addition, pantethine helps prevent some of the complications associated with diabetes such as retinopathy and neuropathy.

Exercise and Diabetes

Exercise has been shown to have a positive impact on diabetes. The connection between physical activity, blood sugar levels, and weight is well understood by the medical community. Research has demonstrated that regular exercise can help individuals with type-2 diabetes control their blood glucose levels and manage their weight. While there are no mandatory guidelines for managing type-2 diabetes, exercise can be an important part of achieving health benefits for people with this chronic condition.

Physical activity and diabetes are strongly connected. The benefits of physical activity include: improved glucose utilization; better insulin sensitivity; improved lipid profile; decreased risk of chronic diseases such as heart disease, stroke, and hypertension; increased life expectancy at any given age; improved fitness and quality of life; reduced mortality rate from all causes. People with diabetes who are physically active have lower levels of HbA1c (a marker for average blood sugar concentration over the preceding 3 months) than those who are inactive. In addition, exercise may result in less medication usage, lower overall health care costs, and fewer physician visits.

People with type 2 diabetes should follow a program designed to meet their individual needs. The American Diabetes Association recommends that individuals with type 2 diabetes engage in at least 150 minutes (2 hours and 30 minutes) per week of moderate-intensity aerobic activity, such as brisk walking (3.0 to 3.9 miles per hour) or swimming laps at a pool or a frequency of 3 days per week for 20 minutes, each of high-intensity aerobic activity such as jogging, a fast walk or running, to achieve fitness and weight loss goals. Low-impact aerobics, cycling, and stair climbing are also good choices. Strength training is also recommended. Individuals with diabetes should not engage in high-impact activities such as sprinting, jumping, or dancing. These activities increase the risk of injury in people with type 2 diabetes.

Aerobic exercise is part of a healthy lifestyle to help manage type 2 diabetes. Type 2 diabetes affects approximately 90 million people worldwide, and millions more suffer from prediabetes or a related condition that doesn't quite fit the category of full-blown type 2 diabetes yet poses a great risk for developing this disease in the future. New research from Columbia University revealed that participants were more likely to stick to an exercise routine if they knew they would be rewarded with a t-shirt every time they logged their activity on Fitbit.com.

Aerobic exercise has been shown to improve a number of factors for people with diabetes. For example, regular physical activity is associated with a lower incidence of cardiovascular disease, lower risk of metabolic syndrome, and excess body fat, and it helps delay the development and progression of diabetic complications such as retinopathy. Exercise also may have direct effects on blood glucose levels in people with type 2 diabetes by promoting beta-cell function or decreasing insulin resistance (the process that causes the body to become less sensitive to the hormone insulin) or both. Although it remains unclear exactly how exercise affects blood glucose levels in people with type 2 diabetes, studies have found that exercise may help regulate blood glucose levels through several mechanisms.

Studies have shown that the benefits of exercise may be limited to those who are physically active, which means that individuals who are not physically active are less likely to benefit from the health benefits of exercise.

Tips for Counting Carbs

We are often told that a low-carb diet is good for type 2 diabetes. But how many carbs are appropriate for someone with diabetes? What does "low-carb" mean? What counts as "low-carb"? How to count carbohydrates and calories from carbs accurately? This book will give you some tips on counting carbohydrates for your type-2 diabetic diet.

We understand that it can be challenging because there is so much information out there. However, you will find this book very helpful in figuring out what to eat, what not to eat, and what is the best carbohydrate intake if you have type 2 diabetes.

In addition, I will also provide you with a top 5 list of foods high in carbohydrates and the foods low in carbohydrates that may be helpful to follow.

The word "carbohydrate" comes from the Greek word "karbousa" which means sugar or honey. So, no surprise that grains and starchy vegetables are high in carbohydrates (grain products are referred to as empty calories). The recommended daily allowance (RDA) for carbohydrates is no more than 130 grams per day (for women and men). One gram of carbohydrate equals 4 calories.

Tips in Counting; Carbohydrates for Type-2 Diabetic Diet

Following a high carbohydrate diet is harder than it sounds with food labels that often don't list carbohydrates at all!

Getting the most healthy foods into your diet on a daily basis requires you to keep track of your macros (macros = mw + cd), which refers to the breakdown of your daily calories over fat, protein, and carbs. The main macro's you want to pay attention to are fat (F) and carbs (C).

To make this easier for you we've put together this guide to help you incorporate a balanced diet into your routine.

Macro-Ratios:

Fat: 35% Carbohydrate 30% Protein: 15%

1. Fat: Calories vs. Protein: and Carbohydrate Calories

Although some people do need to watch their fat intake, most diabetics can safely eat up to 40–50% of their calories from protein and carbs, which is what our diets consist of normally. This means that for each meal you should consume a 1:1 ratio of protein/carbs, or around 200 calories worth per meal (this is not including snacks).

If you are eating more than that, try to cut down on your fat calories and vice versa if you are eating less.

2. Pay Attention to Portions

Although we all want a cheat day every now and then, most of us want to stay within our allotted calorie ranges. To accomplish this, use a measuring cup to measure out the servings of grains in your meals so that you aren't guessing how much 5 oz is, or calculating without those numbers in front of you!

For example, if your carb portion is ¾ cup cooked rice, that is 6 oz by weight — which translates into 3 oz in volume (¾ cup x 1 ¼), or 2 and ½ cups fluffed rice.

3. Avoiding Low Carb Diet Pitfalls

Eating the right amount of carbohydrates is very important in managing type 2 diabetes. Carbohydrates are our main energy source and if we don't consume enough, then our bodies will divert them from muscle tissue (such as your heart) to use as energy. Additionally, most people cut carbohydrates to lose weight, which can also be a problem for diabetics. Maintaining insulin levels, which are very important in preventing high blood sugars, is compromised in people eating low-carb diets, therefore lowering your glucose levels. If your glucose level is too high or too low, then your body will use it as fuel. This can lead to neuropathy (wasting away of the nerves), blurry vision, and even coma.

4. The Ideal Carbohydrates for Type-2 Diabetics

The ideal carbohydrates for diabetics are complex carbohydrates that won't spike your blood sugar levels (i.e. they won't cause a rapid rise and fall like simple carbohydrates). Examples of complex carbohydrates are bread (whole grain and wheat bread), cereal with whole grain, pasta, brown rice, and potatoes. The trick is to consume foods that have a low glycemic index, which means that they will have a slower rise in glucose levels.

5. Make Your Own Carbohydrate Counting App

A great way to count carbohydrates is by making an excel spreadsheet that has all of these food categories listed on it. You can then input the serving size and total carbohydrates in one cell, and calculate the glycemic index in another.

Stocking a Diabetes-Friendly Kitchen

If you have diabetes or know someone who does, you understand that food can be just as important to your health as the medicines doctors prescribe. You also understand that it's not always easy to find healthy options that don't break the bank. You're likely aware of some ideas for stocking a "diabetes-friendly" kitchen, but here are some tips on how to make looking for healthy recipes and foods easier and more affordable.

1) Shop at discount supermarkets — Helpful sources include Aldi, Trader Joe's (all items are under $5 per pound), and Wegmans (sales end at 4 p.m., each trip costs about $30).

2) Buy fresh produce at peak freshness — You can find some items as much as 30% off in peak season.

3) Buy frozen foods — One of the biggest advantages to buying frozen versus fresh is that you can purchase extra and divide them into portions at the time of cooking. Frozen fruits and vegetables are often much cheaper than fresh FRUIT, while in certain cases, you may even opt to buy frozen fruits and vegetables in bulk, whether they're canned or freeze-dried, as you'll be able to use those portions for other meals.

4) Shop at the farmers' market — While this is not a way to stock any kind of pantry for long-term storage (in fact, it's not even necessary), it's a fun way to shop for some fresh produce for the week or months ahead. The best times to go are in the summer when you can get fresh and very inexpensive produce, and in the fall when you can get more seasonal items.

5) Grow your own — It's not a simple matter of digging up some soil and planting a seed. We aren't talking about little plastic pots on your balcony, but an investment in larger containers and even a greenhouse or garden shed. You'll be amazed at how much of your grocery bill will be used to buy fresh produce from growers once you grow your own.

6) Buy bulk food (and freeze it) — If you can afford it, buying large amounts of food in bulk and freezing what you don't eat is a great way to cut costs. It's also a good way to store some of your staples for the year, like oats and beans, which freeze well. As a bonus, you'll be able to do a single large batch rather than two smaller ones for the same amount of money.

7) Read the labels — You should become familiar with the different names of foods, as well as their different packaging, sizes, and amounts. While you still need to use your eyes, it's a good idea to keep a list of what you're buying and how

much goes into each meal. It can help you quickly determine if you have extras that can be frozen or used up in another way. And it will help you avoid buying more of something than you'll need.

8) Prepare meals ahead — While this isn't exactly food storage for the year ahead, it does make meal preparation easier and less expensive in the long term. It's easier to cut up a few veggies and cook a small portion of ground beef in advance than it is to do it all when you're hungry. If you have time in the morning, preparing some of your lunch for the day ahead can also make it easier to leave the house or get out of bed.

9) Buy large bags of nuts — They're not only healthy, but they last longer than other nuts thanks to their lower fat content. However, keep them in an air-tight container, as they don't last long enough to eat if left open.

10) Buy flavored rice cakes — They don't have much protein or fiber but are great for those that need a simple snack on the go. (And they're a good way to introduce children to fruits and veggies.)

11) Buy rice cakes and nuts together — Often in the case of some rice cakes and nuts, you can share the same dry pack for a few dollars more than if each were purchased separately.

12) Buy in season — Do you know when certain foods are in season? Delicacies like asparagus, apples, and peaches are often best during their peak seasons. By stocking your kitchen with these items now, you can save money when they're in season at their lowest prices. In fact, many of these items are worth their weight in gold during off-peak seasons as well. Here's a full list of seasonal fruits and vegetables.

13) Purchase at least one large box of pasta each month — This traditional standby offers a wide variety of low-fat and lower-carbohydrate options for meals that are still filling.

14) Make your own stock — You can make soup from a variety of different foods as well as from organs like hearts or bones. Either way, adding some homemade stock to your meals is a great way to add flavor and healing properties while saving money.

15) Don't buy "great deals" — There are certain things you don't need in order to eat healthy, like protein powder or canned fruits in syrup year-round, but there are others that you'd be better off without. If you tend to purchase many of these items, you may want to avoid the "great deals" on them instead.

16) Keep a list of your favorite healthy meals — It's often easy to forget what you like and don't like. Instead of relying on memory alone, write down what you've tried. You may find that there's something new out there for you if it's carefully organized.

17) Buy in bulk — However, if it isn't something that freezes well or can be stored for long periods (such as some canned goods), then buying in bulk isn't really a good way to save money. It may end up costing more than buying the same amount in smaller amounts over a month or two.

18) Avoid prepackaged and canned goods — Cans often add cost as well as pesticides and unhealthy preservatives to what's inside. Look for bulk options and select the items that look the freshest.

Putting the Guidelines into Practice: Building a Complete Meal

One of the many guidelines for managing Type 2 diabetes is to cycle carbohydrates around twice a day. When on a carbohydrate-free diet, this cycle can be achieved by omitting breakfast and rebalancing your meals with lunch and dinner. This book will discuss why these guidelines are necessary and how they can be applied in order to meet the macronutrient goals of the diet, as well as how this applies to other food groups such as fats, proteins, and fruits/vegetables.

The cycle of carbohydrates is important to control blood sugar levels and prevent reactive hypoglycemia. This can be achieved by matching the number of carbohydrates eaten at each meal with the ability of the body to digest them. The body can only digest carbohydrates to a certain degree while the rest is excreted through urine. Therefore, eating most of your carbohydrates in one meal will cause large swings in blood sugar, since you are eating more carbohydrates per unit of time than the body can utilize. These swings will not only cause energy swings (hunger and fatigue), but they will also cause longer-term issues such as insulin resistance, putting you at risk for Type 2 diabetes. This can be avoided by cycling carbohydrates. By spreading out carbohydrate intake and omitting breakfast, it is possible to achieve this.

These principles can be applied to other food groups as well in order to meet the goals of the carbohydrate-free diet. The goal of this diet is not to lose weight, but instead to improve metabolic health and prevent reactive hypoglycemia (low blood sugar). It has been shown that it is possible to achieve these goals without losing weight and people often have an increased amount of energy despite working out regularly on a low-carbohydrate diet. This makes sense since your body will burn protein for energy in place of carbohydrates when the body lacks glucose from carbohydrates. Therefore, you will have increased energy without gaining weight. Fats and proteins are necessary for weight loss, but the carbohydrate-free diet aims to improve metabolic health as a whole. Therefore, fats and proteins must be eaten in moderation as well. The entire carbohydrate-free diet is very flexible in terms of food selection and macronutrient distribution. Each person must find their own balance between what they need for metabolic health and function and is able to maintain a caloric deficit without losing weight.

Benefits of the Plate Method; The Breakfast Equation

Many of us are tempted to begin our day with a quick sugar high in the form of a muffin, bagel, or doughnut. But this action may lead to an energy crash and an unhealthy craving for sugar that we can't seem to shake. And those without type 2 diabetes are not immune.

A better idea is what I call plate method eating — a technique based on the same principle as portion control but with no need for scales or measuring cups. No one needs to feel guilty about eating carbs, but portion sizes matter! Consider your breakfast: it should consist of protein and healthy fat first, then a carb like fruit or oatmeal second (if desired), followed by additional healthy fats like avocado. Unfortunately, most people eat the carbs first, then have a hard time eating anything else.

Why is this so important? The typical American breakfast is made up of a carb (bread, cereal, juice) and sugar (honey, syrup). Eating these carbs triggers a rise in blood sugar and insulin that can set off a cascade of symptoms including tiredness and moodiness. Instead, fill your plate or bowl with protein first — such as eggs or Greek yogurt — and add healthy fats like avocado or nuts. This will help prevent spikes in blood sugars while giving you lasting energy and satisfaction.

The plate method is a revolutionary new diet that has the potential to reverse type 2 diabetes by reducing blood sugar and cholesterol, burning fat, and improving cardiovascular health. The breakfast equation for Type 2 Diabetes is a specific meal plan for those with Type 2 diabetes to help them live healthy lives with diabetes on a whole new level.

The Breakfast Equation is a meal plan that is based on the idea that breakfast is the most important meal of the day. It has literally changed my life and many others who have tried it.

This meal plan was created to help those with Type 2 diabetes live long, full lives without medication or insulin injections. Burning fat naturally will help you reverse your diabetes and allow you to live a long healthy life with Type 2 Diabetes without long-term complications.

In addition to being an effective meal plan for reversing Type 2 Diabetes, this meal plan can also be used as a weight loss program because it helps control appetite, improves energy levels, and regulates hunger. This allows you to eat the amount of food that you want (you will not be starving, and you will not be feeling deprived) while still losing weight, even if you are just walking around in your daily life.

This meal plan is ideal for those with Type 2 Diabetes. It is also great for those who are overweight or who have a metabolic disorder because it allows the body to function at its full potential and burn fat instead of storing it. It can also benefit those who want to lose weight or have high cholesterol because it helps regulate blood sugar and cholesterol levels, which makes this meal plan ideal for type 2 diabetics, pre-diabetics, people with metabolic disorders, and those who are overweight or obese.

The Breakfast Equation meal plan is also ideal for diabetics because it allows them to overcome the challenges that come with diabetes. Traditional nutrition methods like carb counting and tracking blood sugar levels become difficult and overwhelming when you have diabetes because of the challenges they present. Carb counting and tracking blood sugar are both tasks that require a lot of daily commitment, which often leads to the frustration of having difficulty adhering to these methods consistently. This can lead to feelings of failure, low self-esteem, and many other issues that can make living with diabetes extremely challenging.

The Breakfast Equation meal plan was created to be able to help people with Type 2 Diabetes live a long, healthy life without feeling like they can't! By eliminating carb counting and tracking blood sugar levels, this meal plan allows you to focus on living your life instead of worrying about what you're going to eat and when. You will feel satisfied, full, and energized because the protein content of this meal plan satisfies hunger while allowing the body to burn fat instead of storing it.

The Breakfast Equation meal plan is specifically designed to reverse Type 2 Diabetes and allow you to live a long, healthy life with diabetes. A typical breakfast on the Breakfast Equation plan consists of 3 oz of lean protein, ½ cup of non-starchy vegetables, and one serving of starch. Starch is the most important part because it tricks the body into switching from burning glucose (fat) for fuel to burning fat (the stored kind) for fuel. This means that you will have more energy, feel fuller longer, and be better able to control your appetite when eating this meal plan.

A Special Request

Hello and thank you for purchasing the book!

Your brief amazon review could help me.

You know, this is very easy to do, go to the **ORDERS** section of your Amazon account and click on the
"Write a review for the product" button.
It will automatically take you to the review section.
or
Scan the QR-CODE **NOW** !

It will take you to my Amazon author page!

CHAPTER 4: BREAKFAST RECIPES

1. Breakfast Cheese Bread Cups

Preparation Time: 10 minutes
Cooking Time: 15 minutes
Cooking Level: Easy
Servings: 2
Ingredients:

- 2 eggs
- 2 tbsp cheddar cheese, grated
- Salt and pepper, to taste
- 1 ham slice, cut into 2 pieces
- 4 bread slices, flatten with a rolling pin

Directions:

1. Spray the inside of 2 ramekins with cooking spray. Place 2 flat pieces of bread into each ramekin. Add ham slice pieces into each ramekin.
2. Crack an egg in each ramekin, then sprinkle with cheese. Season with salt and pepper. Place the ramekins into the air fryer at 300°F for 15 minutes. Serve warm.

Nutrition: Low GL Calories: 162; Total Fat: 8 g; Carbs: 10 g; Protein: 11 g; Fiber: 7 g; Sugar: 2 g; Cholesterol: 87 mg; Sodium: 372 mg; Potassium: 419 mg

2. Breakfast Cod Nuggets

Preparation Time: 10 minutes
Cooking Time: 10 minutes
Cooking Level: Easy
Servings: 4
Ingredients:

- 1 lb. cod

For breading:

- 2 eggs, beaten
- 2 tbsp olive oil
- 1 cup almond flour
- ¾ cup breadcrumbs
- 1 tsp dried parsley
- Pinch sea salt
- ½ tsp black pepper

Directions:

1. Preheat the air fryer to 390°F. Cut the cod into strips about 1-inch by 2-inches. Blend breadcrumbs, olive oil, salt, parsley and pepper in a food processor.
2. In three separate bowls, add breadcrumbs, eggs and flour. Place each piece of fish into flour, then the eggs and the breadcrumbs. Add pieces of cod to the air fryer basket and cook for 10 minutes. Serve warm.

Nutrition: Low GL Calories: 213; Total Fat: 12.6 g; Carbs: 9.2 g; Protein: 13.4 g; Fiber: 7 g; Sugar: 2 g; Cholesterol: 73 mg; Sodium: 417 mg; Potassium: 342 mg

3. Vegetable Egg Pancake

Preparation Time: 10 minutes
Cooking Time: 15 minutes
Cooking Level: Easy
Servings: 2
Ingredients:

- 1 cup almond flour
- ½ cup milk
- 1 tbsp parmesan cheese, grated
- 3 eggs
- 1 potato, grated
- 1 beet, peeled and grated
- 1 carrot, grated
- 1 zucchini, grated
- 1 tbsp olive oil

Directions:

1. Preheat your air fryer to 390°F. Mix zucchini, potato, beet, carrot, eggs, milk, almond flour and parmesan
2. Place olive oil into an oven-safe dish. Form patties with vegetable mix and flatten to form patties. Place the patties into an oven-safe dish and cook in the air fryer for 15 minutes. Serve with sliced tomatoes, sour cream, and toast.

Nutrition: Low GL Calories: 223; Total Fat: 11.2 g; Carbs: 10.3 g; Proteins: 13.4 g; Fiber: 4 g; Sugar: 1 g; Cholesterol: 67 mg; Sodium: 362 mg; Potassium: 234 mg

4. Oriental Omelet

Preparation Time: 10 minutes
Cooking Time: 12 minutes
Cooking Level: Easy
Servings: 2
Ingredients:

- ½ cup fresh Shimeji mushrooms, sliced
- 2 eggs, whisked
- Salt and pepper, to taste
- 1 clove garlic, minced
- A handful sliced tofu
- 2 tbsp onion, finely chopped
- Cooking spray

Directions:

1. Spray a baking dish with cooking spray. Add onions and garlic. Air fry at 355°F for 4 minutes.
2. Place the tofu and mushrooms over the onions, and add salt and pepper to taste. Whisk the eggs and pour over the tofu and mushrooms. Air fry again for 20 minutes. Serve warm.

Nutrition: Low GL Calories: 210; Total Fat: 11.2 g; Carbs: 8.6 g; Protein: 12.2 g; Fiber: 4 g; Sugar: 2 g; Cholesterol: 97 mg; Sodium: 377 mg; Potassium: 278 mg

5. Pumpkin Pie French toast

Preparation Time: 10 minutes
Cooking Time: 20 minutes
Cooking Level: Easy
Servings: 4
Ingredients:

- 2 larges, beaten eggs
- 4 slices cinnamon swirl bread
- ¼ cup milk
- ¼ cup pumpkin puree
- ¼ tsp pumpkin spices
- ¼ cup butter

Directions:

1. Mix milk, eggs, pumpkin puree and pie spice. Whisk until the mixture is smooth. In the egg mixture, dip the bread on both sides.
2. Place a rack inside the air fryer's cooking basket. Place 2 slices of bread onto the rack. Set the temperature to 340°F for 10 minutes. Serve the pumpkin pie toast with butter.

Nutrition: Low GL Calories: 212; Total Fat: 8.2 g; Carbs: 7 g; Protein: 11.3 g; Fiber: 4 g; Sugar: 2 mg; Cholesterol: 89 mg; Sodium: 382 mg; Potassium: 312 mg

6. Crispy Breakfast Avocado Fries

Preparation Time: 10 minutes
Cooking Time: 8 minutes
Cooking Level: Easy
Servings: 2
Ingredients:

- 2 eggs, beaten
- 2 large avocados, peeled, pitted, cut into 8 slices each
- ¼ tsp pepper
- ½ tsp cayenne pepper
- Salt, to taste
- Juice ½ a lemon
- ½ cup whole-wheat flour
- 1 cup whole-wheat breadcrumbs
- Greek yogurt, to serve

Directions:

1. Add flour, salt, pepper and cayenne pepper to a bowl and mix. Add breadcrumbs into another bowl. Beat eggs in a third bowl. First, dredge the avocado slices in the flour mixture. Next, dip them into the egg mixture, and finally dredge them in the breadcrumbs. Place avocado fries into the air fryer basket.
2. Preheat air fryer to 390°F. Place the air fryer basket into the air fryer and cook for 6 minutes. When Cooking Time is completed, transfer the avocado fries onto a serving platter. Sprinkle with lemon juice and serve with Greek yogurt.

Nutrition: Low GL Calories: 272 Total Fat: 13.4 g; Carbs: 11.2 g; Protein: 15.4 g; Fiber: 6 g; Sugar: 2 g; Cholesterol: 89 mg; Sodium: 394 mg; Potassium: 253 mg

7. Cheese and Egg Breakfast Sandwich

Preparation Time: 10 minutes
Cooking Time: 6 minutes
Cooking Level: Easy
Servings: 2
Ingredients:

- 1–2 eggs
- 1–2 slices cheddar or Swiss cheese
- A bit butter
- 1 roll sliced in half (your choice, Kaiser Bun, English muffin, etc.)

Directions:

1. Butter your sliced roll on both sides. Place the eggs in an oven-safe dish and whisk. Add seasoning if you wish such as dill, chives, oregano and salt. Place egg dish, roll and cheese into the air fryer.
2. Make assured the buttered sides of the roll are in front of upwards. Set the air fryer to 390°F with a Cooking Time of 6 minutes. Remove the ingredients when the cooking time is completed by the air fryer.

3. Place egg and cheese between the pieces of roll and serve warm. You might like to try adding slices of avocado and tomatoes to this breakfast sandwich!

Nutrition: Low GL Calories: 212; Total Fat: 11.2 g; Carbs: 9.3 g; Protein: 12.4 g; Fiber: 5 g; Cholesterol: 109 mg; Sodium: 324 mg; Potassium: 326 mg

8. Baked Mini Quiche

Preparation Time: 10 minutes
Cooking Time: 15 minutes
Cooking Level: Easy
Servings: 2
Ingredients:

- 2 eggs
- 1 large yellow onion, diced
- 1 ¾ cups whole-wheat flour
- 1 ½ cups spinach, chopped
- ¾ cup cottage cheese
- Salt and black pepper, to taste
- 2 tbsp olive oil
- ¾ cup butter
- ¼ cup milk

Directions:

1. Preheat the air fryer to 355°F. Add flour, butter, salt and milk to the bowl, and knead the dough until smooth and refrigerate for 15 minutes. Abode a frying pan over medium heat and add oil to it. When the oil is heated, add onions into the pan and sauté them. Transfer spinach to a pan and cook until it wilts.
2. Drain excess moisture from spinach. Whisk the eggs together and add cheese to the bowl and mix. Proceeds the dough out of the fridge and divides it into 8 equal parts. Roll the dough into a round that will fit into the bottom of quiche mound. Place rolled dough into molds. Place spinach filling over dough.
3. Place the molds into the air fryer basket, place the basket inside of the air fryer, and cook for 15 minutes. Remove quiche from molds and serve warm or cold.

Nutrition: Low GL Calories: 262; Total Fat: 8.2 g; Carbs: 7.3 g; Protein: 9.5 g; Fiber: 5 g; Sugar: 1 g; Cholesterol: 78 mg; Sodium: 434 mg; Potassium: 216 mg

9. Peanut Butter and Banana Breakfast Sandwich

Preparation Time: 10 minutes
Cooking Time: 6 minutes
Cooking Level: Easy
Servings: 2
Ingredients:

- 2 slices whole-wheat bread
- 1 tsp sugar-free maple syrup
- 1 sliced banana
- 2 tbsp peanut butter

Directions:

1. Evenly coat both sides of the slices of bread with peanut butter. Add the sliced banana and drizzle with some sugar-free maple syrup.
2. Heat in the air fryer to 330°F for 6 minutes. Serve warm.

Nutrition: Low GL Calories: 211; Total Fat: 8.2 g; Carbs: 6.3 g; Protein: 11.2 g; Fiber: 3 g; Sugar: 2 g; Cholesterol: 94 mg; Sodium: 394 mg; Potassium: 246 mg

10. Eggs and Cocotte on Toast

Preparation Time: 10 minutes
Cooking Time: 15 minutes
Cooking Level: Easy
Servings: 2
Ingredients:

- ⅛ tsp black pepper
- ¼ tsp salt

- ½ tsp Italian seasoning
- ¼ tsp balsamic vinegar
- ¼ tsp sugar-free maple syrup
- 1 cup sausages, chopped into small pieces
- 2 eggs
- 2 slices whole-wheat toast
- 3 tbsp cheddar cheese, shredded
- 6-slices tomatoes
- Cooking spray
- A little mayonnaise, to serve

Directions:
1. Spray a baking dish with cooking spray. Place the bread slices at the bottom of the dish. Sprinkle the sausages over the bread. Lay the tomatoes over it. Sprinkle the top with cheese. Beat the eggs and then pour over the top of the bread slices.
2. Drizzle vinegar and maple syrup over eggs. Flavor with Italian seasoning, salt and pepper, then sprinkle some more cheese on top. Place the baking dish in the air fryer basket that should be preheated at 320°F and cooked for 10 minutes. Remove from the air fryer, add a spot of mayonnaise, and serve.

Nutrition: Low GL Calories: 232; Total Fat: 7.4 g; Carbs: 6.3 g; Protein: 14.2 g; Fiber: 7 g; Sugar: 0 g; Cholesterol: 87 mg; Sodium: 327 mg; Potassium: 351 mg

11. Crunchy Fried French toast Sticks

Preparation Time: 6 minutes
Cooking Time: 10–14 minutes
Cooking Level: Easy
Servings: 2
Ingredients:

- 3 slices low-Cholesterol: 89 mg; Sodium: whole-wheat bread, each cut into 4 strips
- 1 tbsp unsalted butter, melted
- 1 egg
- 1 egg white
- 1 tbsp 2% milk
- 1 tbsp honey
- 1 cup sliced fresh strawberries
- 1 tbsp freshly squeezed lemon juice

Directions:
1. Place the bread strips on a plate and drizzle with the melted butter. In a shallow bowl, beat the egg, egg white, milk and honey. Dip the bread
2. Air fry half of the bread strips at 380°F (193°C) for 5 to 7 minutes, turning the strips with tongs once during cooking, until golden brown. Repeat with the remaining strips.
3. Mash strawberries and lemon juice. Serve strawberry sauce with the French toast sticks.

Nutrition: High GL Calories: 145; Fat: 5 g; Carbs: 18 g; Protein: 7 g; Fiber: 3 g; Sugar: 7 g; Cholesterol: 92 mg; Sodium: 120 mg; Potassium: 212 mg

12. Pumpkin Oatmeal with Raisins

Preparation Time: 10 minutes
Cooking Time: 10 minutes
Cooking Level: Easy
Servings: 2
Ingredients:

- 1 cup rolled oats
- 2 tbsp raisins
- ¼ tsp ground cinnamon
- Pinch kosher salt
- ¼ cup pumpkin purée
- 2 tbsp pure maple syrup
- 1 cup low-fat milk

Directions:
1. Combine the rolled oats, raisins, ground cinnamon and kosher salt, then stir pumpkin purée, maple syrup and low-fat milk.
2. Spray a baking pan with cooking spray, then pour the oatmeal mixture into the pan and bake at 300°F or 149°C for 10 minutes.
3. Remove the oatmeal from the fryer and allow it to cool in the pan on a wire rack for 5 minutes before serving.

Nutrition: Moderate GL Calories: 304; Fat: 4 g; Carbs: 57 g; Protein: 10 g; Fiber: 6 g; Sugar: 26 g; Cholesterol: 85 mg; Sodium: 140 mg; Potassium: 345 mg

13. Mushroom and Black Bean Burrito

Preparation Time: 10 minutes
Cooking Time: 15 minutes
Cooking Level: Easy
Servings: 2
Ingredients:

- 2 tbsp canned black beans
- ¼ cup sliced baby portobello mushrooms
- 1 tsp olive oil
- Pinch kosher salt
- 1 large egg
- 1 slice low-fat Cheddar cheese
- 1 (8-inch) whole-grain flour tortilla
- Hot sauce (optional)

Directions:

1. Spray a baking pan with cooking spray, then place black beans and baby portobello mushrooms in the pan, season
2. Bake at 360°F (182°C) for 5 minutes, then pause the fryer to crack the egg on top of the beans and mushrooms. Bake for 8 more minutes or until the egg is cooked as desired.
3. Pause the fryer again, top the egg with cheese, and bake for 1 more minute.
4. Remove the pan from the fryer, then use a spatula to place the bean mixture on the whole-grain flour tortilla. Fold in the sides and roll from front to back. Serve warm with the hot sauce on the side (if using).

Nutrition: Low GL Calories: 276; Fat: 12 g; Carbs: 26 g; Protein: 16 g; Fiber: 6 g; Sugar: 2 g; Cholesterol: 78 mg; Sodium: 306 mg; Potassium: 292 mg

14. Yogurt Raspberry Cake

Preparation Time: 10 minutes
Cooking Time: 8 minutes
Cooking Level: Easy
Servings: 2
Ingredients:

- ½ cup whole-wheat pastry flour
- ⅛ tsp kosher salt
- ¼ tsp baking powder
- ½ cup whole milk vanilla yogurt
- 2 tbsp canola oil
- 2 tbsp pure maple syrup
- ¾ cup fresh raspberries

Directions:

1. Combine wheat pastry flour, kosher salt and baking powder, then stir the whole milk vanilla yogurt, canola oil and maple syrup, and gently fold in the raspberries.
2. Spray the baking pan with cooking spray, then pour cake batter into the pan, and bake at 300°F or 149°C for 8 minutes.
3. Remove the cake from the fryer and allow it to cool

Nutrition: Low GL Calories: 168; Fat: 8 g; Carbs: 21 g; Protein: 3 g; Fiber: 3 g; Sugar: 8 g; Cholesterol: 85 mg; Sodium: 82 mg; Potassium: 312 mg

15. Spinach and Tomato Egg Cup

Preparation Time: 5 minutes
Cooking Time: 10 minutes
Cooking Level: Easy
Servings: 2
Ingredients:

- 2 egg whites, beaten
- 2 tbsp chopped tomato
- 2 tbsp chopped spinach
- Pinch kosher salt
- A pinch Red pepper flakes (optional)

Directions:

1. Spray a 3-inch ramekin with nonstick cooking spray, then combine the egg whites, tomato, spinach, red pepper flakes salt in the ramekin.
2. Place the ramekin in the fryer, bake at 300°F or 149°C for 10 minutes or until the eggs have set.
3. Remove the ramekin from the fryer and allow it to cool on a wire rack for 5 minutes before serving.

Nutrition: Low GL Calories: 32; Fat: 0 g; Carbs: 1 g; Protein: 7 g; Fiber: 1 g; Sugar: 1 g; Cholesterol: 89 mg; Sodium: 184 mg; Potassium: 334 mg

16. Egg Muffins with Bell Pepper

Preparation Time: 5 minutes
Cooking Time: 10 minutes
Cooking Level: Easy
Servings: 2

Ingredients:

- 4 large eggs
- ½ bell pepper, finely chopped
- 1 tbsp finely chopped red onion
- ¼ tsp kosher salt
- ¼ tsp pepper, to taste
- 2 tbsp shredded Cheddar cheese

Directions:

1. Whisk the eggs, then stir bell pepper, red onion, kosher salt and black pepper.
2. Spray the ramekins with cooking spray, then pour half the egg mixture into each ramekin and place ramekins in the fryer basket. Bake at 390°F (199°C) for 8 minutes.
3. Pause the fryer, sprinkle 1 tbsp of shredded Cheddar cheese on top of each cup, and bake for 2 more minutes.
4. Remove from the fryer, allow to cool on a wire rack for 5 minutes, then turn the omelet cups out on plates and sprinkle some black pepper on top before serving.

Nutrition: Low GL Calories: 172; Fat: 12 g; Protein: 14 g; Carbs: 2 g; Fiber: 0 g; Sugar: 1 g; Cholesterol: 93 mg; Sodium: 333 mg; Potassium: 367 mg

17. Egg-in-a-Hole

Preparation Time: 5 minutes
Cooking Time: 5–7 minutes
Cooking Level: Easy
Servings: 2

Ingredients:

- 1 slice whole-grain bread
- 1 large egg
- ⅛ tsp kosher salt
- ¼ cup diced avocado
- ¼ cup diced tomato
- Pinch Pepper, to taste

Directions:

1. Spray a baking pan with cooking spray, then use a ring mold or a sharp knife to cut a hole in the center of the whole-grain bread. Place the bread slice and the circle in the pan.
2. Crack the egg into the hole, then season with the kosher salt. Bake at 360°F (182°C) for 5 to 7 minutes or until the egg is cooked as desired.
3. Remove from the fryer, allow to cool before transferring the toast to a plate, then sprinkle the avocado, tomato and black pepper on top before serving.

Nutrition: Low GL Calories: 220; Fat: 12 g; Carbs: 18 g; Protein: 10 g; Fiber: 5 g; Sugar: 4 g; Cholesterol: 102 mg; Sodium: 406 mg; Potassium: 262 mg

18. Egg and Cheese Pockets

Preparation Time: 10 minutes
Cooking Time: 35 minutes
Cooking Level: Easy
Servings: 2

Ingredients:

- 1 large egg, beaten
- Pinch kosher salt
- ½ sheet puff pastry
- 1 slice Cheddar cheese, divided into 4 pieces

Directions:

1. Pour the egg into a baking pan, season with the kosher salt, and bake at 330°F (166°C) for 3 minutes. Pause the fryer, gently scramble the egg, and bake for 2 more minutes. Remove the egg from the fryer, keeping the fryer on, and set the egg aside to slightly cool.
2. Roll the puff pastry out flat and divide into 4 pieces. Place a piece of cheddar cheese and ¼ of the egg on one side of a piece of pastry, fold the pastry over the egg and cheese and use a fork to press the edges closed. Repeat this process with the remaining pieces.
3. Place 2 pockets in the fryer and bake for 15 minutes or until golden brown. Repeat this process with the other 2 pockets.
4. Remove the pockets from the fryer and allow them to cool on a wire rack for 5 minutes before serving.

Nutrition: Low GL Calories: 215; Fat: 15 g; Carbs: 14 g; Protein: 6 g; Fiber: 0 g; Sugar: 0 g; Cholesterol: 79 mg; Sodium: 143 mg; Potassium: 338 mg

19. Huevos Rancheros

Preparation Time: 20 minutes
Cooking Time: 25 minutes
Cooking Level: Easy
Servings: 2

Ingredients:

- 4 large eggs
- ¼ tsp kosher salt
- ¼ cup masa harina (corn flour)
- 1 tsp olive oil
- ¼ cup warm water
- ½ cup salsa
- ¼ cup crumbled queso fresco or feta cheese

Directions:

1. Crack the eggs into a baking pan, season with the kosher salt, and bake at 330°F (166°C) for 3 minutes. Pause the fryer, gently scramble the eggs, and bake for 2 more minutes. Remove the eggs from the fryer, keeping the fryer on, and set the eggs aside to slightly cool. (Clean the baking pan before making the tortillas.)
2. Increase the temperature to 390°F or 199°C. Combine masa harina, olive oil, and ¼ tsp of kosher salt by hand, then slowly pour in the water, stirring until a soft dough forms.
3. Divide the dough into 4 equal balls, then place each ball between 2 pieces of parchment paper and use a pie plate or a rolling pin to flatten the dough.
4. Spray the baking pan with nonstick cooking spray, then place one flattened tortilla in the pan and air fry for 5 minutes. Repeat this process with the remaining tortillas. Remove the tortillas from the fryer and place on a serving plate, then top each tortilla with the scrambled eggs, salsa, and cheese before serving.

Nutrition: Low GL Calories: 136; Fat: 8 g; Carbs: 8 g; Protein: 8 g; Fiber: 1 g; Sugar: 2 g; Cholesterol: 100 mg; Sodium: 333 mg; Potassium: 318 mg

20. Jalapeño Potato Hash

Preparation Time: 10 minutes
Cooking Time: 19–20 minutes
Cooking Level: Easy
Servings: 2
Ingredients:

- 2 large sweet potatoes
- ½ small red onion,
- 1 green bell pepper,
- 1 jalapeño pepper, seeded and sliced
- ½ tsp kosher salt
- ¼ tsp pepper, to taste
- 1 tsp olive oil
- 1 large egg, poached

Directions:

1. Cook the sweet potatoes on high in the microwave until softened but not completely cooked (3 to 4 minutes), then set aside to cool for 10 minutes. Remove the skins from the sweet potatoes, then cut the sweet potatoes into large chunks.
2. Combine the sweet potatoes, red onion, green bell pepper, jalapeño pepper, kosher salt, black pepper and olive oil, tossing gently. Spray the fryer with cooking spray, then pour the mixture into the basket and air fry at 360°F or 182°C for 8 minutes.
3. Pause the fryer to shake the basket, then air fry for 8 more minutes or until golden brown.
4. Remove the hash from the fryer, place on a plate lined with a paper towel, and allow to cool, then add a poached egg, sprinkle black pepper on top, and serve.

Nutrition: High GL Calories: 131; Fat: 3 g; Carbs: 22 g; Protein: 4 g; Fiber: 4 g; Sugar: 7 g; Cholesterol: 82 mg; Sodium: 174 mg; Potassium: 285 mg

21. Shrimp Rice Frittata

Preparation Time: 15 minutes
Cooking Time: 14–18 minutes
Cooking Level: Easy
Servings: 2
Ingredients:

- 4 eggs
- Pinch salt
- ½ tsp dried basil
- Nonstick cooking spray
- ½ cup cooked rice
- ½ cup chopped cooked shrimp
- ½ cup baby spinach
- ½ cup grated Monterey Jack or Cojack cheese

Directions:

1. Whisk eggs with basil and salt. Spray the baking pan with cooking spray.
2. Combine the spinach, shrimp and rice in the pan. Pour the eggs in and sprinkle with the cheese.
3. Bake at 320°F (160°C) for 14 to 18 minutes or until the frittata is puffed and golden brown.

Nutrition: Low GL Calories: 227; Fat: 9 g; Carbs: 19 g; Protein: 16 g; Fiber: 0 g; Sugar: 1 g; Cholesterol: 89 mg; Sodium: 232 mg; Potassium: 312 mg

22. Vegetable Frittata

Preparation Time: 10 minutes
Cooking Time: 8–12 minutes
Cooking Level: Easy
Servings: 2
Ingredients:

- ½ cup chopped red bell pepper
- 1/3 cup minced onion
- 1/3 cup grated carrot
- 1 tsp olive oil
- 6 egg whites
- 1 egg
- 1/3 cup 2% milk
- 1 tbsp grated Parmesan cheese

Directions:

1. In a baking pan, stir together the red bell pepper, onion, carrot and olive oil. Put the pan into the air fryer. Bake at 350°F (177°C) for 4 to 6 minutes, shaking the basket once, until the vegetables are tender.
2. Whisk egg, egg whites and milk until combined.
3. Pour the egg mixture over the vegetables in the pan. Sprinkle with the Parmesan cheese. Return the pan to the air fryer.
4. Bake 4 to 6 minutes more, or until the frittata is puffy and set. Cut into 4 wedges and serve.

Nutrition: Low GL Calories: 78; Fat: 3 g; Carbs: 5 g; Protein: 8 g; Fiber: 1 g; Sugar: 3 g; Cholesterol: 77 mg; Sodium: 116 mg; Potassium: 382 mg

23. Ginger Blackberry Bliss Smoothie Bowl

Preparation Time: 5 minutes
Cooking Time: 0 minutes
Cooking Level: Easy
Servings: 2
Ingredients:

- ½ cup frozen blackberries
- 1 cup plain Greek yogurt
- 1 cup baby spinach
- ½ cup unsweetened almond milk
- ½ tsp peeled and grated fresh ginger
- ¼ cup chopped pecans

Directions:

1. Blend blackberries, yogurt, spinach, almond milk and ginger until smooth.
2. Spoon the mixture into two bowls.
3. Top each bowl with 2 tbsp of chopped pecans and serve.

Nutrition: Low GL Calorie: 202; Fat: 15 g; Carbohydrates: 15 g; Protein: 7 g; Fiber: 4 g; Sugar: 3 g; Cholesterol: 101 mg; Sodium: 104 mg; Potassium: 347 mg

24. Heart-Healthy Yogurt Parfaits

Preparation Time: 10 minutes
Cooking Time: 5 minutes
Cooking Level: Easy
Servings: 2
Ingredients:

- 1 cup fresh pineapple chunks
- 1 cup plain Greek yogurt
- ¼ cup canned coconut milk
- ¼ cup flaxseed
- 2 tbsp unsweetened toasted coconut flakes
- 2 tbsp chopped macadamia nuts

Directions:

1. Preheat the oven broiler to high. Spread the pineapple chunks in a single layer on a rimmed baking sheet.
2. Broil until the pineapple begins to brown; 4 to 5 minutes.
3. Whisk together the yogurt, coconut milk and flaxseed. Spoon the mixture into two bowls. Top with the pineapple chunks.
4. Serve with the coconut flakes and chopped macadamia nuts sprinkled over the top.

Nutrition: High GL Calorie: 402; Fat: 31 g; Carbohydrates: 26 g; Protein: 10 g; Fiber: 9 g; Sugar: 2 g; Cholesterol: 88 mg; Sodium: 71 mg; Potassium: 347 mg

25. Toads in Holes

Preparation Time: 5 minutes
Cooking Time: 5 minutes
Cooking Level: Easy
Servings: 2
Ingredients:

- 2 tbsp butter
- 2 slices whole-wheat bread
- 2 large eggs
- Salt and pepper, to taste

Directions:

1. Heat butter until it bubbles.
2. As the butter heats, cut a 3-inch hole in the middle of each piece of bread. Discard the centers.
3. Place the bread pieces in the butter in the pan. Carefully crack an egg into the hole of each piece of bread. Cook until the bread crisps and the egg whites set, about 3 minutes.
4. Flip and cook just until the yolk is almost set, 1 to 2 minutes more. Season

Nutrition: Low GL Calorie: 241; Fat: 17 g; Carbohydrates: 12 g; Protein: 10 g; Fiber: 2 g; Sugar: 1 g; Cholesterol: 96 mg; Sodium: 307 mg; Potassium: 312 mg

26. Canadian bacon and Egg Muffin Cups

Preparation Time: 5 minutes
Cooking Time: 20 minutes
Cooking Level: Easy
Servings: 2
Ingredients:

- Cooking spray (for greasing)
- 6 large slices Canadian bacon
- 12 large eggs, beaten
- 1 tsp Dijon mustard
- ½ tsp sea salt
- Dash hot sauce
- 1 cup shredded Swiss cheese

Directions:

1. Preheat the oven to 350°F. Spray 6 nonstick muffin cups with cooking spray.
2. Line each cup with 1 slice of Canadian bacon.
3. Whisk eggs, mustard, salt and hot sauce. Fold in the cheese. Spoon the mixture into the muffin cups.
4. Bake until the eggs set, about 20 minutes.

Nutrition: Low GL Calorie: 259; Fat: 17 g; Carbohydrates: 3 g; Protein: 24 g; Fiber: 0 g; Sugar: 0 g; Cholesterol: 93 mg; Sodium: 781 mg; Potassium: 242 mg

27. Sausage and Pepper Breakfast Burrito

Preparation Time: 10 minutes
Cooking Time: 15 minutes
Cooking Level: Easy
Servings: 2
Ingredients:

- 8 oz bulk pork breakfast sausage
- ½ onion, chopped
- 1 green bell pepper, seeded and chopped
- 8 large eggs, beaten
- 4 (6-inch) low-carb tortillas
- 1 cup shredded pepper Jack cheese
- ½ cup sour cream (optional, for serving)
- ½ cup prepared salsa (optional, for serving)

Directions:

1. In a large nonstick skillet on medium-high heat, cook the sausage, crumbling it with a spoon, until browned, about 5 minutes. Add onion and bell pepper. Cook the veggies until soft, about 3 minutes. Add eggs and cook until eggs are set, about 3 minutes more.
2. Spoon the egg mixture onto the 4 tortillas. Top each with the cheese and fold it into a burrito shape.
3. Serve with salsa or sour cream, if desired.

Nutrition: Low GL Calorie: 486; Fat: 36 g; Carbohydrates: 13 g; Protein: 32 g; Fiber: 8 g; Sugar: 2 g; Cholesterol: 104 mg; Sodium: 810 mg; Potassium: 372 mg

28. Pumpkin Walnut Smoothie Bowl

Preparation Time: 5 minutes
Cooking Time: 0 minutes
Cooking Level: Easy
Servings: 2
Ingredients:

- 1 cup plain Greek yogurt
- ½ cup canned pumpkin purée (not pumpkin pie mix)
- 1 tsp pumpkin pie spice
- 2 (1-gram) packets stevia
- ½ tsp vanilla extract
- Pinch sea salt
- ½ cup chopped walnuts

Directions:

1. In a bowl, whisk together the yogurt, pumpkin purée, pumpkin pie spice, stevia, vanilla and salt (or blend in a blender).
2. Spoon into two bowls. Serve topped with chopped walnuts.

Nutrition: Low GL Calorie: 292; Fat: 23 g; Carbohydrates: 15 g; Protein: 9 g; Fiber: 4 g; Sugar: 0 g; Cholesterol: 89 mg; Sodium: 85 mg; Potassium: 377 mg

29. Melon sandwich

Preparation Time: 8 minutes
Cooking Time: 0 minutes
Cooking Level: Easy
Servings: 2
Ingredients:

- 4 slices toast bread (50 g)
- 6 slices smoked ham
- ½ cup net melon
- 4 tsp sour cream
- 4 leaves lettuce

Directions:

1. Toast. Remove the greasy edges from the ham slices.
2. Slice the melon. Cut the pulp into thin slices.
3. Brush one side of the toast with sour cream. Then cover the slices with the melon slice, ham and salad.
4. Brush the second toast slice with sour cream and place it on the topped slice.

Nutrition: Low GL Calorie: 350; Fat: 10 g; Carbohydrates: 31 g; Protein: 21 g; Fiber: 6 g; Sugar: 1 g; Cholesterol: 78 mg; Sodium: 143 mg; Potassium: 328 mg

30. Buttermilk lentil

Preparation Time: 30 minutes
Cooking Time: 10 minutes
Cooking Level: Easy
Servings: 2
Ingredients:

- 2 eggs
- ¼ cup semolina
- 120 ml buttermilk
- Salt, lemon juice, sweetener (liquid)
- 4 tbsp low-fat quark
- 1 cup strawberries
- 2 tsp nuts
- 3 tsp oil

Directions:

1. Separate the egg yolks. Mix the egg yolks with the buttermilk, the semolina and two pinches of salt, and leave to soak for about 10 minutes.
2. Season the quark with lemon juice and the liquid sweetener. Wash the strawberries. Remove the stems. Halve the fruit. Whisk egg whites until stiff. Fold the mixture into the semolina.
3. Heat some oil. Use a ladle to pour semolina into the hot pan and let it brown. Turn around with a dog. Fry about 4 pancakes in this way.

4. Fill the pancakes with quark cream and add some strawberries. Serve on a plate.

Nutrition: Low GL Calorie: 330; Fat: 8 g; Carbohydrates: 31 g; Protein: 22 g; Fiber: 4 g; Sugar: 1 g; Cholesterol: 94 mg; Sodium: 163 mg; Potassium: 349 mg

31. Stracciatella Omelet

Preparation Time: 30 minutes
Cooking Time: 15 minutes
Cooking Level: Easy
Servings: 2
Ingredients:

- 2 eggs
- 4 tsp flour
- ½ cocoa powder
- 1 lemon
- 5 tsp dark chocolate
- ½ cup whipped cream

Directions:

1. Grate the lemon peel. Separate the yolks from one egg. Beat the egg white until stiff. Stir egg yolk and lemon zest.
2. Preheat the oven. Place parchment paper on a baking sheet. Spread the mixture with a spoon in two circles and bake for 10 minutes.
3. Remove the baking mixture from the baking paper, place it on a plate, and let cool down.
4. Grate the chocolate into grates. Whip cream until stiff add chocolate. Put everything in a piping bag and apply it to the omelets. Dust the omelets with the cocoa and chill for a quarter of an hour.

Nutrition: Low GL Calorie: 390; Fat: 30 g; Carbohydrates: 22 g; Protein: 9 g; Fiber: 8 g; Sugar: 1 g; Cholesterol: 96 mg; Sodium: 143 mg; Potassium: 283 mg

32. Plum muffins

Preparation Time: 10 minutes
Cooking Time: 50 minutes
Cooking Level: Moderate
Servings: 2
Ingredients:

- 5 tsp walnut kernels
- 1 cup plums (pitted)
- 6 tsp butter
- 1 egg
- 2 tsp sugar
- 30 ml milk
- 60 grams flour
- 4 tsp apricot jam
- Salt and baking powder, as needed

Directions:

1. Roughly cut the nuts. Wash the plums, stone them if necessary and cut them into small pieces.
2. Mix egg and milk. Add flour, ½ tsp baking powder and a pinch of salt. Mix in the nuts and plums. Put 4–6 paper sleeves into each other. Preheat the oven.
3. Place the mixture in the Papier-mâché tablets. The cuffs should be ⅝ full.
4. Place the cuffs on a baking sheet and bake for 40 minutes. Let the muffins cool down and then brush with the jam.

Nutrition: Low GL Calorie: 250; Fat: 9 g; Carbohydrates: 28 g; Protein: 7 g; Fiber: 6 g; Sugar: 1 g; Cholesterol: 79 mg; Sodium: 143 mg; Potassium: 312 mg

33. Easy Buckwheat Crêpes

Preparation Time: 5 minutes
Cooking Time: 15 minutes
Cooking Level: Easy
Servings: 2
Ingredients:

- 1 cup buckwheat flour
- 1 ¾ cups milk
- ⅛ tsp kosher salt
- 1 tbsp extra-virgin olive oil
- ½ tbsp ground flaxseed (optional)

Directions:

1. Combine the buckwheat flour, milk, salt, extra-virgin olive oil and flaxseed (if using) in a bowl, and whisk thoroughly, or in a blender and pulse until well combined.
2. Heat a nonstick medium skillet over medium heat. Once it's hot, add a ¼ cup of batter to the skillet, spreading it out evenly. Cook until bubbles appear and the edges crisp like a pancake, 1 to 3 minutes, then flip and cook for another 2 minutes.
3. Layer parchment paper or tea towels between the crêpes to keep them from sticking to one another while also keeping them warm until you're ready to eat.
4. Serve with the desired fillings.

Nutrition: Low GL Calorie: 130; Fat: 5 g; Carbohydrates: 18 g; Protein: 5 g; Fiber: 2 g; Sugar: 2 g; Cholesterol: 89 mg; Sodium: 96 mg; Potassium: 347 mg

34. Shakshuka

Preparation Time: 5 minutes
Cooking Time: 25 minutes
Cooking Level: Easy
Servings: 2
Ingredients:

- 2 tbsp extra-virgin olive oil
- 1 onion, diced
- 2 tbsp tomato paste
- 2 red bell peppers, diced
- 2 tbsp Harissa (optional)
- 4 garlic cloves, minced
- 2 tsp ground cumin
- ½ tsp ground coriander (optional)
- 1 tsp smoked paprika
- 2 (14-oz) cans diced tomatoes
- 4 large eggs
- ½ cup plain Greek yogurt
- Bread, for dipping (optional)

Directions:

1. Heat olive oil. When it starts to shimmer, add onion and cook until translucent, about 3 minutes.
2. Add tomato paste, peppers, harissa (if using), garlic, cumin, coriander (if using), paprika and tomatoes. Bring to a simmer and cook for 10 to 15 minutes, until the peppers are cooked and the sauce is thick. Adjust the seasoning as desired.
3. Make four wells in the mixture with the back of a large spoon and gently break one egg into each well. Cover the saucepan and simmer gently until the egg whites are set but the yolks are still runny; 5 to 8 minutes.
4. Remove from heat and spoon the tomato mixture and one cooked egg into each of the four bowls. Top with the Greek yogurt and serve with bread (if using).

Nutrition: Low GL Calorie: 259; Fat: 14 g; Carbohydrates: 22 g; Protein: 12 g; Fiber: 6 g; Sugar: 1 g; Cholesterol: 101 mg; Sodium: 88 mg; Potassium: 312 mg

35. Eggplant Breakfast Sandwich

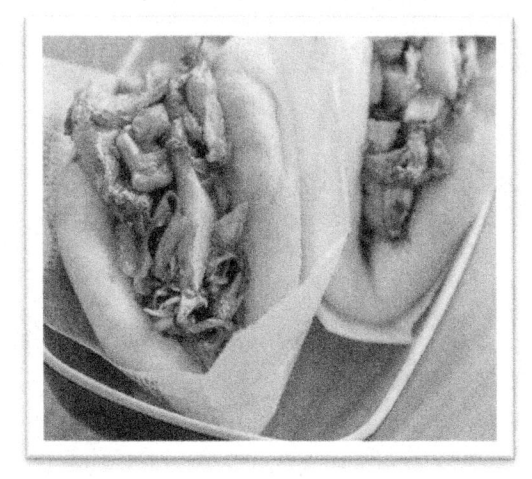

Preparation Time: 5 minutes
Cooking Time: 20 minutes
Cooking Level: Easy
Servings: 2
Ingredients:

- 2 tbsp extra-virgin olive oil, divided
- 1 eggplant, cut into 8 (½-inch-thick) rounds
- ¼ tsp kosher salt
- ¼ tsp Freshly ground black pepper, to taste
- 4 large eggs
- 1 garlic clove, minced
- 4 cups fresh baby spinach
- Hot sauce or Harissa (optional)

Directions:

1. Heat 1 tbsp of extra-virgin olive oil in a large skillet over medium heat. Add eggplant in a single layer and cook until tender and browned on both sides; 4 to 5 minutes per side. Transfer the eggplant from the skillet to a plate and season it with salt and pepper. Wipe out the skillet and set it aside.
2. Meanwhile, place a large saucepan filled three-quarters full with water over medium-high heat and bring it to a simmer. Carefully break the eggs into small, individual bowls and pour slowly into a fine-mesh strainer over another bowl. Allow the excess white to drain, then lower the strainer into the water. Tilt the egg out into the water. Repeat with the remaining eggs. Swirl the water occasionally as the eggs cook and whites set, about 4 minutes. Remove the eggs with a slotted spoon, transfer to a paper towel, and drain them.
3. Heat the remaining 1 tbsp of extra-virgin olive oil over medium heat in the large skillet and add garlic and spinach.
4. Place one eggplant round on each of four plates and evenly divide the spinach among the rounds. Top the spinach with a poached egg on each sandwich and place the remaining eggplant round on the egg. Serve with hot sauce or harissa (if using).

Nutrition: Low GL Calorie: 362; Fat: 25 g; Carbohydrates: 21 g; Protein: 17 g; Fiber: 10 g; Sugar: 1 g; Cholesterol: 89 mg, Sodium: 138 mg; Potassium: 298 mg

36. Perfect Egg Scramble with Simple Salad

Preparation Time: 17 minutes
Cooking Time: 5 minutes
Cooking Level: Easy
Servings: 2
Ingredients:

- 8 large eggs
- 3 tbsp milk
- Kosher salt
- 6 cups arugula
- 1 tbsp extra-virgin olive oil
- 2 tbsp minced red onion
- 1 bunch radishes, thinly sliced
- 2 tbsp unsalted butter

Directions:

1. Whisk the milk and eggs with a pinch of salt until blended. Set aside for 15 minutes.
2. Mix arugula with the extra-virgin olive oil, red onion, radishes and a pinch of salt
3. Melt butter in a medium nonstick skillet over medium-high heat. Add the eggs and cook by scraping the bottom very slowly, then folding. Repeat until the eggs have formed solid, moist curds. Portion the scrambled eggs evenly among the plates and serve immediately.

Nutrition: Low GL Calorie: 262; Fat: 20 g; Carbohydrates: 6 g; Protein: 14 g; Fiber: 2 g; Sugar: 1 g; Cholesterol: 79 mg; Sodium: 128 mg; Potassium: 298 mg

37. Blueberry-Chia Smoothie

Preparation Time: 5 minutes
Cooking Time: 0 minutes
Cooking Level: Easy
Servings: 2
Ingredients:

- 2 cups frozen blueberries
- ½ medium frozen banana
- 2 tbsp peanut butter
- 2 tbsp chia seeds
- 12 oz unsweetened soy milk, plus extra if needed

Directions:

1. Combine the blueberries, banana, peanut butter, chia seeds and soy milk in a blender, and blend on high speed until smooth.
2. Serve immediately. If it's too thick, add more soy milk or water by the tablespoonful until you've reached the desired consistency.

Nutrition: Low GL Calorie: 360; Fat: 16 g; Carbohydrates: 46 g; Protein: 12 g; Fiber: 14 g; Sugar: 1 g; Cholesterol: 89 mg; Sodium: 333 mg; Potassium: 312 mg

CHAPTER 5: VEGETABLE RECIPES

38. Spinach, Artichoke, and Goat Cheese Bake

Preparation Time: 10 minutes
Cooking Time: 35 minutes
Cooking Level: Moderate
Servings: 2
Ingredients:

- Nonstick cooking spray
- 1 (10-oz) package frozen spinach,
- 1 (14-oz) can artichoke hearts, drained
- ¼ cup finely chopped red bell pepper
- 2 garlic cloves, minced
- 8 eggs, lightly beaten
- ¼ cup unsweetened plain almond milk
- ½ tsp salt
- ½ tsp Freshly ground black pepper to taste
- ½ cup crumbled goat cheese

Directions:

1. Preheat the oven to 375°F. Spray a baking dish with cooking spray.
2. Combine the spinach, artichoke hearts, bell pepper, garlic, eggs, almond milk, salt and pepper. Stir well to combine.
3. Transfer the mixture to the baking dish. Sprinkle with the goat cheese.
4. Bake eggs until set, about 35 minutes. Serve warm.

Option tip: Spice things up for breakfast by adding a scant tsp of red pepper flakes to this dish.

Nutrition: Low GL Calorie: 104; Fat: 5 g; Carbohydrates: 6 g; Protein: 9 g; Fiber: 2 g; Sugars: 1 g; Cholesterol: 89 mg; Sodium: 488 mg; Potassium: 234 mg

39. Roasted Broccoli with Sesame Seeds

Preparation Time: 15 minutes
Cooking Time: 4 minutes
Cooking Level: Easy
Servings: 2

Ingredients

- 1 pound broccoli florets
- 2 tbsp sesame oil
- ½ tsp shallot powder
- ½ tsp porcini powder
- 1 tsp garlic powder
- Salt and pepper, to taste
- ½ tsp cumin powder
- ¼ tsp paprika
- 2 tbsp sesame seeds

Directions:

1. Preheat the fryer to 400°F.
2. Blanch the broccoli in salted boiling water until al dente, about 3 to 4 minutes. Drain well and transfer to the lightly greased Air Fryer basket.
3. Add sesame oil, shallot powder, porcini powder, garlic powder, salt, black pepper, cumin powder, paprika and sesame seeds.
4. Cook for 6 minutes,

Nutrition: Low GL Calorie 320; Fat: 16 g; Carbohydrates: 30 g; Protein: 13 g; Fiber: 6 g; Sugar: 1 g; Cholesterol: 89 mg; Sodium: 143 mg; Potassium: 365 mg

40. Corn on the Cob with Herb Butter

Preparation Time: 15 minutes
Cooking Time: 12 minutes
Cooking Level: Easy
Servings: 2

Ingredients

- 2 ears fresh corn
- 2 tbsp butter, room temperature
- 1 tsp granulated garlic
- ½ tsp fresh ginger, grated
- Salt and pepper, to taste
- 1 tbsp fresh rosemary, chopped
- 1 tbsp fresh basil, chopped
- 2 tbsp fresh chives, roughly chopped

Directions:

1. Spritz the corn with cooking spray. Cook at 395°F for 6 minutes, turning them over halfway through the cooking time.
2. Mix butter with granulated garlic, ginger, salt, black pepper, rosemary and basil.
3. Spread the butter mixture all over the corn on the cob. Cook in the preheated fryer for an additional 2 minutes. Bon appétit!

Nutrition: Low GL Calorie: 331; Fat: 4 g; Carb: 4.6 g; Protein: 29 g; Fiber: 7 g; Sugars: 7 g; Cholesterol: 100 mg; Sodium: 403 mg; Potassium: 298 mg

41. Rainbow Vegetable Fritters

Preparation Time: 20 minutes
Cooking Time: 12 minutes
Cooking Level: Easy
Servings: 2

Ingredients

- 1 zucchini, grated and squeezed
- 1 cup corn kernels
- ½ cup canned green peas
- 4 tbsp all-purpose flour
- 2 tbsp fresh shallots, minced
- 1 tsp fresh garlic, minced
- 1 tbsp peanut oil
- Salt and pepper, to taste
- 1 tsp cayenne pepper

Directions:

1. Thoroughly combine all the ingredients until everything is well incorporated.
2. Shape the mixture into patties. Spray the fryer basket with oil
3. Cook in the preheated fryer at 365°F for 6 minutes on each side
4. Serve immediately and enjoy!

Nutrition: Low GL Calories: 15; Fat: 2 g; Carbs: 1 g; Protein: 2 g; Fiber: 7 g; Sugars: 4 g; Cholesterol: 92 mg; Sodium: 373 mg; Potassium: 333 mg

42. Roasted Veggies with Yogurt-Tahini Sauce

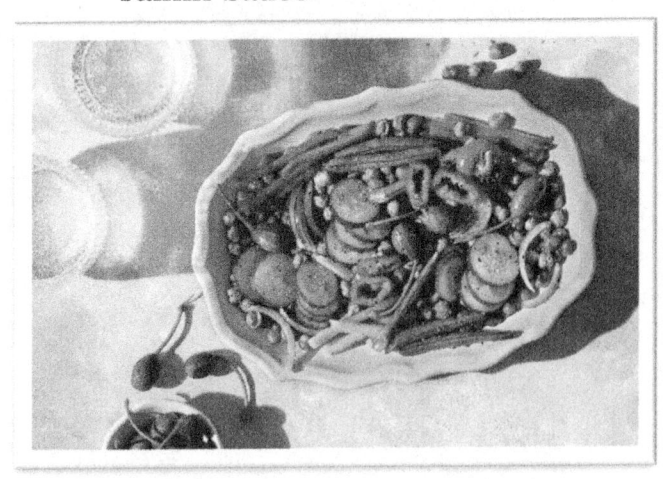

Preparation Time: 20 minutes
Cooking Time: 10 minutes
Cooking Level: Easy
Servings: 2
Ingredients:

- 1 pound Brussels sprouts
- 1 pound button mushrooms
- 2 tbsp olive oil
- ½ tsp white pepper
- ½ tsp dried dill weed
- ½ tsp cayenne pepper
- ½ tsp celery seeds
- ½ tsp mustard seeds
- Salt, to taste

Yogurt Tahini Sauce:

- 1 cup plain yogurt
- 2 heaping tbsp tahini paste
- 1 tbsp lemon juice
- 1 tbsp extra-virgin olive oil
- ½ tsp Aleppo pepper, minced

Directions:

1. Toss the Brussels sprouts and mushrooms with olive oil and spices. Preheat your Air Fryer to 380°F.
2. Add the Brussels sprouts to the cooking basket and cook for 10 minutes.
3. Add mushrooms; turn the temperature to 390°F and cook for 6 minutes more.
4. Make the sauce while cooking the vegetables. Serve warm vegetables with the sauce on the side. Bon appétit!

Nutrition: Low GL Calorie: 266; Fat: 10 g; Carb: 4.7 g; Protein: 5 g; Fiber: 11 g; Sugars: 7 g; Cholesterol: 82 mg; Sodium: 403 mg; Potassium: 323 mg

43. Avocado-Tofu Scramble with Roasted Potatoes

Preparation Time: 5 minutes
Cooking Time: 25 minutes
Cooking Level: Easy
Servings: 2
Ingredients

- 1 ½ pounds small potatoes, cut into bite-size pieces
- 4 tbsp plant-based oil (safflower, olive, or grape seed), divided
- Kosher salt
- Freshly ground black pepper, to taste
- 1 oz water
- 2 tsp ground cumin
- 2 tsp turmeric
- ¼ tsp paprika
- 1 yellow onion, finely chopped
- 1 bell pepper, finely chopped
- 3 cups kale, torn into bite-size pieces
- 3 oz firm tofu, drained and crumbled
- 1 avocado, diced, for garnish

Directions:

1. Preheat the oven to 425°F. Line a baking sheet with parchment paper. Combine the potatoes with 2 tbsp of oil and a pinch each of salt and pepper to taste on the baking sheet, and then toss to coat. Roast for 20 to 25 minutes or until tender and golden brown.
2. Meanwhile, stir together the water, cumin, turmeric and paprika until well mixed to make the sauce. Set aside. Heat the remaining oil. Add bell pepper and onion; sauté for 3 to 5 minutes. Season with salt and pepper. Add kale, cover, and allow the steam to cook the kale for about 2 minutes.
3. Remove the lid and, using a spatula, push the vegetables to one side of the skillet and place the tofu and sauce on the empty side. Stir tofu and vegetables.
4. Serve tofu scramble with the roasted potatoes on the side and garnished with avocado.

Nutrition: Low GL Calorie: 256; Fat: 10 g; Carbohydrates: 36 g; Protein: 7 g; Fiber: 7 g; Sugar: 4 g; Cholesterol: 95 mg; Sodium: 114 mg; Potassium: 278 mg

44. Easy Sweet Potato Hash Browns

Preparation Time: 10 minutes
Cooking Time: 45 minutes
Cooking Level: Moderate
Servings: 2
Ingredients

- 1 pound sweet potatoes, peeled and grated
- 2 eggs, whisked
- ¼ cup scallions, chopped
- 1 tsp fresh garlic, minced
- Salt and pepper, to taste
- ¼ tsp ground allspice
- ½ tsp cinnamon
- 1 tbsp peanut oil

Directions:

1. Allow the sweet potatoes to soak for 25 minutes in cold water. Drain the water; dry the sweet potatoes with a kitchen towel.
2. Add the remaining ingredients
3. Preheat the fryer to 395°F and cook for 20 minutes. Shake the basket once or twice. Serve with ketchup.

Nutrition: Low GL Calorie: 18; Fat: 2 g; Carbs: 7 g; Protein: 2 g; Fiber: 7 g; Sugars: 2 g; Cholesterol: 77 mg; Sodium: 343 mg; Potassium: 287 mg

45. Skinny Pumpkin Chips

Preparation Time: 10 minutes
Cooking Time: 13 minutes
Cooking Level: Easy
Servings: 2
Ingredients

- 1 pound pumpkin, cut into sticks
- 1 tbsp coconut oil
- ½ tsp rosemary
- ½ tsp basil
- Salt and ground black pepper, to taste

Directions:

1. Preheat the fryer to 395°F. Brush pumpkin sticks with coconut oil; add spices
2. Cook for 13 minutes.

Nutrition: Low GL Calories: 247; Fat: 21 g; Carbs: 8 g; Protein: 3 g; Fiber: 9 g; Sugars: 2 g; Cholesterol: 101 mg; Sodium: 227 mg; Potassium: 297 mg

46. Cheese Stuffed Roasted Peppers

Preparation Time: 10 minutes
Cooking Time: 15 minutes
Cooking Level: Easy
Servings: 2
Ingredients

- 2 red bell peppers, tops and seeds removed
- 2 yellow bell peppers, tops and seeds removed
- Salt and pepper, to taste
- 1 cup cream cheese
- 4 tbsp mayonnaise
- 2 pickles, chopped

Directions:

1. Arrange the peppers in the lightly greased cooking basket. Preheat the fryer to 400°F and cook for 15 minutes, turning them over halfway through the cooking time.
2. Season with salt and pepper.
3. Combine the cream cheese with the mayonnaise and chopped pickles. Stuff the pepper with the cream cheese mixture and serve. Enjoy!

Nutrition: Low GL Calorie: 347; Fat: 32 g; Carbs: 8 g; Protein: 8 g; Fiber: 11 g; Sugars: 7 g; Cholesterol: 102 mg; Sodium: 348 mg; Potassium: 323 mg

47. Sweet Potato Chips with Greek Yogurt Dip

Preparation Time: 5 minutes
Cooking Time: 30 minutes
Cooking Level: Moderate
Servings: 2
Ingredients

- 4 sweet potatoes, sliced
- 2 tbsp olive oil
- Salt and pepper, to taste
- 1 tsp paprika

Dipping Sauce:

- ½ cup Greek-style yogurt
- 1 clove garlic, minced
- 1 tbsp fresh chives, chopped

Directions:

1. Soak the sweet potato slices in icy cold water for 20 to 30 minutes. Drain the sweet potatoes and pat them dry with kitchen towels.
2. Combine the sweet potato with olive oil, salt, black pepper and paprika.
3. Place in the lightly greased cooking basket. Cook in the preheated fryer at 360°F for 14 minutes.
4. Meanwhile, make the sauce by whisking the remaining ingredients. Serve sweet potato chips with the sauce for dipping and enjoy!

Nutrition: Low GL Calorie: 310; Fat: 34 g; Carbs: 14 g; Protein: 3 g; Fiber: 8 g; Sugars: 7 g; Cholesterol: 89 mg; Sodium: 386 mg; Potassium: 312 mg

48. Greek-Style Roasted Tomatoes with Feta

Preparation Time: 10 minutes
Cooking Time: 12 minutes
Cooking Level: Easy
Servings: 2
Ingredients

- 3 medium-sized tomatoes, cut into four slices, pat dry
- 1 tsp dried basil
- 1 tsp dried oregano
- ¼ tsp red pepper flakes, crushed
- ½ tsp sea salt
- 3 slices Feta cheese

Directions:

1. Spritz the tomatoes with cooking oil and transfer them to the Air Fryer basket. Sprinkle with seasonings.
2. Cook at 350°F for approximately 8 minutes turning them over halfway through the cooking time.
3. Top with the cheese and cook an additional 4 minutes. Bon appétit!

Nutrition: Low GL Calorie: 130; Fat: 5 g; Carbohydrates: 18 g; Protein: 5 g; Fiber: 2 g; Sugar: 2 g; Cholesterol: 101 mg; Sodium: 89 mg; Potassium: 282 mg

49. Sweet Corn Fritters with Avocado

Preparation Time: 10 minutes
Cooking Time: 15 minutes
Cooking Level: Easy
Servings: 2
Ingredients

- 2 cups sweet corn kernels

- 1 small-sized onion, chopped
- 1 garlic clove, minced
- 2 eggs, whisked
- 1 tsp baking powder
- 2 tbsp fresh cilantro, chopped
- Salt and pepper, to taste
- 1 avocado, peeled, pitted and diced
- 2 tbsp sweet chili sauce

Directions:
1. Thoroughly combine the corn, onion, garlic, eggs, baking powder, cilantro, salt and black pepper.
2. Shape the corn mixture into 6 patties and transfer them to the lightly greased Air Fryer basket.
3. Cook in the preheated Air Fry at 370°F for 8 minutes; turn them over and cook for 7 minutes longer.
4. Serve fritters with avocado and chili sauce.

Nutrition: Low GL Calories: 110; Fat: 5 g; Carbohydrates: 12 g; Protein: 7 g; Fiber: 2 g; Sugar: 2 g; Cholesterol: 85 mg; Sodium: 76 mg; Potassium: 372 mg

50. Greek-Style Vegetable Bake

Preparation Time: 15 minutes
Cooking Time: 20 minutes
Cooking Level: Easy
Servings: 2
Ingredients

- 1 eggplant, peeled and sliced
- 2 bell peppers, seeded and sliced
- 1 red onion, sliced
- 1 tsp fresh garlic, minced
- 4 tbsp olive oil
- 1 tsp mustard
- 1 tsp dried oregano
- 1 tsp smoked paprika
- Salt and ground black pepper, to taste
- 1 tomato, sliced
- 6 oz halloumi cheese, sliced lengthways

Directions:
1. Preheat the fryer to 370°F. Spritz a baking pan with nonstick cooking spray.
2. Place eggplant, peppers, onion and garlic on the bottom of the baking pan. Add olive oil, mustard and spices. Transfer to the cooking basket and cook for 14 minutes.
3. Top with the tomatoes and cheese; increase the temperature to 390°F and cook for 5 minutes more until bubbling. Cool before serving.
4. Bon appétit!

Nutrition: Low GL Calories: 130; Fat: 5 g; Carbohydrates: 18 g; Protein: 5 g; Fiber: 2 g; Sugar: 2 g; Cholesterol: 89 mg; Sodium: 89 mg; Potassium: 312 mg

51. Pureed Peas

Preparation Time: 10 minutes
Cooking Time: 15 minutes
Cooking Level: Easy
Servings: 2
Ingredients:

- ¼ Cup Heavy Cream
- 1 Cup Peas, Frozen
- 1 tbsp Butter
- Sea Salt and Black Pepper, to Taste

Directions:
1. Add your peas into a pot of boiling water. Boil for 5 minutes before draining the water away.
2. Transfer them to a food processor, processing until smooth.

Nutrition: Low GL Calories: 106; Fat: 9 g;; Protein: 2 g; Fiber: 9 g; Sugar: 2 g; Cholesterol: 92 mg; Sodium: 258 mg; Potassium: 287 mg

52. Tomato Toasts

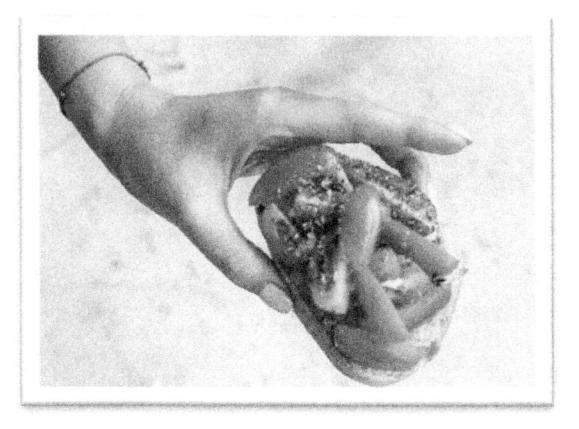

Preparation Time: 5 minutes
Cooking Time: 5 minutes
Cooking Level: Easy
Servings: 2
Ingredients:

- 4 slices sprouted bread toast
- 2 tomatoes, sliced
- 1 avocado, mashed
- 1 tsp olive oil

- 1 pinch salt
- ¾ tsp ground black pepper

Directions:
1. Blend the olive oil, mashed avocado, salt and ground black pepper.
2. When the mixture is homogenous, spread it over the sprouted bread.
3. Then place the sliced tomatoes over the toast.
4. Enjoy!

Nutrition: Low GL Calories: 125; Fat: 11.1 g; Carbohydrates: 7.0 g; Protein: 1.5 g; Fiber: 8 g; Sugar: 6 g; Cholesterol: 109 mg; Sodium: 120 mg; Potassium: 289 mg

53. Collard Greens

Preparation Time: 10 minutes
Cooking Time: 10 minutes
Cooking Level: Easy
Servings: 2
Ingredients:

- 4 Cups Collard Greens
- 2 tbsp Butter
- 2 tsp Cayenne Pepper
- 1 Clove Garlic, Minced
- 1 tsp Sea Salt, Fine

Directions:
1. Start by rinsing your collard greens, and pat them dry using a paper towel. Stem them, and then cut them into small strips.
2. Melt your butter in a skillet, adding all the ingredients. Sauté until wilted, which will take up to 10 minutes.

Nutrition: Low GL Calories: 64; Fat: 6 g; Carbs: 1 g; Protein: 1 g; Fiber: 4 g; Sugar: 2 g; Cholesterol: 89 mg; Sodium: 158 mg; Potassium: 312 mg

54. Keto "hummus"

Preparation Time: 10 minutes
Cooking Time: 15 minutes
Cooking Level: Easy
Servings: 2
Ingredients:

- 3 tbsp Olive Oil
- 1 tsp Smoked Paprika
- 2 Cloves Garlic
- 3 tbsp Lemon Juice, Fresh
- 3 Cups Cauliflower, Chopped into Florets
- 4 tbsp tahini
- 1 Zucchini, Seeded and Chopped
- ¼ Cup Heavy Cream
- 1 tbsp Butter
- Sea Salt and Black Pepper, to Taste

Directions:
1. Start by heating your butter up, and then add in your cauliflower florets. Sauté until they turn tender.
2. Blend the cauliflower and add in the remaining ingredients. Blend for 2 minutes or until creamy and smooth. If your mixture becomes too thick, add a little water until you reach your desired consistency.
3. Refrigerate for a half hour before serving chilled.

Nutrition: Low GL Calories: 265; Fat: 25 g; Carbs: 6 g; Protein: 5 g; Fiber: 9 g; Sugar: 2 g; Cholesterol: 92 mg; Sodium: 258 mg; Potassium: 297 mg

55. Sweet Potato Fritters

Preparation Time: 10 minutes
Cooking Time: 20 minutes
Cooking Level: Easy
Servings: 2
Ingredients:

- ¼ Cup Flaxseed Meal
- 1 Egg
- ½ tsp Garlic Powder
- ¼ tsp Cumin
- ¼ Cup Almonds, Chopped Fine
- 1 Sweet Potato, Small and Peeled
- ¼ tsp Turmeric
- 2 tbsp Butter
- Sea Salt and Black Pepper, to Taste

Directions:
1. Shred your sweet potato using a food processor or a grater.
2. **Take** out a bowl and whisk your turmeric, salt, a tbsp of butter and egg together.
3. Mix in the shredded sweet potato, flaxseed meal and almonds. Season with salt and pepper, and mix again.
4. Place a frying pan over medium heat, melting your remaining butter.
5. When your butter is hot, drop in the sweet potato mixture using a large spoon. Fry for 5 minutes, flip, and then fry for 3 more minutes. Continue until you're out of batter. Serve warm.

Nutrition: Low GL Calories: 196; Fat: 15 g; Carbs: 6 g; Protein: 6 g; Net Fiber: 9 g; Sugar: 2 g; Cholesterol: 100 mg; Sodium: 318 mg; Potassium: 302 mg

56. Red Cabbage Mix

Preparation Time: 10 minutes
Cooking Time: 5 minutes
Cooking Level: Easy
Servings: 2
Ingredients

- 4 tbsp coconut oil
- 1 tsp butter
- 2 garlic cloves
- 6 cups red cabbage, shredded
- Salt and black pepper, to taste
- ⅜ cup water

Directions:

1. Turn on the sauté mode of the instant pot. Add coconut oil and butter to the instant pot.
2. Heat butter to let it melt. Add salt, pepper and garlic cloves.
3. Cook until aroma comes. Add cabbage and pour water.
4. Once the timer beeps, release the steam naturally. Serve and enjoy.

Nutrition: Low GL Calories: 609; Fat: 29.66 g; Carbohydrates: 4.39 g; Protein: 81.01 g; Fiber: 7 g; Sugar: 2 g; Cholesterol: 72 mg; Sodium: 198 mg; Potassium: 292 mg

57. Beets Dijon

Preparation Time: 10 minutes
Cooking Time: 14 minutes
Cooking Level: Easy
Servings: 2
Ingredients

- 1 pound beets, peeled, cubed (½-inch)
- ⅜ cup finely chopped onion
- ⅜ cup sour cream
- 2 tbsp Dijon mustard
- 2–3 tsp lemon juice
- Salt and white pepper, to taste

Directions:

1. Combine beets, onions, Dijon mustard, lemon juice, salt and black pepper in a bowl, and set aside. Pour water into the instant pot and set trivet inside the pot.
2. Place a heatproof bowl, having beets on a trivet, and lock the lid. Set timer to 12 minutes. Once the timer beeps, release the steam quickly.
3. Remove the beets bowl from the instant pot. Drain water from the pot and turn on sauté mode.
4. Transfer the beet to the pot and add sour cream. Cook for 2 minutes and then serve.

Nutrition: Low GL Calories: 297; Fat: 13.24 g; Carbohydrates: 38.71 g; Protein: 9.24 g; Fiber: 2.9 g; Sugar: 3 g; Cholesterol: 62 mg; Sodium: 345.32 mg; Potassium: 288 mg

58. Cilantro Lime Chicken Salad

Preparation Time: 10 minutes
Cooking Time: 5 minutes
Cooking Level: Easy
Servings: 2
Ingredients:

- 1 ½ cups cooked chicken, shredded
- 2 tbsp fresh lime juice
- 2 tbsp fresh cilantro, chopped
- 2 tbsp green onion, sliced
- 1 tsp chili powder
- Salt and pepper, to taste

Directions:

1. Add all the ingredients into the medium bowl and mix well. Season with pepper and salt.

Nutrition: Low GL Calorie: 113; Fat: 2 g; Carbohydrates: 1 g; Protein: 20 g; Fiber: 7 g; Sugar: 0.5 g; Cholesterol: 89 mg; Sodium: 255 mg; Potassium: 312 mg

59. Fennel and Trout Parcels

Preparation Time: 10 minutes
Cooking Time: 15 minutes
Cooking Level: Easy
Servings: 2
Ingredients:

- ½ pound (227 g) deboned trout, butterflied
- Salt and black pepper, to season

- 3 tbsp olive oil plus extra for tossing
- 4 sprigs rosemary
- 4 sprigs thyme
- 4 butter cubes
- 1 cup thinly sliced fennel
- 1 medium red onion, sliced
- 8 lemon slices
- 3 tsp capers, to garnish

Directions:
1. Preheat the oven to 400°F (205°C). Cut out a parchment paper wide enough for each trout. In a bowl, toss the fennel and onion with a little bit of olive oil and share into the middle parts of the paper.
2. Place fish on each veggie mound, top with a drizzle of olive oil each, a pinch of salt and black pepper, a sprig of rosemary and thyme, and 1 cube of butter. Also, lay the lemon slices on the fish. Wrap and close the fish packets securely, and place them on a baking sheet. Bake for 15 minutes, and remove once ready. Plate them, garnish the fish with capers, and serve with a squash mash.

Nutrition: Low GL Calories: 235; Fat: 9.1 g; Carbs: 3.7 g; Protein: 17.1 g; Fiber: 1.0 g; Sugar: 2.7 g; Cholesterol: 89 mg; Sodium: 178 mg; Potassium: 310 mg

60. Slow "Roasted" Tomatoes

Preparation Time: 5 minutes
Cooking Time: 1 hour 15 minutes
Cooking Level: Difficult
Servings: 2
Ingredients:

- ½ tbsp balsamic vinegar
- 1 large firm under-ripe tomato, halved crosswise
- 1 garlic clove, minced
- 1 tsp olive oil
- ½ tsp dried basil, crushed
- ½ cup breadcrumbs, coarse, soft whole-wheat
- Dried rosemary, crushed
- 1 tbsp Parmesan cheese, grated
- Salt
- ¼ tsp dried oregano, crushed
- Chopped fresh basil, optional

Directions:
1. Using cooking spray, coat the unheated slow cooker lightly. Then add tomatoes to the bottom of the slow cooker, and cut side up.
2. In a bowl, combine vinegar together with garlic, oil, rosemary, dried basil and salt, and then spoon the mixture over the tomatoes in the slow cooker evenly. Close the lid and cook for either 2 hours on low, or 1 hour on high.
3. Over medium heat, preheat a skillet, and then add breadcrumbs. Cook as you stir constantly until lightly browned, for about 2–3 minutes. Remove from heat when done and then stir parmesan.
4. When through, remove tomatoes from the slow cooker and put them on the serving plates, and then drizzle over tomatoes with the cooking liquid. Then sprinkle with the breadcrumb mixture and let rest for 10 minutes in order to absorb the flavors. Garnish with basil if need be and then serve. Enjoy!

Nutrition: Calorie: Low GL Calories: 96; Fat: 4 g; Carbohydrates: 13 g; Protein: 3 g; Fiber: 9 g; Sugar: 2 g; Cholesterol: 64 mg; Sodium: 254.78 mg; Potassium: 234.12 mg

61. Brussels Sprout Hash and Eggs

Preparation Time: 15 minutes
Cooking Time: 15 minutes
Cooking Level: Easy
Servings: 2
Ingredients:

- 3 tsp extra-virgin olive oil, divided
- 1 pound Brussels sprouts, sliced
- 2 garlic cloves, thinly sliced
- ¼ tsp salt
- Juice 1 lemon
- 4 eggs

Directions:
1. In a large skillet, heat 1 ½ tsp of oil over medium heat. Add Brussels sprouts and toss. Cook, stirring regularly, for 6 to 8 minutes until browned and softened. Add garlic and continue to cook until fragrant, about 1 minute. Season with salt and lemon juice. Transfer to a serving dish.
2. Heat the remaining 1 ½ tsp of oil over medium-high heat in the same pan. Crack the eggs into the pan. Fry for 2 to 4 minutes, flip, and continue cooking to desired doneness. Serve over the bed of hash.

Make-ahead tip: Brussels sprouts, like other brassica vegetables, are easy to prep in advance and hold up well both raw and cooked. Prep the Brussels sprouts up to 5 days in advance by slicing them when you have a free moment.

Nutrition: Low GL Calories: 158; Fat: 9 g; Carbohydrates: 12 g; Protein: 10 g; Fiber: 4 g; Sugars: 4 g; Cholesterol: 95 mg; Sodium: 234 mg; Potassium: 278 mg

62. Parsley-Lemon Salmon

Preparation Time: 10 minutes
Cooking Time: 20 minutes
Cooking Level: Easy
Servings: 2
Ingredients:

- 4 salmon fillets
- ½ cup heavy cream
- 1 tbsp mayonnaise
- ½ tbsp parsley, chopped
- ½ lemon, zested and juiced
- Salt and black pepper, to season

- 1 tbsp Parmesan cheese, grated

Directions:
1. In a bowl, mix heavy cream, parsley, mayonnaise, lemon zest, lemon juice, salt and pepper, and set aside. Season fish with salt and black pepper, drizzle lemon juice on both sides of the fish and arrange them on a parchment paper-lined baking sheet. Spread the parsley mixture and sprinkle with parmesan cheese. Bake for 15 minutes at 400°F (205°C). Great served with steamed broccoli.

Nutrition: Low GL Calories: 555; Fat: 30.3 g; Carbs: 2.2 g; Protein: 56.1 g; Fiber: 0.1 g; Sugar: 2.1 g; Cholesterol: 84 mg; Sodium: 167 mg; Potassium: 237 mg

63. Greek Tuna Salad

Preparation Time: 10 minutes
Cooking Time: 0 minutes
Cooking Level: Easy
Servings: 2
Ingredients:

- 2 cans tuna
- ¼ small red onion, finely chopped
- 1 celery stalks, finely chopped
- ½ avocado, chopped
- 1 tbsp chopped fresh parsley
- 1 cup Greek yogurt
- 2 tbsp butter
- 2 tsp Dijon Mustard
- ½ tbsp vinegar
- Salt and black pepper, to taste

Directions:
1. The ingredients listed must be added to a salad bowl and mixed until well combined.
2. Serve afterward.

Nutrition: Low GL Calories: 376; Fat: 10.4 g; Carbohydrates: 3.9 g; Protein: 18.4 g; Fiber: 11.9 g; Sugar: 2 g; Cholesterol: 89 mg; Sodium: 173 mg; Potassium: 312 mg

64. Glazed Carrots and Cauliflower

Preparation Time: 10 minutes
Cooking Time: 5 minutes
Cooking Level: Easy
Servings: 2
Ingredients:

- ⅜ pound baby carrot
- 1 cauliflower head, small and chopped
- ¾ cup lime juice
- 3 tbsp butter/olive oil
- ⅜ cup stevia
- ¼ tsp ground cinnamon
- Salt and black pepper, to taste

Directions:
1. Combine all the ingredients in the instant pot.
2. When the timer beeps, release the steam quickly. Open the instant pot lid. Stir and serve.

Nutrition: Low GL Calories: 122; Fat: 4.91 g; Carbohydrates: 23.3 g; Protein: 2.51 g; Fiber: 4.8 g; Sugar: 2 g; Cholesterol: 58 mg; Sodium: 132.43 mg; Potassium: 211 mg

65. Broth-Braised Cabbage

Preparation Time: 10 minutes
Cooking Time: 5 minutes
Cooking Level: Easy
Servings: 2
Ingredients:

- 1 head of cabbage, sliced
- 1 small onion
- 2 garlic cloves, minced
- ⅜ tsp star anise seeds
- ¼ cup vegetable broth
- 2 slices diced bacon
- 2 tsp olive oil
- Salt and black pepper, to taste

Directions:
1. Turn on the sauté mode of the instant pot. Add oil and heat it.
2. Then add bacon and cook until crisp. Then add small onions and garlic cloves, and cook until aroma comes.
3. Add salt, pepper and anise seed. At the end, add cabbage and pour the broth.
4. Cook on high for 3 minutes. Then quickly release the steam. Serve and enjoy.

Nutrition: Low GL Calories: 135; Fat: 7.73 g; Carbohydrates: 14.81 g; Protein: 4.2 g; Fiber: 4.6 g; Sugar: 2 g; Cholesterol: 62 mg; Sodium: 382.78 mg; Potassium: 246 mg

66. Feta Brussels sprouts and Scrambled Eggs

Preparation Time: 5 minutes
Cooking Time: 15 minutes
Cooking Level: Easy
Servings: 2

Ingredients:

- 4 slices low-Cholesterol: 89 mg; Sodium: turkey bacon
- 20 Brussels sprouts, halved lengthwise
- 8 large eggs, whisked
- ¼ cup crumbled feta cheese, for garnish

From the Cupboard:

- Avocado oil cooking spray

Directions:

1. Heat a skillet until hot. Coat the skillet with cooking spray. Fry the bacon slices for about 8 minutes until evenly crisp, flipping occasionally.
2. Drain the bacon on a paper towel and cool. Leave the bacon grease in the skillet. Add Brussels sprouts to the bacon grease in the skillet and cook as you stir for about 6 minutes until browned on both sides.
3. Push the Brussels sprouts to one side of the skillet, add whisked eggs, and scramble for about 3 to 4 minutes until almost set.
4. Once the bacon is cooled, crumble it into small pieces. Divide Brussels sprouts and scrambled eggs among 4 serving plates. Scatter the tops with crumbled bacon pieces and garnish with feta cheese before serving.

Nutrition: Low GL Calorie: 255; Fat: 15.3 g; Carbs: 10.2 g; Protein: 21.3 g; Fiber: 4.2; Sugar: 4.2 g; Cholesterol: 92 mg; Sodium: 340 mg; Potassium: 272 mg;

67. Baked Feta with Delicious Vegetables

Preparation Time: 60 minutes
Cooking Time: 20 minutes
Cooking Level: Easy
Servings: 2
Ingredients:

- 1 cup feta; Max. 45% fat
- 4 organic cocktail tomatoes
- 1 tbsp olive oil
- 1 tbsp fresh herbs (e.g. marjoram, thyme, rosemary, basil)
- Sea salt and black pepper
- 4 onions, red
- 2 peppers, yellow
- 1 red pepper
- 1 tbsp rapeseed oil
- 1–2 tbsp balsamic vinegar, light
- 1 tsp paprika powder, noble sweet
- 1 tsp linden blossom honey
- ½ organic lemon
- Basil for garnish

Directions:

1. Preheat the oven to 200°C. Quarter the feta cheese. Place a piece of baking paper approx. 30 × 50 cm on a baking sheet, Place feta cheese on top.
2. Wash, dry and slice cocktail tomatoes; wash, dry and chop herbs. Mix olive oil with the herbs, and season with sea salt and pepper to taste and distribute evenly over the cheese. Cover the baking paper with the cheese at the ends like a piece of candy and seal (not completely). Then bake the parcels in the oven (middle rack) for about 15 minutes.
3. In the meantime, peel and halve the onions and cut them into thin slices. Quarter the peppers, remove the stones and stem, wash and cut into fine strips. Squeeze the lemon.
4. Sauté the onions for about 5 minutes. Add peppers and fry for another 5 minutes. Season the finished vegetables with balsamic vinegar, spices, herbs, honey and lemon juice. Remove the feta from the baking paper, arrange it on two plates with the vegetables, and garnish with basil.

Nutrition: High GL Calories: 407; Fat: 38.43 g; Carbohydrates: 16.09 g; Protein: 2.9 g; Fiber: 8 g; Sugar: 2 g; Cholesterol: 68 mg; Sodium: 188.12 mg; Potassium: 219 mg

68. Cauliflower Avocado Mash with Chicken Breast

Preparation Time: 25 minutes
Cooking Time: 3 minutes
Cooking Level: Easy
Servings: 2
Ingredients:

- 2½ cups cauliflower
- Rock salt
- 1 small onion, light
- 5 tsp dried tomatoes
- 1 tbsp rapeseed oil
- Black pepper
- 2 chicken breast fillets (½ cup each)
- 1 organic lemon
- Milk (3.5% fat), to taste
- Vegetable broth, as needed
- ¼ avocado, ripe
- 3 tbsp feta
- Chives, for garnish

Directions:

1. Clean the cauliflower, cut into florets, wash thoroughly and cook in salted water for approx. 8–10 minutes until soft (over medium heat), drain.
2. Chop onion and tomatoes, then sauté briefly, season with rock salt and pepper, and remove from the pan. Wash, dry, and chop the chives.

3. Season the chicken with salt and pepper. Heat oil. Fry the meat for about 5–8 minutes on both sides. Squeeze the lemon and drizzle with lemon juice, put the pan aside, and simmer the meat (covered).
4. Warm the milk together with the vegetable stock. Remove the stone and peel from the avocado, put the cauliflower and avocado in a container, and mash them gradually stirring in the milk; season with salt and freshly ground pepper. Serve mash with the chicken breast. Crumble the feta. Finally, spread the onion and tomato mixture and the feta over the top and garnish with chives.

Note: The avocado is one of the superfoods, it can lower blood sugar and insulin levels at the same time. It tastes excellent and is very versatile.

Nutrition: Low GL Calories: 126; Fat: 7.95 g; Carbohydrates: 11.6 g; Protein: 4.86 g; Fiber: 5 g; Sugar: 4 g; Cholesterol: 89 mg; Sodium: 332.12 mg; Potassium: 287 mg

69. Tomato-Herb Omelet

Preparation Time: 10 minutes
Cooking Time: 10 minutes
Cooking Level: Easy
Servings: 2
Ingredients:

- 1 tbsp coconut oil, divided
- 2 scallions, green and white parts, chopped
- 1 tsp minced garlic
- 2 tomatoes, chopped, liquid squeezed out
- 6 eggs, beaten
- ½ tsp chopped fresh thyme
- ½ tsp chopped fresh basil
- ½ tsp chopped fresh chives
- ½ tsp chopped fresh oregano
- ⅛ tsp sea salt
- Pinch ground nutmeg
- Pinch Pepper, to taste
- Chopped fresh parsley, for garnish

Directions:

1. Put a small saucepan over medium heat before adding 1 tsp of coconut oil. Sauté the scallions and garlic for about 3 minutes, until the vegetables are softened.
2. Add tomatoes and sauté for 3 minutes. Remove the saucepan from the heat and set aside. Whisk together the eggs, thyme, basil, chives, oregano, salt, nutmeg and pepper in a medium bowl.
3. Put a large skillet over medium-high heat before adding the remaining 2 tsp of oil. Swirl the oil until it coats the skillet. Pour in the egg mixture, and swirl until the eggs start to firm up — do not stir eggs. Lift the edges of the firmed eggs to let the uncooked egg flow at the bottom.
4. When the eggs are almost done, spoon the tomato mixture onto one-half of the eggs. Fold the uncovered side over the tomato mixture and cook for a minute longer. Cut the omelet in half, sprinkle with parsley, and serve.

Nutrition: Low GL Calories: 306; Fat: 21 g; Carbohydrates: 13 g; Protein: 19 g; Fiber: 6 g; Sugar: 3 g; Cholesterol: 72 mg; Sodium: 312 mg; Potassium: 312 mg

CHAPTER 6: MEAT RECIPES

70. Cheesy Stuffed Chicken

Preparation Time: 15 minutes
Cooking Time: 20 minutes
Cooking Level: Easy
Servings: 2
Ingredients:

- 1 lb. chicken breasts, boneless and butterflied
- 2 cups fresh spinach, chopped
- 4 oz. low-fat cream cheese, soft
- ¼ cup mozzarella cheese, grated

What You'll Need From The Store Cupboard:

- ¼ cup reduced-fat Parmesan cheese
- 1 tbsp garlic, diced fine
- 1 tbsp olive oil
- 1 tsp chili powder
- 1 tsp Italian seasoning
- ¾ tsp black pepper, divided
- ½ tsp salt

Directions:

1. Combine the spinach, cream cheese, parmesan, mozzarella, garlic, ½ tsp salt and ½ tsp pepper; stir to combine.
2. Stir together the chili powder, Italian seasoning, salt and pepper; use it to season both sides of the chicken. Spoon ¼ of the cheese mixture into the middle of the chicken and fold over to seal it inside.
3. Cook the chicken, cover and cook 9–10 minutes per side, or until cooked through. Serve.

Nutrition: Low GL Calorie: 256; Fat: 14 g; Carbs: 2 g; Protein: 29 g; Fiber: 1 g; Sugar: 0 g; Cholesterol: 89 mg; Sodium: 187 mg; Potassium: 252 mg

71. Beefy Pie

Preparation Time: 15 minutes
Cooking/Baking Time: 50 minutes
Cooking Level: Moderate
Servings: 2
Ingredients:

- ½ cup shredded reduced-fat sharp cheddar cheese, divided
- ¾ cup beef broth
- ¾ cup fat-free sour cream

- 1 lb. 95%-lean ground beef
- 1¼ lb. red potatoes, unpeeled and cut into chunks
- 2 tbsp flour
- 2 tbsp ketchup
- 3 cloves garlic
- 2 cups fresh vegetables of your choice

Directions:

1. Cook potatoes and garlic in 1½-inch boiling water for approximately 20 minutes, or until potatoes are soft. In the meantime, brown beef in a big nonstick frying pan. Mix in flour. Cook for 1 minute.
2. Mix in vegetables, broth and ketchup. Cover. Cook for 10 minutes, stirring regularly. Drain cooked potatoes and garlic. Throw them back into their pan. Mix in sour cream and mash potatoes
3. Stir ¼ cup cheddar cheese into mashed potatoes. Spoon the meat mixture into a thoroughly oil-coated 8×8-inch baking dish.
4. Add a layer of mashed potatoes on top. Bake at 375°F for 18 minutes. Top with residual cheddar cheese. Bake until cheese is melted.

Nutrition: Low GL Calorie: 310; Fat: 7 gm; Carb: 41 gm; Protein: 24 gm; Fiber: 5 gm; Sugars: 7 gm; Cholesterol: 89 mg; Sodium: 360 mg; Potassium: 312 mg

72. Mediterranean Feta Chicken

Preparation Time: 20 minutes
Cooking Time: 15 minutes
Cooking Level: Easy
Servings: 2
Ingredients:

- 2 tbsp olive oil
- 1 cup crumbled feta cheese
- 2 (6-oz) boneless and skinless chicken breast halves
- 1 tsp Greek seasoning
- ⅜ cup chopped sun-dried tomatoes

Directions:

1. Preheat the oven to 375°F–190°C. Line a baking pan with parchment paper. Grease it with some avocado oil. (You can also use cooking spray)
2. Mix the feta cheese and tomatoes in a mixing bowl.
3. Coat the chicken with olive oil and season with the seasoning. Add the cheese mixture and roll up the chicken breasts. Secure with a toothpick, pinning them.
4. Place the chicken into the pan; bake for 25–30 minutes. Remove the toothpicks and serve warm.

Nutrition: Low GL Calorie: 204; Fat: 14 g; Carbohydrates: 9 g; Protein: 19 g; Fiber: 1 g; Sugar: 2 g; Cholesterol: 89 mg; Sodium: 289 mg; Potassium: 309 mg

73. Greek Turkey Burgers

Preparation Time: 10 minutes
Cooking Time: 15 minutes
Cooking Level: Easy
Servings: 2
Ingredients:

- ⅜ cup feta cheese, crumbled
- 1 tsp dill
- 1 egg white
- 7 oz roasted red bell peppers, sliced
- ½ cup breadcrumbs
- 4 whole-wheat buns
- ¾ cup mint, chopped
- 1 cup red onion, sliced
- 1 pound ground turkey
- 2 tbsp lemon juice
- Canola oil as needed
- 4 Iceberg salad leaves

Directions:

1. Beat the egg whites. Add mint, breadcrumbs, onions, feta cheese, lemon juice, dill and turkey; combine well. Form 4 patties from the mixture.
2. Over medium stove flame, heat oil in a skillet or saucepan (preferably of medium size).
3. Add patties and cook them until evenly brown on both sides.
4. Serve patties in the buns, topping them with roasted peppers and iceberg leaves.

Nutrition: Low GL Calorie: 362; Fat: 13 g; Carbohydrates: 38 g; Protein: 33 g; Fiber: 4 g; Sugar: 2 g; Cholesterol: 72 mg; Sodium: 327 mg; Potassium: 286 mg

74. Roasted Leg Lamb

Preparation Time: 15 minutes
Cooking Time: 2 ½ Hours
Cooking Level: Difficult
Servings: 12
Ingredients:

- 2 to 4 oz bone-in lamb leg, trimmed
- 1 cup chicken broth

Marinade:

- ⅜ cup fresh minced rosemary
- 2 tbsp Dijon mustard
- 2 tbsp olive oil
- 8 minced garlic cloves
- 1 tsp soy sauce reduced-Cholesterol: 89 mg; Sodium:
- ½ tsp salt
- ½ tsp pepper

Directions:

1. Preheat the oven to 325°F. Combine the marinade ingredients and coat the lamb. Refrigerate with cover overnight.
2. Place the lamb on a rack using a shallow roasting pan with the fat side up. Bake without cover for 1 ½ hour.
3. Pour broth then cover loosely using foil. Bake for another 1 ½ hours or until meat turns to your desired doneness (Medium-rare 135°F; medium 140°F; and medium-well 145°F using a kitchen thermometer).
4. Cool lamb for 10 to 15 minutes before slicing.

Nutrition: Low GL Calories: 246; Fats: 11 g; Carbohydrates: 2 g; Protein: 33 g; Fiber: 0 g; Sugar: 2 g; Cholesterol: 57 mg; Sodium: 320 mg; Potassium: 289 mg

75. Lamb Chops Curry

Preparation Time: 10 minutes
Cooking Time: 30 minutes
Cooking Level: Moderate
Servings: 2
Ingredients:

- 4 4-oz bone-in loin chops of lamb
- 1 tbsp canola oil
- ¾ cup orange juice
- 2 tbsp teriyaki sauce reduced-Cholesterol: 89 mg; Sodium:
- 2 tsp grated orange zest
- 1 tsp curry powder
- 1 garlic clove, minced
- 1 tsp cornstarch
- 2 tbsp cold water

Directions:

1. Brown the lamb chops on both sides over canola oil.
2. Combine the next 5 ingredients and pour over the skillet. Simmer for 20 minutes or until the lamb turns tender. Remove from heat and keep warm.
3. Combine the last 2 ingredients until smooth. Stir in the pan drippings and bring to boil for 2 minutes or until it thickens.
4. Serve with steamed rice if desired.

Nutrition: Low GL Calories: 337; Fats: 17 g; Carbohydrates: 15 g; Protein: 3 g; Fiber: 1 g; Sugar: 2 g; Cholesterol: 79 mg; Sodium: 402 mg; Potassium: 28 mg

76. Pork Cutlets in Cucumber Sauce

Preparation Time: 4 Hours 15 minutes
Cooking Time: 15 minutes
Cooking Level: Easy
Servings: 2
Ingredients:

Marinate:

- 16 oz pork tenderloin, cut into ½-inch thick slices
- 1 small chopped onion
- 2 tbsp lemon juice
- 1 tbsp fresh minced parsley
- 2 minced garlic cloves
- ¾ tsp dried thyme
- ⅛ tsp pepper

Cucumber Sauce:

- 1 small seeded and chopped tomato
- ⅝ cup plain yogurt, reduced-fat
- ½ cup seeded cucumber, chopped

- 1 tbsp onion, finely chopped
- ½ tsp lemon juice
- ⅛ tsp garlic powder

Directions:
1. Marinate the chops for 4 hours (or overnight). Cover and refrigerate.
2. Combine all the cucumber sauce ingredients and mix. Cover and refrigerate.
3. Drain and discard the marinade. Place the chops on a greased broiler pan. Broil for 6 to 8 minutes each side 4-inch from the heat.
4. Serve with cucumber sauce.

Nutrition: Low GL Calories: 177; Fats: 5 g; Carbohydrates: 8 g; Protein: 25 g; Fiber: 1 g; Sugar: 1 g; Cholesterol: 89 mg; Sodium: 77 mg; Potassium: 312 mg

77. Grilled Lamb Chops

Preparation Time: 4 Hours 15 minutes
Cooking Time: 15 minutes
Cooking Level: Easy
Servings: 2
Ingredients:

- 8-3 oz lamb loin chops

Marinade:

- 1 small sliced onion
- 2 tbsp red wine vinegar
- 1 tbsp lemon juice
- 1 tbsp olive oil
- 2 tsp fresh minced rosemary (substitute ¾ tsp crushed dried)
- 2 tsp Dijon mustard
- 1 minced garlic clove
- ½ tsp pepper
- ¼ tsp salt
- ¼ tsp ground ginger

Directions:
1. Coat the lamb chops with the combined marinade mixture. Cover and refrigerate for 4 hours or overnight.
2. Drain and discard the marinade. Lightly oil your grill rack.
3. Grill the lamb chops for 4 to 7 minutes on each side over medium heat.
4. Grill until it reaches your desired doneness (medium-rare, 135°F; medium, 140°F medium-well, 145°F temperature reading on your kitchen thermometer)

Nutrition: Low GL Calories: 164; Fats: 8 g; Carbohydrates: 0 g; Protein: 21 g; Fiber: 0 g; Sugar: 2 g; Cholesterol: 95 mg; Sodium: 112 mg; Potassium: 328 mg

78. Beef Moroccan Kebabs

Preparation Time: 8 Hours 25 minutes
Cooking Time: 10 minutes
Cooking Level: Easy
Servings: 2
Ingredients:

- 32 oz top sirloin steak beef, cut into 1-inch slices

Marinade:

- 1 cup fresh parsley, chopped
- 1 cup fresh cilantro, chopped
- ¼ cup onion. grated
- 3 tbsp lemon juice
- 2 tbsp olive oil
- 1 tbsp ground cumin
- 1 tbsp ground coriander
- 1 tbsp paprika
- 1 tbsp cider vinegar
- 1 tbsp ketchup
- 2 minced garlic cloves,
- 1 tsp fresh ginger root, minced
- 1 tsp Thai-style red chili paste
- Dash pepper and salt

Directions:
1. Marinate for at least 8 hours.
2. Thread the beef cubes into skewers, and then follow Steps 3 to 4 of Grilled Lamb Chops.

Nutrition: Low GL Calories: 185; Fats: 9 g; Carbohydrates: 3 g; Protein: 22 g; Fiber: 1 g; Sugar: 1 g; Cholesterol: 89 mg; Sodium: 91 mg; Potassium: 312 mg

79. Lamb Kebabs

Preparation Time: 8 Hours 10 minutes
Cooking Time: 10 minutes
Cooking Level: Easy
Servings: 2
Ingredients:

Marinade/Basting Sauce:

- ½ cup lemon juice
- 2 tbsp dried oregano
- 4 tsp olive oil
- 6 minced garlic cloves

Kebabs:

- 16 oz boneless lamb, cut 1-inch cubes
- 16 cherry tomatoes
- 1 large size green pepper, cut into 1-inch pieces
- 1 large size onion, cut into 1-inch wedges

Directions:

1. Follow the directions from Beef Moroccan Kebabs
2. Reserved 1 cup of the sauce for basting while grilling. Alternately, arrange veggies and meat in skewers.
3. Serve

Nutrition: Low GL Calories: 226; Fats: 9 g; Carbohydrates: 13 g; Protein: 25 g; Fiber: 2 g; Sugar: 2 g; Cholesterol: 57 mg; Sodium: 83 mg; Potassium: 245 mg

80. Pork Medallion in Lemon Caper Sauce

Preparation Time: 5 minutes
Cooking Time: 30 minutes
Cooking Level: Moderate
Servings: 2
Ingredients:

- 1-16 oz pork tenderloin, cut into 12 slices and flatten ¼-inch thick
- ½ cup all-purpose flour
- ½ tsp salt
- ¼ tsp pepper
- 1 tbsp butter
- 1 tbsp olive oil

Sauce:

- 1 cup chicken broth, reduced-Cholesterol: 89 mg; Sodium:
- ¼ cup white wine (or ¼ cup reduced-Cholesterol: 89 mg; Sodium: chicken broth)
- 1 minced garlic clove, minced
- 1 tbsp drained capers
- 1 tbsp lemon juice
- ½ tsp crushed dried rosemary

Directions:

1. Coat the pork slices in flour, pepper and salt mixture. Cook the pork slices in batches using oil and butter mixture until juices cleared. Remove from skillet and keep warm.
2. Combine the first three ingredients in the same pan. Stir to loosen brown bits. Bring to a boil until reduced in half. Stir the remaining ingredients until heated through. Serve with pork.

Nutrition: Low GL Calories: 232; Fats: 10 g; Carbohydrates: 7 g; Protein: 24 g; Fiber: 0 g; Sugar: 1 g; Cholesterol: 67 mg; Sodium: 589 mg; Potassium: 23 mg

81. Roasted Pork with Currant Sauce

Preparation Time: 10 minutes
Cooking Time: 1 hour
Cooking Level: Difficult
Servings: 2
Ingredients:

- 1 boneless pork loin roast (2 pounds)

Marinade:

- 1-½ cups orange juice
- ¼ cup lemon juice
- 2 tsp minced fresh ginger root
- 1 tsp minced garlic
- 1 tsp dried oregano
- 1 tsp ground cinnamon
- ½ tsp ground coriander
- 1 small onion, sliced

Currant Sauce:

- 1 shallot, chopped
- 1 tsp minced garlic
- 1 tbsp butter
- 1 tbsp all-purpose flour
- ½ cup reduced-Cholesterol: 89 mg; Sodium: chicken broth
- ½ cup red currant jelly

Directions:

1. Follow Steps 1 and 2 from Grilled Lamb Chops. Reserve 1 cup of the marinade.
2. Bake 1 hour at 350°F or until inserted kitchen thermometer reads 160°F. Cool before slicing. Set aside.
3. Sauté shallots and garlic in butter for a minute. Sprinkle flour and stir until blended. Gradually add the remaining ingredients and bring to a boil. Stir-cook for 2 minutes or until thick.
4. Serve with pork.

Nutrition: Low GL Calories: 307; Fats: 9 g; Carbohydrates: 26 g; Protein: 30 g; Fiber: 0 g; Sugar: 2 g; Cholesterol: 54 mg; Sodium: 115 mg; Potassium: 242 mg

82. Roasted Steak and Tomato Salad

Preparation Time: 20 minutes
Cooking Time: 20 minutes
Cooking Level: Easy
Servings: 2
Ingredients

- 2 (8 oz.) beef tenderloin steaks, trimmed
- 1 tsp cracked black pepper
- ¼ tsp kosher salt
- 6 small tomatoes, halved
- 2 tsps olive oil
- ¼ cup shredded parmesan cheese
- ½ tsp dried oregano, crushed
- 8 cups torn romaine lettuce
- 1 (14-oz.) can artichoke hearts, drained and quartered
- ⅜ cup red onion slivers
- 3 tbsp balsamic vinegar
- 1 tbsp olive oil

Directions:

1. Preheat the oven to 400°F. Season the meat. Let it stand at room temperature. Arrange the tomato on a baking sheet (cut side down). Heat 2 tsps oil in a skillet. Add the steak and cook until well browned on all sides, about 8 minutes. Transfer meat to the other side of the baking sheet.
2. Roast for 8 to 10 minutes for medium (145°F). Remove the meat from the oven. Cover with foil and let stand. Move oven rack for broiling.
3. Turn oven to broil. Turn tomatoes and cut sides up. Combine oregano and Parmesan. Sprinkle over tomatoes. Broil until cheese is melted and golden.
4. In a bowl, combine onion, artichoke hearts, and lettuce. Drizzle with vinegar and 1 tbsp oil. Toss to coat. Arrange on plates. Slice steak and arrange over lettuce with tomato halves.

Nutrition: Low GL Calories: 299; Fat: 14 g; Carb: 16 g; Protein: 29 g; Fiber: 2 g; Sugar: 1 g; Cholesterol: 62 mg; Sodium: 267 mg; Potassium: 224 mg

83. Beef-Vegetable Ragout

Preparation Time: 30 minutes
Cooking Time: 8 Hours
Cooking Level: Difficult
Servings: 2
Ingredients

- 1 ½ lb. Beef chuck roast
- 3 cups Sliced fresh button or cremini mushrooms
- 1 cup Chopped onion
- 4 cloves Garlic, minced
- ½ tsp Salt
- ½ tsp Black pepper
- ¼ cup Quick-cooking tapioca, crushed
- 2 (14.5 oz.) cans 50% less-Cholesterol: 89 mg; Sodium: beef broth
- ½ cup Dry sherry
- 4 cups Sugar: snap pea pods
- 2 cups Cherry tomatoes, halved
- 4 cups Hot cooked multigrain noodles

Directions:

1. Cut the meat into ¾-inch pieces. Coat a skillet with cooking spray. Cook the meat, until browned.
2. Combine the next five ingredients (through pepper) in a slow cooker. Sprinkle with tapioca. Add meat and pour in broth and dry sherry.
3. Cover and cook for 8 to 10 hours (low) for 4 to 5 hours (high).
4. Stir sugar snap peas. Cover and cook for 5 minutes. Stir cherry tomatoes. Serve the meat mixture over hot cooked noodles.

Nutrition: Low GL Calories: 208; Fat: 4 g; Carb: 19 g; Protein: 24 g; Fiber: 6 g; Sugar: 2 g; Cholesterol: 89 mg; Sodium: 53 mg; Potassium: 274 mg

84. Greek Flat Iron Steaks

Preparation Time: 10 minutes
Cooking Time: 15 minutes
Cooking Level: Easy
Servings: 2
Ingredients

- 1 Lemon
- 2 (6 to 8 oz.) Boneless beef shoulder top blade steaks (flat iron)
- ¼ tsp Salt
- ¼ tsp Black pepper
- 1 tsp Dried rosemary, crushed
- 4 tsp Olive oil
- 2 cups Grape tomatoes, halved
- 2 cloves Garlic, minced
- ⅜ cup Pitted green olives, halved
- ¼ cup Crumbled feta cheese
- Lemon wedges

Directions:

1. Remove 1 tsp zest from the lemon. Set the zest aside. Cut steaks and season. Sprinkle rosemary on both sides of the steaks.
2. Heat 2 tsps oil in a skillet. Add the steaks and cook until medium-rare, about 8 to 10 minutes. Turning once. Remove and set aside.
3. Add remaining 2 tsps oil to the skillet. Add garlic and tomatoes. Cook until the tomatoes are soft and burst, for about 3 minutes. Remove from the heat. Stir lemon zest and olives.
4. Serve steaks with tomato relish. Sprinkle with cheese and serve with the reserved lemon wedges.

Nutrition: Low GL Calories: 223; Fat: 14 g; Carb: 6 g; Protein: 20 g; Fiber: 3 g; Sugar: 2 g; Cholesterol: 89 mg; Sodium: 197 mg; Potassium: 322 mg

85. Pork Chops with Grape Sauce

Preparation Time: 15 minutes
Cooking Time: 25 minutes
Cooking Level: Easy
Servings: 2
Ingredients:

- Cooking spray
- 4 pork chops
- ¼ cup onion, sliced
- 1 clove garlic, minced
- ½ cup low-Cholesterol: 89 mg; Sodium: chicken broth
- ¾ cup apple juice
- 1 tbsp cornstarch
- 1 tbsp balsamic vinegar
- 1 tsp honey
- 1 cup seedless red grapes,

Directions:

1. Spray oil on your pan. Put it over medium heat. Add the pork chops to the pan. Cook for 5 minutes per side.
2. Remove and set it aside. Add onion and garlic. Cook for 2 minutes. Pour in the broth and apple juice. Bring to a boil. Reduce the heat to simmer. Put the pork chops back into the skillet.
3. Simmer for 4 minutes. In a bowl, mix cornstarch, vinegar and honey. Add to the pan.
4. Cook until the sauce has thickened. Add grapes. Pour the sauce over the pork chops before serving.

Nutrition: High GL Calorie: 188; Fat: 4 g; Carbohydrate: 18 g; Protein: 19 g; Fiber: 1 g; Sugar: 0.2 g; Cholesterol: 89 mg; Sodium: 117 mg; Potassium: 312 mg

86. Roasted Pork and Apples

Preparation Time: 15 minutes
Cooking Time: 30 minutes
Cooking Level: Moderate
Servings: 2
Ingredients:

- Salt and pepper, to taste
- ½ tsp dried, crushed
- 1 lb. pork tenderloin
- 1 tbsp canola oil
- 1 onion, sliced into wedges
- 3 cooking apples, sliced into wedges
- ⅝ cup apple cider
- Sprigs fresh sage

Directions:

1. In a bowl, mix salt, pepper and sage. Season both sides of the pork with this mixture. Place a pan over medium heat. Brown both sides.
2. Transfer to a roasting pan. Add onion on top and around the pork. Drizzle oil on top of the pork and apples.
3. Roast in the oven at 425°F for 10 minutes. Add apples and roast for another 15 minutes.
4. In a pan, boil the apple cider and then simmer for 10 minutes. Pour the apple cider sauce over the pork before serving.

Nutrition: Low GL Calorie: 239; Fat: 6 g; Carbohydrate: 22 g; Protein: 24 g; Fiber: 3 g; Sugar: 4 g; Cholesterol: 74 mg; Sodium: 455 mg; Potassium: 265 mg

87. Irish Pork Roast

Preparation Time: 40 minutes
Cooking Time: 1 hour
Cooking Level: Difficult
Servings: 2
Ingredients:

- 1 ½ lb. parsnips, peeled and sliced into small pieces
- 1 ½ lb. carrots, sliced into small pieces
- 3 tbsp olive oil, divided
- 2 tsp fresh thyme leaves, divided
- Salt and pepper, to taste
- 2 lb. pork loin roast
- 1 tsp honey
- 1 cup dry hard cider
- Applesauce

Directions:

1. Preheat the oven to 400°F. Drizzle half of the oil over the parsnips and carrots. Season with salt and pepper and half of the thyme. Arrange on a roasting pan. Rub the pork with the remaining oil. Season with the remaining thyme.
2. Season with salt and pepper. Put it on the roasting pan on top of the vegetables.
3. Roast for 65 minutes. Let it cool before slicing. Transfer the carrots and parsnips to a bowl and mix with honey.
4. Add cider. Place in a pan and simmer over low heat until the sauce has thickened. Serve the pork with vegetables and applesauce.

Nutrition: High GL Calorie: 272; Fat: 8 g; Carbohydrate: 23 g; Protein: 24 g; Fiber: 6 g; Sugar: 2 g; Cholesterol: 89 mg; Sodium: 287 mg; Potassium: 312 mg

88. Sesame Pork with Mustard Sauce

Preparation Time: 25 minutes
Cooking Time: 25 minutes
Cooking Level: Easy
Servings: 2
Ingredients:

- 2 tbsp low-Cholesterol: 89 mg; Sodium: teriyaki sauce
- ¼ cup chili sauce
- 2 cloves garlic, minced
- 2 tsp ginger, grated
- 2 pork tenderloins
- 2 tsp sesame seeds
- ¼ cup low-fat sour cream
- 1 tsp Dijon mustard
- Salt, to taste
- 1 scallion, chopped

Directions:

1. Preheat the oven to 425°F. Mix teriyaki sauce, chili sauce, garlic and ginger. Put the pork on a roasting pan.

2. Brush sauce on both sides of the pork. Bake for 15 minutes. Brush with more sauce.
3. Top with sesame seeds. Roast for 10 more minutes.
4. Mix the rest of the ingredients. Serve pork with mustard sauce.

Nutrition: Low GL Calorie: 135; Fat: 3 g; Carbohydrate: 7 g; Protein: 20 g; Fiber: 1 g; Sugars: 15 g; Cholesterol: 78 mg; Sodium: 255 mg; Potassium: 233 mg

89. Steak with Mushroom Sauce

Preparation Time: 20 minutes
Cooking Time: 5 minutes
Cooking Level: Easy
Servings: 2
Ingredients:

- 12 oz. sirloin steak, sliced and trimmed
- 2 tsp grilling seasoning
- 2 tsp oil
- 6 oz. broccoli, trimmed
- 2 cups frozen peas
- 3 cups fresh mushrooms, sliced
- 1 cup beef broth (unsalted)
- 1 tbsp mustard
- 2 tsp cornstarch
- Salt, to taste

Directions:

1. Preheat the oven to 350°F. Season meat with grilling seasoning. In a pan over medium-high heat, cook the meat and broccoli for 4 minutes. Sprinkle the peas around the steak.
2. Bake for 8 minutes. Remove both meat and vegetables from the pan. Add mushrooms to the pan.
3. Cook for 3 minutes. Mix broth, mustard, salt and cornstarch. Add to the mushrooms.
4. Cook for 1 minute. Pour the sauce over the meat and vegetables before serving.

Nutrition: Low GL Calorie: 226; Fat: 6 g; Carbohydrate: 16 g; Fiber: 5 g; Protein: 26 g; Sugar: 1 mg; Potassium: 312 mg; Cholesterol: 58 mg; Sodium: 356 mg; Potassium: 282 mg

90. Steak with Tomato and Herbs

Preparation Time: 30 minutes
Cooking Time: 30 minutes
Cooking Level: Moderate
Servings: 2
Ingredients:

- 8 oz. beef loin steak, sliced in half
- Salt and pepper, to taste
- Cooking spray
- 1 tsp fresh basil, snipped
- ¼ cup green onion, sliced
- ½ cup tomato, chopped

Directions:

1. Season the steak with salt and pepper. Spray oil on your pan. Put the pan over medium-high heat.
2. Once hot, add the steaks. Reduce the heat to medium. Cook for 10 to 13 minutes for medium, turning once.
3. Add basil and green onion. Cook for 2 minutes. Add tomato.
4. Cook for 1 minute. Let it cool a little before slicing.

Nutrition: Low GL Calorie: 170; Fat: 6 g; Carbohydrate: 3 g; Protein: 25 g; Fiber: 1 g; Sugars: 5 g; Cholesterol: 89 mg; Sodium: 266 mg; Potassium: 312 mg

91. Barbecue Beef Brisket

Preparation Time: 25 minutes
Cooking Time: 10 Hours
Cooking Level: Difficult
Servings: 2
Ingredients:

- 4 lb. beef brisket (boneless), trimmed and sliced
- 1 bay leaf
- 2 onions, sliced into rings
- ½ tsp dried thyme, crushed
- ¼ cup chili sauce

- 1 clove garlic, minced
- Salt and pepper, to taste
- 2 tbsp light brown sugar
- 2 tbsp cornstarch
- 2 tbsp cold water

Directions:
1. Put the meat in a slow cooker. Add bay leaf and onion. In a bowl, mix thyme, chili sauce, salt, pepper and sugar.
2. Pour the sauce over the meat. Mix well. Seal the pot and cook on low heat for 10 hours.
3. Discard the bay leaf. Pour cooking liquid into a pan. Add mixed water and cornstarch.
4. Simmer until the sauce has thickened. Pour the sauce over the meat.

Nutrition: Low GL Calorie: 182; Fat: 6 g; Carbohydrate: 9 g; Protein: 20 g; Fiber: 1 g; Sugars: 4 g; Cholesterol: 89 mg; Sodium: 383 mg; Potassium: 218 mg

92. Beef and Asparagus

Preparation Time: 15 minutes
Cooking Time: 10 minutes
Cooking Level: Easy
Servings: 2
Ingredients:

- 2 tsp olive oil
- 1 lb. lean beef sirloin, trimmed and sliced
- 1 carrot, shredded
- Salt and pepper, to taste
- 12 oz. asparagus, trimmed and sliced
- 1 tsp dried herbes de Provence, crushed
- ½ cup Marsala
- ¼ tsp lemon zest

Directions:
1. Cook the beef and carrot.
2. Season with salt and pepper. Cook for 3 minutes.
3. Add asparagus and herbs. Cook for 2 minutes.
4. Add Marsala and lemon zest. Cook for 5 minutes, stirring frequently.

Nutrition: Low GL Calorie: 327; Fat: 7 g; Carbohydrate: 29 g; Protein: 28 g; Fiber: 2 g; Sugars: 3 g; Cholesterol: 305 mg; Sodium: 269 mg; Potassium: 09 mg

93. Braised Lamb with Vegetables

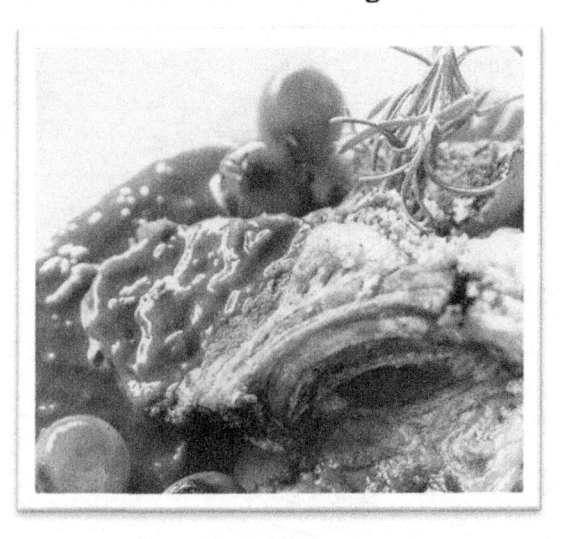

Preparation Time: 30 minutes
Cooking Time: 2 Hours and 15 minutes
Cooking Level: Difficult
Servings: 2
Ingredients:

- Salt and pepper, to taste
- 2 ½ lb. boneless lamb leg, trimmed and sliced into cubes
- 1 tbsp olive oil
- 1 onion, chopped
- 1 carrot, chopped
- 14 oz. canned diced tomatoes
- 1 cup low-Cholesterol: 89 mg; Sodium: beef broth
- 1 tbsp fresh rosemary, chopped
- 4 cloves garlic, minced
- 1 cup pearl onions
- 1 cup baby turnips, peeled and sliced into wedges
- 1 ½ cups baby carrots
- 1 ½ cups peas
- 2 tbsp fresh parsley, chopped

Directions:
1. Sprinkle salt and pepper to taste on both sides of the lamb. Pour oil into a deep skillet. Cook the lamb for 6 minutes. Transfer the lamb to a plate. Add onion and carrot.
2. Cook for 3 minutes. Stir tomatoes, broth, rosemary and garlic. Simmer for 5 minutes. Add the lamb back to the skillet.
3. Reduce the heat to low. Simmer for 1 hour and 15 minutes. Add pearl onion, baby carrot and baby turnips. Simmer for 30 minutes.
4. Add peas. Cook for 1 minute. Garnish with parsley before serving.

Nutrition: Low GL Calorie: 420; Fat: 14 g; Carbohydrate: 16 g; Protein: 43 g; Fiber: 4 g; Sugar: 3 g; Cholesterol: 89 mg; Sodium: 126 mg; Potassium: 312 m

94. Rosemary Lamb

Preparation Time: 15 minutes
Cooking Time: 2 Hours
Cooking Level: Difficult
Servings: 2
Ingredients:

- Salt and pepper, to taste
- 2 tsp fresh rosemary, snipped
- 5 lb. whole leg lamb, trimmed and cut with slits on all sides
- 3 cloves garlic, slivered
- 1 cup water

Directions:

1. Preheat the oven to 375°F. Mix salt, pepper and rosemary
2. Sprinkle the mixture all over the lamb. Insert slivers of garlic into the slits.
3. Put the lamb on a roasting pan.
4. Add water to the pan. Roast for 2 hours.

Nutrition: Low GL Calorie: 136; Fat: 4 g; Cholesterol: 68 mg; Protein: 23 g; Sugar: 7 g; Cholesterol: 89 mg; Sodium: 218 mg; Sodium: 248 mg; Potassium: 282 mg

95. Mediterranean Lamb Meatballs

Preparation Time: 10 minutes
Cooking Time: 20 minutes
Cooking Level: Easy
Servings: 2
Ingredients:

- 12 oz. roasted red peppers
- 1 ½ cups whole-wheat breadcrumbs
- 2 eggs, beaten
- ⅜ cup tomato sauce
- ½ cup fresh basil
- ¼ cup parsley, snipped
- Salt and pepper, to taste
- 2 lb. lean ground lamb

Directions:

1. Preheat the oven to 350°F.
2. Mix all the ingredients and then form meatballs.
3. Put the meatballs on a baking pan.
4. Bake for 20 minutes.

Nutrition: Low GL Calorie: 94; Fat: 3 g; Carbohydrate: 2 g; Protein: 14 g; Fiber: 1 g; Sugar: 0 g; Cholesterol: 89 mg; Sodium: 170 mg; Potassium: 312 mg

96. Cranberry Pork Roast

Preparation Time: 20 minutes
Cooking Time: 8–10 Hours
Cooking Level: Difficult
Servings: 2
Ingredients:

- ⅛ tsp ground cloves
- ⅛ tsp ground nutmeg
- 1 cup ground, or finely chopped, cranberries
- 1 tsp grated orange peel
- 2¾-lb. boneless pork roast, trimmed of fat
- 3 tbsp honey

Directions:

1. Place the roast in the Crock-Pot.
2. Mix the residual ingredients. Pour over the roast.
3. Cover. Cook on low for approximately 8–10 hours.

Nutrition: High GL Calorie: 214; Fat: 9 gm; Carb: 7 gm; Protein: 25 gm; Fiber: 1 gm; Sugars: 7 gm; Cholesterol: 89 mg; Sodium: 37 mg; Potassium: 312 mg

97. Crock Pork Tenderloin

Preparation Time: 5–15 minutes
Cooking Time: 4 Hours
Cooking Level: Difficult
Servings: 2
Ingredients:

- ¾ cup red wine
- 1 cup water
- 1 envelope salt-free onion soup mix
- 2-lb. pork soft loin, cut in half lengthwise, visible fat removed
- 3 tbsp light soy sauce
- 6 cloves garlic, peeled and chopped
- freshly ground pepper

Directions:
1. Place pork soft loin pieces in the Crock-Pot. Pour water, wine and soy sauce over the pork.
2. Turn the pork over in liquid several times to totally moisten.
3. Drizzle with dry onion soup mix. Top with chopped garlic and pepper.
4. Cover. Cook on low for approximately 4 hours.

Nutrition: Low GL Calorie: 220; Fat: 4 gm; Carb: 6 gm; Protein: 37 gm; Fiber: 0 gm; Sugars: 2 gm; Cholesterol: 57 mg; Sodium: 370 mg; Potassium: 287 mg

98. Conventional Beef Pot Roast

Preparation Time: ½ Hour
Cooking Time: 10–12 Hours
Cooking Level: Difficult
Servings: 2
Ingredients:

- ½ cup boiling water
- ½ tsp pepper
- 1 moderate onion, sliced
- 1 bouillon cube
- 1 tsp salt
- 3–4-lb. rump roast, or pot roast,
- 4 moderate carrots, sliced
- 4 moderate potatoes, cubed

Directions:
1. Put the vegetables and meat in the Crock-Pot. Sprinkle with salt and pepper to taste and stir until mixed.
2. Dissolve the bouillon cube in water, and then pour over the rest of the ingredients.
3. Cover. Cook on low for approximately 10–12 hours.

Nutrition: Low GL Calorie: 246; Total Fat: 6 gm; Carb: 20 gm Protein: 27 gm; Fiber: 3 gm; Sugar: 0.6 g; Cholesterol: 54 mg; Sodium: 485 mg; Potassium: 308 mg

99. Applesauce Meatloaf

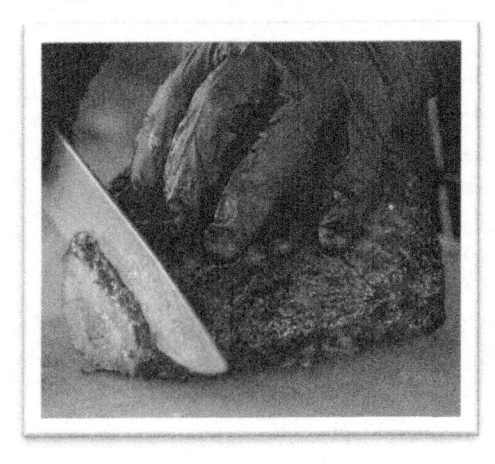

Preparation Time: 15 minutes
Baking Time: 40–60 minutes
Cooking Level: Moderate–Difficult
Servings: 2
Ingredients:

- ¼ cup chopped onion
- ¼ cup egg substitute
- ½ cup unsweetened applesauce
- ¾ cup dry oatmeal
- 1 tsp salt
- 1½ tbsp chili powder
- 2 lbs. 95%-lean ground beef
- Dash pepper

Directions:
1. Mix ground beef, dry oatmeal, egg substitute, applesauce, onion, salt, pepper and chili powder in a good-sized mixing vessel.
2. Shape into a loaf. Place in 5×9-inch oil-coated loaf pan.
3. Bake at 350°F for approximately 40–60 minutes, or until the meat thermometer shows 160°F in the center of the loaf.
4. Let it stand before slicing to allow the meat to gather its juices and firm up.

Nutrition: Low GL Calorie: 200; Total Fat: 6 gm; Carb: 8 gm; Protein: 26 gm; Fiber: 2 gm; Sugar: 0.6 g; Cholesterol: 45 mg; Sodium: 395 mg; Potassium: 288 mg

100. Ham in Cider

Preparation Time: 20 minutes
Cooking Time: 8 ½–10 ½ Hours
Cooking Level: Difficult
Servings: 2
Ingredients:

- ¼ cup brown sugar substitute to equal ¼ cup sugar
- 1 cup golden raisins
- 1 tsp ground cloves
- 2 tsp dry mustard
- 3-lb. boneless, precooked extra-lean, lower-Cholesterol: 89 mg; Sodium: ham, trimmed of fat
- 4 cups sweet cider, or apple juice

Directions:
1. Place the ham and cider in the Crock-Pot. Cover. Cook on low for approximately 8–10 hours.
2. Take out the ham from the cider and place it in a baking pan.

3. Prepare a paste of sugar, mustard, cloves and a little hot cider. Coat over the ham. Pour ½ cup of juice from the Crock-Pot into the baking pan. Mix in raisins.
4. Bake at 375°F for approximately half an hour, until the paste has turned into a glaze.

Nutrition: Moderate GL Calorie: 255; Fat: 3 gm; Carb: 31 gm; Protein: 27 gm; Fiber: 1 gm; Sugar: 6 g; Cholesterol: 89 mg; Sodium: 1194 mg; Potassium: 312 mg

101. Roasted Pork Loin

Preparation Time: 5 minutes
Cooking Time: 40 minutes
Cooking Level: Moderate
Servings: 2
Ingredients:

- 1 pound (454 g) pork loin
- 1 tbsp extra-virgin olive oil, divided
- 2 tsp honey
- ¼ tsp Pepper, to taste
- ½ tsp dried rosemary
- 2 small gold potatoes, chopped into 2-inch cubes
- 4 (6-inch) carrots, chopped into ½-inch rounds

Directions:

1. Preheat the oven to 350°F (180°C). Rub the pork loin with ½ tbsp of oil and honey. Season with pepper and rosemary.
2. Toss potatoes and carrots in the remaining ½ tbsp of oil.
3. Place pork and the vegetables on a baking sheet in a single layer. Cook for 40 minutes.
4. Let the pork rest before slicing. Divide the pork and vegetables into four equal portions.

Nutrition: High GL Calories: 343; Fat: 10 g; Carbs: 26 g; Protein: 26 g; Fiber: 4 g; Sugars: 6 g; Cholesterol: 63 mg; Sodium: 109 mg; Potassium: 277 mg

102. Grilled Greek Chicken

Preparation Time: 10 minutes
Cooking Time: 12 minutes
Cooking Level: Easy
Servings: 2
Ingredients:

- 1 ½ lb chicken breasts, skinless and boneless
- 1 tbsp garlic, minced
- ¼ tsp cayenne pepper
- 1 tsp fresh thyme
- ½ tsp oregano
- 1 tbsp red wine vinegar
- 3 tbsp olive oil
- 3 tbsp fresh lemon juice
- ½ tsp pepper
- ½ tsp salt

Directions:

1. Add the chicken into the zip-lock bag. Pour the remaining ingredients over the chicken. Seal the bag and shake well.
2. Place the marinated chicken into the refrigerator overnight.
3. Heat the grill over medium-high heat.
4. Grill chicken for 4–6 minutes on each side. Serve and enjoy.

Nutrition: Low GL Calorie: 420; Fat: 23 g; Carbohydrates: 1 g; Protein: 50 g; Fiber: 4 g; Sugar: 0.3 g; Cholesterol: 47 mg; Sodium: 150 mg; Potassium: 198 mg

103. Guacamole Chicken Salad

Preparation Time: 10 minutes
Cooking Time: 10 minutes
Cooking Level: Easy
Servings: 2

Ingredients:
- 2 chicken breasts, cooked and cubed
- 1 cup cilantro, chopped
- 1 tbsp fresh lime juice
- 2 avocados, peeled and pitted
- 2 Serrano chili peppers, chopped
- ½ cup celery, chopped
- ½ cup onion, chopped
- 1 tsp kosher salt

Directions:
1. Add the avocados and lime juice into the bowl and mash using a fork.
2. Add the remaining ingredients into the bowl and stir to combine.
3. Serve and enjoy.

Nutrition: Low GL Calorie: 477; Fat: 33.4 g; Carbohydrates: 15.9 g; Protein: 31.2 g; Sugar: 2 g; Cholesterol: 65 mg; Sodium: 287 mg; Potassium: 245 mg

104. Greek Chicken Salad

Preparation Time: 10 minutes
Cooking Time: 5 minutes
Cooking Level: Easy
Servings: 2
Ingredients:
- 1 cup cooked chicken, shredded
- 2 tsp fresh basil, chopped
- ¼ cup cucumber, diced
- 1 tsp vinegar
- 1 tbsp sour cream
- Salt and pepper, to taste

Directions:
1. Add all the ingredients into a medium bowl and mix well to combine.
2. Season with pepper and salt. Place in the refrigerator for 10 minutes.
3. Serve and enjoy.

Nutrition: Low GL Calorie: 243; Fat: 6.8 g; Carbohydrates: 1.6 g; Protein: 41.2 g; Fiber: 2 g; Sugar: 0.5 g; Cholesterol: 58 mg; Sodium: 113 mg; Potassium: 317 mg

105. Shredded Turkey Breast

Preparation Time: 10 minutes
Cooking Time: 8 Hours
Cooking Level: Difficult
Servings: 20
Ingredients:
- 4 lb turkey breast, skinless, boneless, and halves
- 1 ½ tbsp taco seasoning, homemade
- 12 oz chicken stock
- ½ cup butter, cubed
- Salt and pepper, to taste

Directions:
1. Place the turkey breast into the crockpot.
2. Pour the remaining ingredients over the turkey breast.
3. Cover and cook for 8 hours (low).
4. Shred the turkey breast with a fork. Serve and enjoy.

Nutrition: Low GL Calorie: 327; Fat: 15.4 g; Carbohydrates: 11.8 g; Protein: 34.3 g; Fiber: 7 g; Sugar: 6.5 g; Cholesterol: 71 mg; Sodium: 111 mg; Potassium: 282 mg

106. Chicken Saute

Preparation Time: 10 minutes
Cooking Time: 25 minutes
Cooking Level: Easy
Servings: 2
Ingredients:
- 4 oz chicken fillet
- 4 tomatoes, peeled
- 1 bell pepper, chopped
- 1 tsp olive oil
- 1 cup water
- 1 tsp salt
- 1 chili pepper, chopped
- ½ tsp saffron

Directions:
1. Pour water into the pan and bring it to a boil. Meanwhile, chop the chicken fillet. Add a chicken fillet to the boiling water and cook it for 10 minutes or until the chicken is tender.
2. After this, put the chopped bell pepper and chili pepper in the skillet. Add olive oil and roast the vegetables for 3 minutes. Add chopped tomatoes and mix up well.
3. Cook the vegetables for 2 minutes more. Then add salt and ¾ cup of water from the chicken.

66

4. Add the chopped chicken fillet and mix up. Cook and sauté for 10 minutes over medium heat.

Nutrition: Low GL Calorie: 192; Fat: 7.2 g; Carbs: 14.4 g; Protein: 19.2 g; Fiber: 3.8 g; Sugar: 2 g; Cholesterol: 68 mg; Sodium: 243 mg; Potassium: 265 mg

107. Duck Patties

Preparation Time: 15 minutes
Cooking Time: 10 minutes
Cooking Level: Easy
Servings: 2
Ingredients:

- 1-pound duck breast, skinless, boneless
- 1 tbsp semolina
- ½ tsp cayenne pepper
- 2 eggs, beaten
- 1 tsp salt
- 1 tbsp fresh cilantro, chopped
- 1 tbsp olive oil

Directions:

1. Chop the duck breast into tiny pieces (grind it) and combine them together with semolina, cayenne pepper, salt and cilantro. Mix up well.
2. Then add eggs and stir gently.
3. Place the duck mixture in the oil with the help of the spoon to make the shape of small patties.
4. Roast the patties for 3 minutes from each side over medium heat. Then close the lid and cook the patties for 4 minutes more over low heat.

Nutrition: Low GL Calorie: 106; Fat: 5.2 g; Carbs: 0.4 g; Protein: 13.2 g; Fiber: 0.8 g; Sugar: 2 g; Cholesterol: 55 mg; Sodium: 257 mg; Potassium: 189 mg

108. Grilled Marinated Chicken

Preparation Time: 35 minutes
Cooking Time: 20 minutes
Cooking Level: Easy
Servings: 2
Ingredients:

- 2-pound chicken breast, skinless, boneless
- 2 tbsp lemon juice
- 1 tsp sage
- ½ tsp ground nutmeg
- ½ tsp dried oregano
- 1 tsp paprika
- 1 tsp onion powder
- 2 tbsp olive oil
- 1 tsp chili flakes
- 1 tsp salt
- 1 tsp apple cider vinegar

Directions:

1. Make the marinade: whisk together apple cider vinegar, salt, chili flakes, olive oil, onion powder, paprika, dried oregano, ground nutmeg, sage and lemon juice.
2. Then rub the chicken with the marinade carefully and leave for 25 minutes to marinate.
3. Meanwhile, preheat the grill to 385°F. Place the marinated chicken breast on the grill and cook it for 10 minutes from each side.
4. Cut the cooked chicken into the needed servings.

Nutrition: Low GL Calorie: 218; Fat: 8.2 g; Carbs: 0.4 g; Protein: 32.2 g; Fiber: 0.8 g; Sugar: 1 g; Cholesterol: 81 mg; Sodium: 312 mg; Potassium: 283 mg

CHAPTER 7: FISH AND SEAFOOD

109. Shrimp and Artichoke Skillet

Preparation Time: 5 minutes
Cooking Time: 10 minutes
Cooking Level: Easy
Servings: 2
Ingredients:

- 1 ½ cups shrimp, peel and devein
- 2 shallots, diced
- 1 tbsp margarine

What You'll Need from the Store Cupboard

- 2 12 oz. jars artichoke hearts, drain and rinse
- 2 cups white wine
- 2 cloves garlic, diced fine

Directions:

1. Melt margarine in a large skillet over med-high heat. Add shallot and garlic, and cook until they start to brown, stirring frequently.
2. Add artichokes and cook for 5 minutes. Reduce the heat and add wine. Cook for 3 minutes, stirring occasionally.
3. Add shrimp and cook until they turn pink. Serve.

Nutrition: Low GL Calorie: 487; Fat: 5 g; Total Carbs: 26 g; Protein: 64 g; Fiber: 9 g; Sugar: 0 g; Cholesterol: 89 mg; Sodium: 178 mg; Potassium: 312 mg

110. Sardines with Zoodles

Preparation Time: 10 minutes
Cooking Time: 15 minutes
Cooking Level: Easy
Servings: 2
Ingredients:

- 2 tbsp olive oil
- 2 cups zoodles (spiralized zucchini)
- 1 pound (454 g) whole fresh sardines, gutted and cleaned
- ½ cup sundried tomatoes, chopped
- 1 tbsp dill
- 1 garlic clove, minced

Directions:

1. Preheat the oven to 350°F (180°C) and line a baking sheet with parchment paper. Arrange the sardines on the dish, drizzle with olive oil, and sprinkle with salt and pepper. Bake 10 minutes until the skin is crispy.
2. Warm oil in a skillet and stir-fry zucchini, garlic and tomatoes for 5 minutes. Transfer the sardines to a plate and serve with the veggie pasta.

Nutrition: Low GL Calories: 432; Fat: 28.2 g; Carbs: 7.1 g; Protein: 32.3 g; Fiber: 1.7 g; Sugar: 2.4 g; Cholesterol: 59 mg; Sodium: 97 mg; Potassium: 283 mg

111. Chimichurri Grilled Shrimp

Preparation Time: 10 minutes
Cooking Time: 35 minutes
Cooking Level: Moderate
Servings: 2
Ingredients:

- 1 pound (454 g) shrimp, peeled and deveined
- 2 tbsp olive oil
- Juice 1 lime

Chimichurri:

- ½ tsp salt
- ¼ cup olive oil
- 2 garlic cloves
- ¼ cup red onions, chopped
- ¼ cup red wine vinegar
- ½ tsp pepper
- 2 cups parsley
- ¼ tsp red pepper flakes

Directions:

1. Process the chimichurri ingredients in a blender until smooth; set aside. Combine shrimp, olive oil and lime juice in a bowl, and let marinate in the fridge for 30 minutes. Preheat your grill

to medium. Add the shrimp and cook about for 2 minutes per side. Serve the shrimp drizzled with the chimichurri sauce.

Nutrition: Low GL Calories: 284; Fat: 20.4 g; Carbs: 4.8 g; Protein: 15.8 g; Fiber: 1.2 g; Sugar: 3.6 g; Cholesterol: 89 mg; Sodium: 168.17 mg; Potassium: 288 mg

112. Salmon and Cucumber Panzanella

Preparation Time: 15 minutes
Cooking Time: 10 minutes
Cooking Level: Easy
Servings: 2
Ingredients:

- 1 pound (454 g) skinned salmon, cut into 4 steaks each
- 1 cucumber, peeled, seeded, cubed
- Salt and black pepper, to taste
- 8 black olives, pitted and chopped
- 1 tbsp capers, rinsed
- 2 large tomatoes, diced
- 3 tbsp red wine vinegar
- ¼ cup thinly sliced red onion
- 3 tbsp olive oil
- 2 slices zero carb bread, cubed
- ¼ cup thinly sliced basil leaves

Directions:

1. Preheat a grill to 350°F (180°C) and prepare the salad. In a bowl, mix cucumbers, olives, pepper, capers, tomatoes, wine vinegar, onion, olive oil, bread and basil leaves. Let it sit for the flavors to incorporate.
2. Season the salmon steaks with salt and pepper; grill them on both sides for 8 minutes in total. Serve the salmon steaks warm on a bed of veggies salad.

Nutrition: Low GL Calories: 339; Fat: 21.6 g; Carbs: 5.3 g; Protein: 28.6 g; Fiber: 2.1 g; Sugar: 3.2 g; Cholesterol: 81 mg; Sodium: 167 mg; Potassium: 309 mg

113. Blackened Tilapia Tacos

Preparation Time: 10 minutes
Cooking Time: 5 minutes
Cooking Level: Easy
Servings: 2
Ingredients:

- 1 tbsp olive oil
- 1 tsp chili powder
- 2 tilapia fillets
- 1 tsp paprika
- 4 low carb tortillas

Slaw:

- ½ cup red cabbage, shredded
- 1 tbsp lemon juice
- 1 tsp apple cider vinegar
- 1 tbsp olive oil
- Salt and black pepper, to taste

Directions:

1. Season the tilapia with chili powder and paprika. Heat olive oil.
2. Add the tilapia and cook until blackened, about 3 minutes per side. Cut into strips. Divide the tilapia between the tortillas. Combine the slaw ingredients in a bowl and top the fish with it to serve.

Nutrition: Low GL Calories: 269; Fat: 20.1 g; Carbs: 5.3 g; Protein: 13.7 g; Fiber: 1.9 g; Sugar: 3.4 g; Cholesterol: 57 mg; Sodium: 167 mg; Potassium: 302 mg

114. Parmesan Shrimp with Curry Sauce

Preparation Time: 10 minutes
Cooking Time: 5 minutes

Cooking Level: Easy
Servings: 2
Ingredients:

- ½ oz (14 g) grated Parmesan cheese
- 1 egg, beaten
- ¼ tsp curry powder
- 2 tsp almond flour
- 12 shrimp, shelled
- 3 tbsp coconut oil

Sauce:

- 2 tbsp curry leaves
- 2 tbsp butter
- ½ onion, diced
- ½ cup heavy cream
- ½ oz (14 g) Cheddar cheese, shredded

Directions:

1. Combine all the dry ingredients for the batter. Melt coconut oil. Dip shrimp in the egg first, then coat with the dry mixture. Fry until golden and crispy.
2. In another skillet, melt butter. Add the onion and cook for 3 minutes. Add curry leaves and cook 30 for seconds. Stir heavy cream and cheddar, and cook until thickened. Add shrimp and coat well. Serve.

Nutrition: Low GL Calories: 561; Fat: 40.9 g; Carbs: 5.0 g; Protein: 24.3 g; Fiber: 0.8 g; Cholesterol: 64 mg; Sodium: 167 mg; Potassium: 213 mg

115. Pistachio Salmon with Shallot Sauce

Preparation Time: 15 minutes
Cooking Time: 20 minutes
Cooking Level: Easy
Servings: 2
Ingredients:

- 2 salmon fillets
- ½ tsp pepper
- 1 tsp salt
- ¼ cup mayonnaise
- ½ cup chopped pistachios

Sauce:

- 1 chopped shallot
- 2 tsp lemon zest
- 1 tbsp olive oil
- A pinch black pepper
- 1 cup heavy cream

Directions:

1. Preheat the oven to 370°F (188°C).
2. Brush the salmon with mayonnaise and season with salt and pepper. Coat with pistachios, place in a lined baking dish, and bake for 15 minutes.
3. In olive oil, sauté the shallot for 3 minutes. Stir the rest of the sauce ingredients. Boil and cook until thickened. Serve the fish with the sauce.

Nutrition: Low GL Calories: 562; Fat: 46.8 g; Carbs: 8.1 g; Protein: 34.1 g; Fiber: 2.2 g; Sugar: 2.9 g; Cholesterol: 67 mg; Sodium: 96 mg; Potassium: 301 mg

116. Sicilian Zoodle and Sardine Spaghetti

Preparation Time: 5 minutes
Cooking Time: 10 minutes
Cooking Level: Easy
Servings: 2
Ingredients:

- 2 cups zoodles (spiraled zucchini)
- 2 oz (57 g) cubed bacon
- 4 oz (113 g) canned sardines, chopped
- ½ cup canned chopped tomatoes
- 1 tbsp capers
- 1 tbsp parsley
- 1 tsp minced garlic

Directions:

1. Pour some of the sardine oil into a pan. Add garlic, and cook for 1 minute. Add bacon and cook for 2 more minutes. Stir tomatoes and let simmer for 5 minutes. Add zoodles and sardines, and cook for 3 minutes.

Nutrition: Low GL Calories: 356; Fat: 31.2 g; Carbs: 8.8 g; Protein: 20.1 g; Fiber: 2.9 g; Sugar: 2.9 g; Cholesterol: 82 mg; Sodium: 96 mg; Potassium: 210 mg

117. Shrimp and Daikon Noodle Panang

Preparation Time: 8 minutes
Cooking Time: 15 minutes
Cooking Level: Easy
Servings: 2
Ingredients:

- 1 tbsp coconut oil
- 3 tbsp red curry paste
- 2 tbsp natural peanut butter (no sugar added)
- 1 (14-oz / 397-g) can full-fat unsweetened coconut milk
- 2 tbsp fish sauce (no sugar added)
- 2 tbsp granulated erythritol
- 1 pound (454 g) large shrimp, peeled and deveined
- 3 cups spiral-sliced daikon noodles (about 10 oz / 283 g)
- ½ cup sliced red bell peppers
- 1 tsp sliced Thai red chili peppers (optional)
- 1 tbsp lime juice
- ¼ cup whole or chopped fresh cilantro leaves, for garnish (optional)

Directions:

1. Heat coconut oil in a large sauté pan over medium heat. Add curry paste and peanut butter, and cook for 2 minutes, stirring constantly. Add coconut milk, fish sauce and sweetener, and cook until the sauce thickened and coats the back of a spoon.
2. Add shrimp, daikon noodles, bell peppers and Thai chili peppers, if using, and cook for 3 minutes, or until the shrimp have just turned pink; don't overcook the shrimp or they will be tough and dry.
3. Remove from the heat. Stir lime juice. Serve hot, garnished with cilantro, if desired.

Nutrition: Low GL Calories: 356; Fat: 27.0 g; Carbs: 8.9 g; Protein: 24.9 g; Fiber: 2.0 g; Sugar: 1.9 g; Cholesterol: 89 mg; Sodium: 234. 96 mg; Potassium: 312 mg

118. Sour Cream Salmon Steaks

Preparation Time: 10 minutes
Cooking Time: 20 minutes
Cooking Level: Easy
Servings: 2
Ingredients:

- 1 cup sour cream
- ½ tbsp minced dill
- ½ lemon, zested and juiced
- Pink salt and black pepper to season
- 2 salmon steaks
- ½ cup grated Parmesan cheese

Directions:

1. Preheat the oven to 400°F (205°C) and line a baking sheet with parchment paper; set aside. In a bowl, mix sour cream, dill, lemon zest, juice, salt and black pepper, and set aside.
2. Season the fish with salt and black pepper, drizzle lemon juice on both sides of the fish, and arrange them on the baking sheet. Spread the sour cream mixture on each fish and sprinkle with Parmesan.
3. Bake the fish for 15 minutes and then broil the top carefully for 2 minutes for a nice brown color. Plate the fish and serve with buttery green beans.

Nutrition: Low GL Calories: 289; Fat: 23.5 g; Carbs: 1.5 g; Protein: 16.1 g; Fiber: 0.2 g; Sugar: 1.3 g; Cholesterol: 85 mg; Sodium: 96 mg; Potassium: 224 mg

119. Coconut Mussel Curry

Preparation Time: 15 minutes
Cooking Time: 20 minutes
Cooking Level: Easy
Servings: 2

Ingredients:
- 2 tbsp cup coconut oil
- 2 green onions, chopped
- 1 pound (454 g) mussels, cleaned, de-bearded
- 1 shallot, chopped
- 1 garlic clove, minced
- ½ cup coconut milk
- ½ cup white wine
- 1 tsp red curry powder
- 2 tbsp parsley, chopped

Directions:
1. Cook the shallots and garlic in the wine over low heat. Stir the coconut milk and red curry powder, and cook for 3 minutes.
2. Add mussels and steam for 7 minutes or until their shells are opened. Then, use a slotted spoon to remove to a bowl leaving the sauce in the pan. Discard any closed mussels at this point.
3. Stir coconut oil into the sauce, turn the heat off, and stir parsley and green onions. Serve sauce immediately with a butternut squash mash.

Nutrition: Low GL Calories: 354; Fat: 20.4 g; Protein: 21.0 g; Carbs: 2.2 g; Sugar: 0.2 g; Fiber: 2.0 g; Cholesterol: 84 mg; Sodium: 246 mg; Potassium: 282 mg

120. Crab Patties

Preparation Time: 10 minutes
Cooking Time: 5 minutes
Cooking Level: Easy
Servings: 2

Ingredients:
- 2 tbsp coconut oil
- 1 tbsp lemon juice
- 1 cup lump crab meat
- 2 tsp Dijon mustard
- 1 egg, beaten
- 1 ½ tbsp coconut flour

Directions:
1. In a bowl, place the crabmeat, add all the ingredients, except for the oil; mix well to combine. Make patties out of the mixture. Melt coconut oil. Add the crab patties and cook for about 2–3 minutes per side.

Nutrition: Low GL Calories: 216; Fat: 11.6 g; Carbs: 3.6 g; Protein: 15.2 g; Fiber: 0.1 g; Sugar: 3.5 g; Cholesterol: 52 mg; Sodium: 292 mg; Potassium: 196 mg

121. Seared Scallops with Chorizo

Preparation Time: 10 minutes
Cooking Time: 10 minutes
Cooking Level: Easy
Servings: 2

Ingredients:
- 2 tbsp butter
- 16 fresh scallops
- 8 oz (227 g) chorizo, chopped
- 1 red bell pepper, seeds removed, sliced
- 1 cup red onions, finely chopped
- 1 cup Asiago cheese, grated
- Salt and black pepper, to taste

Directions:
1. Melt half butter and cook the onion and bell pepper for 5 minutes until tender. Add chorizo and stir-fry for another 3 minutes. Remove and set aside.
2. Pat dry the scallops with paper towels and season with salt and pepper. Add the remaining butter to the skillet and sear the scallops for 2 minutes on each side to have a golden brown color. Add the chorizo mixture back and warm through. Transfer to a serving platter and top with Asiago cheese.

Nutrition: Low GL Calories: 490; Fat: 32.1 g; Carbs: 6.0 g; Protein: 35.8 g; Fiber: 1.1 g; Sugar: 4.9 g; Cholesterol: 49 mg; Sodium: 317 mg; Potassium: 179 mg

122. Creamy Herbed Salmon

Preparation Time: 10 minutes
Cooking Time: 10 minutes
Cooking Level: Easy
Servings: 2

Ingredients:

- 2 salmon fillets
- ¾ tsp dried tarragon
- 2 tbsp olive oil
- ¾ tsp dried dill

Sauce:

- 2 tbsp butter
- ½ tsp dill
- ½ tsp tarragon
- ¼ cup heavy cream
- Salt and black pepper, to taste

Directions:

1. Season the salmon with dill and tarragon. Warm olive oil in a pan over medium heat. Add the salmon and cook for about 4 minutes on both sides. Set aside.
2. To make the sauce: Melt butter and add dill and tarragon. Cook for 30 seconds to infuse the flavors. Whisk heavy cream, season with salt and black pepper, and cook for 2–3 minutes. Serve the salmon topped with the sauce.

Nutrition: Low GL Calories: 467; Fat: 40.1 g; Carbs: 1.9 g; Protein: 22.1 g; Fiber: 0.3 g; Sugar: 1.6 g; Cholesterol: 45 mg; Sodium: 248 mg; Potassium: 219 mg

123. Mussels and Coconut Milk Curry

Preparation Time: 10 minutes
Cooking Time: 20 minutes
Cooking Level: Easy
Servings: 2
Ingredients:

- 3 pounds (1.4 kg) mussels, cleaned, de-bearded
- 1 cup minced shallots
- 3 tbsp minced garlic
- 1 ½ cups coconut milk
- 2 cups dry white wine
- 2 tsp red curry powder
- ⅜ cup coconut oil
- ⅜ cup chopped green onions
- ⅜ cup chopped parsley

Directions:

1. Pour wine into a large saucepan and cook the shallots and garlic over low heat. Stir the coconut milk and red curry powder, and cook for 3 minutes.
2. Add mussels and steam for 7 minutes or until their shells are opened. Then, use a slotted spoon to remove to a bowl, leaving the sauce in the pan. Discard any closed mussels at this point.
3. Stir coconut oil into the sauce, turn the heat off, and stir parsley and green onions. Serve sauce immediately with a butternut squash mash.

Nutrition: Low GL Calories: 355; Fat: 20.5 g; Carbs: 2.5 g; Protein: 21.0 g; Fiber: 2.3 g; Sugar: 0.2 g; Cholesterol: 57 mg; Sodium: 218 mg; Potassium: 276 mg

124. Alaska Cod with Butter Garlic Sauce

Preparation Time: 10 minutes
Cooking Time: 15 minutes
Cooking Level: Easy
Servings: 2
Ingredients:

- 2 tsp olive oil

2 Alaska cod fillets:

- Salt and black pepper to taste
- 4 tbsp salted butter
- 4 cloves garlic, minced
- ⅜ cup lemon juice
- 3 tbsp white wine
- 2 tbsp chopped chives

Directions:

1. Heat oil and season the cod with salt and black pepper. Fry the fillets in the oil for 4 minutes on one side, flip, and cook for 1 minute. Take out, plate, and set aside.
2. In another skillet over low heat, melt butter and sauté the garlic for 3 minutes. Add lemon juice, wine and chives. Season with salt and black pepper, and cook for 3 minutes until the wine slightly reduces. Put the fish in the skillet, spoon sauce over, cook for 30 seconds, and turn the heat off.
3. Divide the fish into 6 plates, top with sauce, and serve with buttered green beans.

Nutrition: Low GL Calorie: 265; Fat: 17.1 g; Carbs: 2.5 g; Protein: 19.9 g; Fiber: 0.1 g; Sugar: 2.4 g; Cholesterol: 89 mg; Sodium: 248 mg; Potassium: 312 mg

125. Seared Tuna with Niçoise Salad

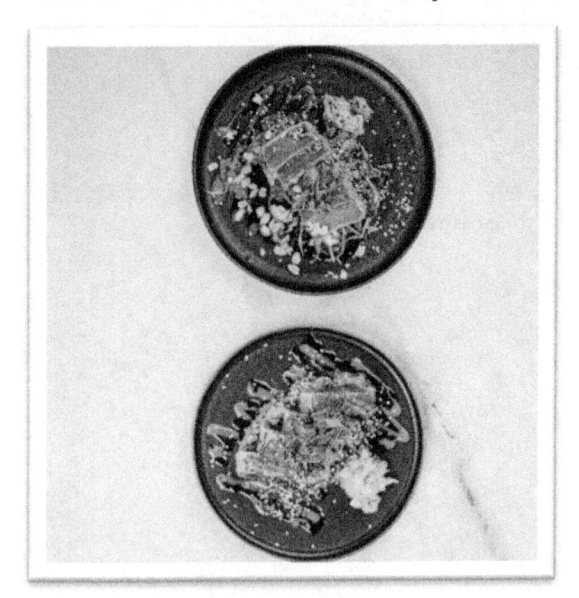

Preparation Time: 10 minutes
Cooking Time: 8 minutes
Cooking Level: Easy
Servings: 2
Ingredients:

- 1 tbsp sugar-free mayonnaise
- 1 tsp Dijon mustard
- ½ tsp kosher salt
- ¼ tsp ground black pepper
- 1 pound (454 g) ahi tuna steaks
- 1 tbsp avocado oil or other light-tasting oil, for the pan
- 2 medium heads red or green leaf lettuce, leaves washed and dried
- 8 hard-boiled eggs, peeled and quartered
- 2 cups cooked cauliflower florets
- 2 cups blanched green beans
- 2 large tomatoes, cut into wedges

Dijon vinaigrette:

- ¼ cup extra-virgin olive oil
- ¼ cup red wine vinegar
- ¼ cup sugar-free mayonnaise
- 1 tbsp Dijon mustard
- ¼ tsp kosher salt
- ⅛ tsp ground black pepper

Directions:

1. Combine the mayonnaise, mustard, salt and pepper in a small bowl. Coat the tuna steaks on all sides with the mixture.
2. Heat oil in a medium-sized nonstick pan over medium-high heat. Add the tuna steaks and sear for about 2 minutes per side for rare or 4 minutes per side to cook them through. Remove from the pan and set aside.
3. Place lettuce leaves on a serving platter or Divide them among 4 individual serving plates. Arrange the eggs, cauliflower, green beans and tomato wedges around the outer edges on top of the lettuce.
4. Place tuna steaks, whole or cut into pieces, in the center of the platter or plates. Whisk the vinaigrette ingredients. Drizzle over the salad just before serving.

Nutrition: Low GL Calories: 547; Fat: 36.9 g; Carbs: 12.0 g; Protein: 15.8 g; Fiber: 6.0 g; Sugar: 1.0 g; Cholesterol: 68 mg; Sodium: 248 mg; Potassium: 272 mg

126. Lemony Paprika Shrimp

Preparation Time: 10 minutes
Cooking Time: 20 minutes
Cooking Level: Easy
Servings: 2
Ingredients:

- ½ cup butter, divided
- 2 pounds (907 g) shrimp, peeled and deveined
- Salt and black pepper, to taste
- ¼ tsp sweet paprika
- 1 tbsp minced garlic
- 3 tbsp water
- 1 lemon, zested and juiced
- 2 tbsp chopped parsley

Directions:

1. Melt half of the butter, season the shrimp with salt, black pepper paprika, and add to the butter. Stir garlic and cook shrimp for 4 minutes on both sides until pink. Remove to a bowl and set aside.
2. Put the remaining butter in the skillet; include the lemon zest, juice and water. Add shrimp and parsley, and adjust the taste with salt and pepper. Cook for 2 minutes. Serve shrimp and sauce with squash pasta.

Nutrition: Low GL Calories: 256; Fat: 22.1 g; Carbs: 2.0 g; Protein: 12.9 g; Fiber: 0.1 g; Sugar: 1.9 g; Cholesterol: 89 mg; Sodium: 248 mg; Potassium: 312 mg

127. Tiger Shrimp with Chimichurri

Preparation Time: 15 minutes
Cooking Time: 35 minutes
Cooking Level: Moderate
Servings: 2
Ingredients:

- 1 pound (454 g) tiger shrimp, peeled and deveined
- 2 tbsp olive oil
- 1 garlic clove, minced
- Juice 1 lime
- Salt and black pepper, to taste

Chimichurri:

- Salt and black pepper, to taste
- ¼ cup extra-virgin olive oil
- 2 garlic cloves, minced
- 1 lime, juiced
- ¼ cup red wine vinegar
- 2 cups parsley, minced
- ¼ tsp red pepper flakes

Directions:

1. Combine the shrimp, olive oil, garlic and lime juice in a bowl, and let marinate in the fridge for 30 minutes. To make the chimichurri dressing, blitz the chimichurri ingredients in a blender until smooth; set aside. Preheat your grill to medium. Add the shrimp and cook about for 2 minutes per side. Serve the shrimp drizzled with the chimichurri dressing.

Nutrition: Low GL Calories: 524; Fat: 30.2 g; Carbs: 8.3 g; Protein: 48.8 g; Fiber: 1.2 g; Sugar: 1.1 g; Cholesterol: 81 mg; Sodium: 318 mg; Potassium: 304 mg

128. Grilled Salmon with Greek Green Salad

Preparation Time: 15 minutes
Cooking Time: 8 minutes
Cooking Level: Easy
Servings: 2
Ingredients:

Salad:

- 2 medium heads romaine lettuce, chopped
- ½ medium cucumber, chopped
- ¾ cup cherry tomatoes, halved
- ¾ cup crumbled Feta cheese
- ½ cup pitted Kalamata olives
- ½ cup thinly sliced red onions
- 1 tsp dried ground oregano
- Pinch salt
- Pinch ground black pepper

Dressing:

- ¼ cup extra-virgin olive oil
- ¼ cup red wine vinegar
- 1 large clove garlic, minced
- 2 tsp onion powder
- 2 tsp dried ground oregano
- Salt and pepper, to taste

Salmon:

- 4 (6-oz / 170-g) skin-on salmon fillets
- 1 tbsp extra-virgin olive oil
- Salt and pepper, to taste
- 1 tbsp avocado oil or other cooking oil of choice, for the grill grates Fresh dill, for garnish (optional)

Directions:

1. Combine all the salad ingredients and toss. Divide the salad among 4 bowls and set it aside.
2. Make the dressing: Place olive oil, vinegar, garlic, oregano and onion powder in a bowl, and whisk to combine. Season and set aside. Rinse the salmon and pat dry. Brush salmon with olive oil and season with salt and pepper. Preheat a grill to medium-high heat, then brush hot grill grates with the avocado oil.
3. Place salmon skin side up on the grill, close the grill lid, and cook for 2 minutes. Flip the salmon and cook skin side down for 5 to 6 minutes, until the internal temperature reaches 145°F (63°C).
4. Allow the salmon to rest for a few minutes, then place a fillet on top of each salad. Whisk the salad dressing again and drizzle

it over the salads. Garnish with fresh dill, if desired, and enjoy!

Nutrition: Low GL Calories: 589; Fat: 41.8 g; Carbs: 10.2 g; Protein: 42.0 g; Fiber: 2.6 g; Sugar: 1.6 g; Cholesterol: 56 mg; Sodium: 98 mg; Potassium: 287 mg

129. Tuna Carbonara

Preparation Time: 5 minutes
Cooking Time: 25 minutes
Cooking Level: Easy
Servings: 2
Ingredients:

- ½ lb. tuna fillet, cut in pieces
- 2 eggs
- 4 tbsp fresh parsley, diced

What You'll Need From Store Cupboard:

- ½ Homemade Pasta, cook and drain,
- ½ cup reduced-fat parmesan cheese
- 2 cloves garlic, peeled
- 2 tbsp extra-virgin olive oil
- Salt and pepper, to taste

Directions:

1. Beat the eggs, parmesan and a dash of pepper.
2. Heat oil in a large skillet over med-high heat. Add garlic and cook until browned. Add the tuna and cook 2–3 minutes, or until tuna is almost cooked through. Discard the garlic.
3. Add pasta and reduce the heat. Stir the egg mixture and cook, stirring constantly, for 2 minutes. If the sauce is too thick, thin with water, a little bit at a time, until it has a creamy texture.
4. Season and serve garnished with parsley.

Nutrition: Low GL Calorie: 409; Fat: 30 g; Total Carbs: 7 g; Protein: 25 g; Fiber: 1 g; Sugar: 0 g; Cholesterol: 89 mg; Sodium: 264 mg; Potassium: 312 mg

130. Flavors Cioppino

Preparation Time: 10 minutes
Cooking Time: 5 minutes
Cooking Level: Easy
Servings: 2
Ingredients:

- 1 lb. codfish, cut into chunks
- 1 ½ lbs. shrimp
- 28 oz. can tomatoes, diced
- 1 cup dry white wine
- 1 bay leaf
- 1 tsp cayenne
- 1 tsp oregano
- 1 shallot, chopped
- 1 tsp garlic, minced
- 1 tbsp olive oil
- ½ tsp salt

Directions:

1. Add oil into the inner pot of the instant pot and set the pot on sauté mode. Add shallot and garlic, and sauté for 2 minutes.
2. Add wine, bay leaf, cayenne, oregano and salt, and cook for 3 minutes. Add the remaining ingredients and stir well.
3. Seal the pot with a lid and select manual, and cook on low for 10 minutes.
4. Once done, release pressure using quick release. Remove lid. Serve and enjoy.

Nutrition: Low GL Calorie: 281; Fat: 5 g; Carbohydrates: 10.5 g; Protein: 40.7 g; Fiber: 3 g; Sugar: 4.9 g; Cholesterol: 68 mg; Sodium: 266 mg; Potassium: 318 mg

131. Mediterranean Fish Fillets

Preparation Time: 10 minutes
Cooking Time: 3 minutes
Cooking Level: Easy
Servings: 2
Ingredients:

- 4 cod fillets
- 1 lb. grape tomatoes, halved
- 1 cup olives, pitted and sliced
- 2 tbsp capers
- 1 tsp dried thyme
- 2 tbsp olive oil
- 1 tsp garlic, minced
- Pepper
- Salt

Directions:

1. Pour 1 cup water in the instant pot then place steamer rack in the pot. Spray heat-safe baking dish with cooking spray.
2. Add half grape tomatoes into the dish and season with pepper and salt. Arrange the fish fillets on top of cherry tomatoes. Drizzle with oil and season with garlic, thyme, capers, pepper and salt.
3. Spread olives and the remaining grape tomatoes on top of fish fillets. Place the dish on top of steamer rack in the pot.

4. Seal the pot with a lid and select manual, and cook on high for 3 minutes. Once done, release pressure using quick release. Remove lid. Serve and enjoy.

Nutrition: Low GL Calorie: 212; Fat: 11.9 g; Carbohydrates: 7.1 g; Protein: 21.4 g; Fiber: 2 g; Sugar: 3 g; Cholesterol: 47 mg; Sodium: 55 mg; Potassium: 317 mg

132. Delicious Shrimp Alfredo

Preparation Time: 10 minutes
Cooking Time: 3 minutes
Cooking Level: Easy
Servings: 2
Ingredients:

- 12 shrimp, remove shells
- 1 tbsp garlic, minced
- ¼ cup parmesan cheese
- 2 cups whole-wheat rotini noodles
- 1 cup fish broth
- 15 oz. alfredo sauce
- 1 onion, chopped
- Salt

Directions:

1. Add all the ingredients except for the parmesan cheese into the instant pot and stir well.
2. Seal the pot and cook on high for 3 minutes.
3. Once done, release the pressure using quick release. Remove the lid.
4. Stir the cheese and serve.

Nutrition: Low GL Calorie: 669; Fat: 23.1 g; Carbohydrates: 6 g; Protein: 37.8 g; Fiber: 2 g; Sugar: 2.4 g; Cholesterol: 89 mg; Sodium: 190 mg; Potassium: 312 mg

133. Tomato Olive Fish Fillets

Preparation Time: 10 minutes
Cooking Time: 8 minutes
Cooking Level: Easy
Servings: 2
Ingredients:

- 2 lbs. halibut fish fillets
- 2 oregano sprigs
- 2 rosemary sprigs
- 2 tbsp fresh lime juice
- 1 cup olives, pitted
- 28 oz. can tomatoes, diced
- 1 tbsp garlic, minced
- 1 onion, chopped
- 2 tbsp olive oil

Directions:

1. Add oil into the inner pot of the instant pot and set the pot on sauté mode. Add onion and sauté for 3 minutes.
2. Add garlic and sauté for a minute. Add lime juice, olives, herb sprig and tomatoes, and stir well. Seal the pot and cook on high for 3 minutes.
3. Once done, release the pressure using quick release. Remove lid. Add the fish fillets, seal the pot again with the lid, and cook on high for 2 minutes.
4. Once done, release the pressure using quick release. Remove lid. Serve and enjoy.

Nutrition: Low GL Calorie: 333; Fat: 19.1 g; Carbohydrates: 3.8 g; Protein: 13.4 g; Fiber: 2 g; Sugar: 8.4 g; Cholesterol: 74 mg; Sodium: 5 mg; Potassium: 2922 mg

134. Halibut Tacos with Cabbage Slaw

Preparation Time: 15 minutes

77

Cooking Time: 6 minutes
Cooking Level: Easy
Servings: 2
Ingredients:

- 1 tbsp olive oil
- 1 tsp chili powder
- 4 halibut fillets, skinless, sliced
- 2 low carb tortillas

Slaw:

- 2 tbsp red cabbage, shredded
- 1 tbsp lemon juice
- Salt, to taste
- ½ tbsp extra-virgin olive oil
- ½ carrot, shredded
- 1 tbsp cilantro, chopped

Directions:

1. Combine the red cabbage with salt in a bowl; massage cabbage to tenderize. Add in the remaining slaw ingredient; toss to coat and set aside.
2. Rub the halibut with olive oil, chili powder and paprika. Heat a grill pan over medium heat.
3. Add the halibut and cook until lightly charred and cooked through, about 3 minutes per side.
4. Divide between the tortillas. Combine all the slaw ingredients
5. Split the slaw among the tortillas.

Nutrition: Low GL Calories: 386; Fat: 25.9 g; Carbs: 6.4 g; Protein: 23.7 g; Fiber: 6.2 g; Sugar: 0.7 g; Cholesterol: 54 mg; Sodium: 212 mg; Potassium: 216 mg

135. Pistachio Nut Salmon with Shallot Sauce

Preparation Time: 15 minutes
Cooking Time: 30 minutes
Cooking Level: Moderate
Servings: 2
Ingredients:

- 4 salmon fillets
- ½ tsp pepper
- 1 tsp salt
- ¼ cup mayonnaise
- ½ cup pistachios, chopped

Sauce:

- 1 shallot, chopped
- 2 tsp lemon zest
- 1 tbsp olive oil
- A pinch pepper
- 1 cup heavy cream

Directions:

1. Preheat the oven to 375ºF (190ºC). Brush the salmon with mayonnaise and season with salt and pepper. Coat with pistachios. Place in a lined baking dish and bake for 15 minutes.
2. Heat olive oil, sauté the shallots for a few minutes. Stir the rest of the sauce ingredients. Boil and cook until thickened. Serve salmon topped with the sauce.

Nutrition: Low GL Calories: 564; Fat: 47.0 g; Carbs: 8.1 g; Protein: 34.0 g; Fiber: 2.1 g; Sugar: 2 g; Cholesterol: 89 mg; Sodium: 98 mg; Potassium: 289 mg

136. Coconut Crab Cakes

Preparation Time: 20 minutes
Cooking Time: 25 minutes
Cooking Level: Easy
Servings: 2
Ingredients:

- 1 tbsp minced garlic
- 2 pasteurized eggs
- 2 tsp coconut oil
- ¾ cup coconut flakes
- ¾ cup chopped spinach
- ¼ pound crabmeat
- ¼ cup chopped leek
- ½ cup extra-virgin olive oil
- ½ tsp pepper
- ¼ onion diced
- Salt, to taste

Directions:

1. Pour crabmeat into a bowl, then add in the coconut flakes and mix well.
2. Whisk the eggs in a bowl, then mix in leek and spinach.
3. Season the egg mixture with pepper, two pinches of salt, and garlic. Then, pour eggs into the crab and stir well.
4. Preheat a pan, heat extra-virgin olive, and fry the crab evenly from each side until golden brown. Remove from pan and serve hot.

Nutrition: Low GL Calories: 254; Fat: 9.5 g; Carbohydrates: 4.1 g; Protein: 8.9 g; Fiber: 5.4 g; Sugar: 1 g; Cholesterol: 85 mg; Sodium: 76 mg; Potassium: 302 mg

137. Tuna Cakes

Preparation Time: 15 minutes
Cooking Time: 10 minutes
Cooking Level: Easy
Servings: 2
Ingredients:

- 1 (15-oz) can water-packed tuna, drained
- ½ celery stalk, chopped
- 2 tbsp fresh parsley, chopped
- 1 tsp fresh dill, chopped
- 2 tbsp walnuts, chopped
- 2 tbsp mayonnaise
- 1 organic egg, beaten
- 1 tbsp butter
- 3 cups lettuce

Directions:

1. For burgers: Add all the ingredients (except the butter and lettuce) in a bowl and mix until well combined.
2. Make two equal-sized patties from the mixture. Melt some butter and cook patties for about 2–3 minutes.
3. Carefully flip the side and cook for about 2–3 minutes.
4. Divide lettuce onto serving plates. Top each plate with one burger and serve.

Nutrition: Low GL Calories: 267; Fat: 12.5 g; Carbohydrates: 3.8 g; Protein: 11.5 g; Fiber: 9.4 g; Sugar: 2 g; Cholesterol: 89 mg; Sodium: 182 mg; Potassium: 273 mg

138. Chili-Lime Tuna Salad

Preparation Time: 10 minutes
Cooking Time: 0 minutes
Cooking Level: Easy
Servings: 2
Ingredients:

- 1 tbsp lime juice
- ⅜ cup mayonnaise
- ¼ tsp salt
- 1 tsp Tajin chili lime seasoning
- ⅛ tsp pepper
- 1 medium stalk celery (finely chopped)
- 2 cups romaine lettuce (chopped roughly)
- 2 tbsp red onion (finely chopped)
- optional: chopped green onion, black pepper, lemon juice
- 2 oz canned tuna

Directions:

1. Using a bowl of medium size, mix some of the ingredients such as lime, pepper and chili-lime
2. Then, add tuna and vegetables to the pot, and stir. You can serve with cucumber, celery, or a bed of greens

Nutrition: Low GL Calories: 259; Fat: 11.3 g; Carbohydrates: 2.9 g; Protein: 12.9 g; Fiber: 7.4 g; Sugar: 2 g; Cholesterol: 89 mg; Sodium: 119 mg; Potassium: 262 mg

139. Lemony Sea Bass Fillet

Preparation Time: 10 minutes
Cooking Time: 10–15 minutes
Cooking Level: Easy

Servings: 2
Ingredients:
Fish:

- 4 sea bass fillets
- 2 tbsp olive oil, divided
- A pinch of chili pepper
- Salt, to taste

Olive Sauce:

- 1 tbsp green olives, pitted and sliced
- 1 lemon, juiced
- Salt, to taste

Directions:

1. Preheat the grill to high heat. Stir together one tbsp olive oil, chili pepper and salt
2. Brush both sides of the fillet generously with the mixture. Grill the fillets on the preheated grill for about 5 to 6 minutes on each side until lightly browned.
3. Meanwhile, warm the left olive oil in a skillet over medium heat. Add green olives, lemon juice and salt.
4. Cook until the sauce is heated through. Transfer the fillets to four serving plates, then pour the sauce over them. Serve warm.

Nutrition: Low GL Calories: 257; Fat: 12.4 g; Carbohydrates: 2 g; Protein: 12.7 g; Fiber: 56 g; Sugar: 2 g; Cholesterol: 89 mg; Sodium: 173 mg; Potassium: 312 mg

140. Curried Fish with Super Greens

Preparation Time: 10 minutes
Cooking Time: 20 minutes
Cooking Level: Easy
Servings: 2
Ingredients:

- 2 tbsp coconut oil
- 2 tsp garlic, minced
- 1 ½ tbsp grated fresh ginger
- ½ tsp ground cumin
- 1 tbsp curry powder
- 2 cups coconut milk
- 16 oz (454 g) firm white fish, cut into 1-inch chunks
- 1 cup kale, shredded
- 2 tbsp cilantro, chopped

Directions:

1. Melt the coconut oil. Add garlic and ginger, and sauté for about 2 minutes until tender.
2. Fold in the cumin and curry powder, then cook for 1 to 2 minutes until fragrant.
3. Put in the coconut milk and boil. Boil then simmer until the flavors mellow, about 5 minutes. Add the fish chunks and simmer for 10 minutes until the fish flakes easily with a fork, stirring once.
4. Scatter the shredded kale and chopped cilantro over the fish, then cook for 2 minutes more until softened.

Nutrition: Low GL Calories: 376; Fat: 19.9 g; Carbohydrates: 6.7 g; Protein: 14.8 g; Fiber: 15.8 g; Sugar: 2 g; Cholesterol: 59 mg; Sodium: 153 mg; Potassium: 302 mg

141. Garlic-Lemon Mahi Mahi

Preparation Time: 15 minutes
Cooking Time: 10 minutes
Cooking Level: Easy
Servings: 2
Ingredients:

- 2 tbsp butter
- 5 tbsp extra-virgin olive oil
- 4 oz mahi-mahi fillets
- 3 minced cloves garlic
- Kosher Salt and pepper, to taste
- 2 pounds asparagus
- 2 sliced lemons
- Zest and juice 2 lemons
- 1 tsp crushed red pepper flakes
- 1 tbsp chopped parsley

Directions:

1. Melt three tbsp of butter and olive oil in a microwave. Heat a skillet and put in mahi-mahi, then sprinkle black pepper.
2. For around 5 minutes per side, cook it. When done, move to a plate. In another skillet, add the remaining oil and add in the asparagus, stir fry for 2–3 minutes. Take out on a plate.
3. In the same skillet, pour in the remaining butter, and add garlic, red pepper, lemon, zest, juice and parsley.
4. Add in the mahi-mahi and asparagus, and stir together. Serve hot.

Nutrition: Low GL Calories: 317; Fat: 8.5 g; Carbohydrates: 3.1 g; Protein: 16.1 g; Fiber: 6.9 g; Sugar: 2 g; Cholesterol: 89 mg; Sodium: 189 mg; Potassium: 192 mg

142. Scallops in Creamy Garlic Sauce

Preparation Time: 15 minutes
Cooking Time: 15 minutes
Cooking Level: Easy
Servings: 2
Ingredients:

- 1 ¼ pounds fresh sea scallops, side muscles removed
- Salt and ground black pepper, as required
- 4 tbsp butter, divided
- 2 garlic cloves, chopped
- ¼ cup homemade chicken broth
- 1 cup heavy cream
- 1 tbsp fresh lemon juice
- 2 tbsp fresh parsley, chopped

Directions:

1. Sprinkle the scallops evenly with salt and black pepper. Melt 2 tbsp of butter in a large pan over medium-high heat and cook the scallops for about 2–3 minutes per side.
2. Flip the scallops and cook for about 2 more minutes. Transfer the scallops onto a plate. Using the same pan, the butter must be melted and sauté the garlic for about 1 minute.
3. Pour broth and bring to a gentle boil. Cook for about 2 minutes. Stir cream and cook for about 1–2 minutes or until slightly thickened.
4. Stir the cooked scallops and lemon juice, and remove from the heat. Garnish with fresh parsley and serve hot.

Nutrition: Low GL Calories: 259; Fat: 8.5 g; Carbohydrates: 2.1 g; Protein: 12.2 g; Fiber: 7.4 g; Sugar: 2 g; Cholesterol: 59 mg; Sodium: 173 mg; Potassium: 288 mg

143. Israeli Salmon Salad

Preparation Time: 10 minutes
Cooking Time: 0 minutes
Cooking Level: Easy
Servings: 2
Ingredients:

- 1 cup flaked smoked salmon
- 1 tomato, chopped
- ½ small red onion, chopped
- 1 cucumber, chopped
- tbsp pitted green olives
- 1 avocado, chopped
- 2 tbsp avocado oil
- 2 tbsp almond oil
- 1 tbsp plain vinegar
- Salt and black pepper, to taste
- 1 cup crumbled feta cheese
- 1 cup grated cheddar cheese

Directions:

1. In a salad bowl, add salmon, tomatoes, red onion, cucumber, green olives and avocado. Mix well.
2. In a bowl, whisk the avocado oil, vinegar, salt and black pepper.
3. Drizzle the dressing over the salad and toss well.
4. Sprinkle some feta cheese and serve the salad immediately.

Nutrition: Low GL Calories: 415; Fat: 11.4 g; Carbohydrates: 3.8 g; Protein: 15.4 g; Fiber: 9.9 g; Sugar: 2 g; Cholesterol: 82 mg; Sodium: 233 mg; Potassium: 310 mg

CHAPTER 8: SNACKS AND APPETIZERS RECIPES

144. Cauliflower Poppers

Preparation Time: 20 minutes
Cooking Time: 30 minutes
Cooking Level: Moderate
Servings: 2
Ingredients:

- 4 C. cauliflower florets
- 2 tsp olive oil
- ¼ tsp chili powder
- Pepper and salt, to taste

Directions:

1. Preheat the oven to 450°F. Grease a roasting pan.
2. In a bowl, add all the ingredients and toss to coat well.
3. Transfer the cauliflower mixture into a prepared roasting pan and spread in an even layer.
4. Roast for about 25–30 minutes. Serve warm.

Nutrition: Low GL Calories: 102; Fat: 8.5 g; Carbohydrates: 2.1 g; Protein: 4.2 g; Fiber: 4.7 g; Sugar: 0.1 g; Cholesterol: 78 mg; Sodium: 212 mg; Potassium: 189 mg

145. Roasted Radishes with Brown Butter Sauce

Preparation Time: 10 minutes
Cooking Time: 15 minutes
Cooking Level: Easy
Servings: 2
Ingredients:

- 2 cups halved radishes
- 1 tbsp olive oil
- Pink Himalayan salt and pepper, to taste
- ½ tbsp butter
- 1 tbsp chopped fresh flat-leaf Italian parsley

Directions:

1. Preheat the oven to 450°F.
2. Toss the radishes in the olive oil and season with Pink Himalayan salt to taste and pepper.
3. Spread the radishes on a baking sheet in a single layer. Roast for 15 minutes, stirring halfway through.
4. Meanwhile, when the radishes have been roasting for about 10 minutes, in a small, light-colored saucepan over medium heat, melt butter completely, stirring frequently, and season with Pink Himalayan salt to taste. When the butter begins to bubble and foam, continue stirring. When the bubbling diminishes a bit, the butter should be a nice nutty brown. The browning process should take about 3 minutes total. Transfer the browned butter to a heat-safe container (I use a mug).
5. Remove the radishes from the oven and divide them between two plates. Spoon the brown butter over the radishes, top with the chopped parsley, and serve.

Nutrition: Low GL Calories: 361; Total Fat: 37 g; Carbs: 3.8 g; Protein: 2 g; Fiber: 4 g; Sugar: 1 g; Cholesterol: 89 mg; Sodium: 327 mg; Potassium: 312 mg

146. Sweet Onion Dip

Preparation Time: 15 minutes
Cooking Time: 25–30 minutes
Cooking Level: Moderate
Servings: 2
Ingredients:

- 3 cup sweet onion chopped
- ½ tsp pepper sauce
- 2 cups Swiss cheese shredded
- Ground black pepper, to taste
- 1 cups mayonnaise
- ¼ cup horseradish

Directions:

1. Take a bowl, add sweet onion, horseradish, pepper sauce, mayonnaise and Swiss cheese; mix them well and transfer into the pie plate.
2. Preheat the oven to 375°F.
3. Now put the plate into the oven and bake for 25 to 30 minutes until the edges turn golden brown.
4. Sprinkle pepper to taste and serve with crackers.

Nutrition: Low GL Calories: 278; Fat: 11.4 g; Carbohydrates: 2.9 g; Protein: 6.9 g; Fiber: 4.1 g; Sugar: 1 g; Cholesterol: 72 mg; Sodium: 248 mg; Potassium: 234 mg

147. Keto Trail Mix

Preparation Time: 5 minutes
Cooking Time: 0 minutes
Cooking Level: Easy
Servings: 2
Ingredients:

- ½ cup salted pumpkin seeds
- ½ cup slivered almonds
- ¾ cup roasted pecan halves
- ¾ cup unsweetened cranberries
- 1 cup toasted coconut flakes

Directions:

1. In a skillet, place the almonds and pecans. Heat for 2–3 minutes and let cool.
2. Once cooled, in a large resealable plastic bag, combine all the ingredients.
3. Seal and shake vigorously to mix.
4. Evenly divide into the suggested servings and store in airtight meal prep containers.

Nutrition: Low GL Calories: 98; Fat: 1.2 g; Carbohydrates: 1.1 g; Protein: 3.2 g; Fiber: 4.1 g; Sugar: 1 g; Cholesterol: 81 mg; Sodium: 268 mg; Potassium: 214 mg

148. Cold Cuts and Cheese Pinwheels

Preparation Time: 20 minutes
Cooking Time: 0 minutes
Cooking Level: Easy
Servings: 2
Ingredients:

- 8 oz cream cheese, at room temperature
- ¼ pound salami, thinly sliced
- 2 tbsp sliced pepperoncini

Directions:

1. Layout a sheet of plastic wrap on a large cutting board or counter. Place the cream cheese in the center of the plastic wrap, and then add another layer of plastic wrap on top. Using a rolling pin, roll the cream cheese until it is even and about ¼ inch thick.
2. Try to make the shape somewhat resemble a rectangle. Pull off the top layer of plastic wrap. Place the salami slices so they overlap to cover the cream cheese layer completely.
3. Place a new piece of plastic wrap on top of the salami layer to flip over your cream cheese-salami rectangle. Flip the layer, so the cream cheese side is up. Remove the plastic wrap and add sliced pepperoncini in a layer on top.
4. Roll the layered ingredients into a tight log, pressing the meat and cream cheese together. (You want it as tight as possible.) Then wrap the roll with plastic wrap and refrigerate for at least 6 hours so it will set. Slice and serve.

Nutrition: Low GL Calories: 141; Fat: 4.9 g; Carbohydrates: 0.3 g; Protein: 8.5 g; Fiber: 2.1 g; Sugar: 1 g; Cholesterol: 89 mg; Sodium: 118 mg; Potassium: 310 mg

149. Zucchini Balls with Capers and Bacon

Preparation Time: 3 Hours
Cooking Time: 20 minutes
Cooking Level: Easy
Servings: 2
Ingredients:

- 2 zucchinis, shredded
- 2 bacon slices, chopped
- ½ cup cream cheese,
- 1 cup fontina cheese
- ¼ cup capers
- 1 clove garlic, crushed
- ½ cup grated Parmesan cheese
- ½ tsp poppy seeds
- ¼ tsp dried dill weed
- ½ tsp onion powder
- Salt and black pepper, to taste
- 1 cup crushed pork rinds

Directions:

1. Preheat the oven to 360°F. Thoroughly mix zucchinis, capers, ½ of Parmesan cheese, garlic, cream cheese, bacon and fontina cheese until well combined.
2. Shape the mixture into balls. Refrigerate for 3 hours.
3. Mix the remaining Parmesan cheese, crushed pork rinds, dill, black pepper, onion powder, poppy seeds and salt.
4. Roll the cheese ball in Parmesan mixture to coat. Arrange in a greased baking dish in a single layer and bake for 15–20 minutes, shaking once.

Nutrition: Low GL Calories: 227; Fat: 12.5 g; Carbohydrates: 4.3 g; Protein: 14.5 g; Fiber: 9.4 g; Sugar: 1 g; Cholesterol: 59 mg; Sodium: 328 mg; Potassium: 277 mg

150. Plantains with Tapioca Pearls

Preparation Time: 15 minutes
Cooking Time: 3 Hours
Cooking Level: Difficult
Servings: 2
Ingredients:

- 5 ripe plantains, sliced into thick disks
- 1 can thick coconut cream
- 1 tsp coconut oil
- ¼ cup tiny tapioca pearls, dried
- 1 cup white sugar
- 2 cups water
- Pinch salt

Directions:

1. Grease the Instant Pot Pressure Cooker with coconut oil.
2. Place the ripe plantains. Top this with tapioca pearls, coconut oil, white sugar and salt. Pour water in the Instant Pot.
3. Lock the lid in place. Press the high pressure and cook for 5 minutes.
4. When the beep sounds, choose the Quick Pressure Release. This will depressurize for 7 minutes. Remove the lid.
5. Tip in in the coconut cream. Allow residual heat cook the last ingredient.
6. To serve, ladle just the right amount of plantains into dessert bowls.

Nutrition: Low GL Calorie: 345; Fat: 8 g; Carbs: 3.5 g; Protein: 20 g; Fiber: 4.5 g; Sugar: 1 g; Cholesterol: 89 mg; Sodium: 98 mg; Potassium: 312 mg

151. Sweet Orange and Lemon Barley Risotto

Preparation Time: 5 minutes
Cooking Time: 45 minutes
Cooking Level: Moderate
Servings: 2
Ingredients:

- 1 ½ cups barley pearls
- ¼ cup raisins
- 1 cup sweet orange, chopped, reserve juice
- 4 cups water
- 4 strips lemon peels
- ¼ cup white sugar, add more if needed

Directions:

1. Combine barley pearls, lemon peels, raisins, water and white sugar into the Instant Pot Pressure Cooker.
2. Lock the lid in place. Press the high pressure and cook for 10 minutes. When the beep sounds, choose the Quick Pressure Release. This will depressurize for 7 minutes. Remove the lid. Discard lemon peels.
3. Add in the sweet orange and juices. Pour coconut cream. Allow the residual heat cook the coconut cream. Adjust the seasoning according to your preferred taste.
4. To serve, ladle equal amounts into dessert bowls. Cool slightly before serving.

Nutrition: Moderate GL Calorie: 124; Fat: 11 g; Fiber: 15 g; Carbs: 3.9 g; Protein: 28 g; Sugar: 1 g; Cholesterol: 57 mg; Sodium: 248 mg; Potassium: 284 mg

152. Homemade Applesauce

Preparation Time: 5 minutes
Cooking Time: 45 minutes
Cooking Level: Moderate
Servings: 2
Ingredients:

- 10 soft-fleshed apples, quartered
- ¼ tsp nutmeg powder
- 1 tsp cinnamon powder
- ¼ cup sugar
- ¼ cup water

Directions:

1. Put together apples, nutmeg powder, cinnamon powder, sugar and water into the Instant Pot Pressure Cooker.
2. Lock the lid in place. Press the high pressure and cook for 15 minutes. When the beep sounds, choose the Quick Pressure Release. This will depressurize for 7 minutes. Remove the lid.
3. Mash the apples until the desired consistency is achieved. Adjust the seasoning according to your preferred taste.
4. Spoon the applesauce into bowls. Store leftovers in the fridge. This is best served cold.

Nutrition: Low GL Calorie: 345; Fat: 12 g; Carbs: 3.4 g; Protein: 28 g; Fiber: 5 g; Sugar: 1 g; Cholesterol: 89 mg; Sodium: 168 mg; Potassium: 199 mg

153. Homemade Beet Hummus

Preparation Time: 5 minutes
Cooking Time: 45 minutes
Cooking Level: Moderate
Servings: 2
Ingredients:

- 5 pieces cucumbers, thickly sliced
- 6 cups water
- 2 lb red beets, peeled
- 1 garlic clove, peeled
- 3 tbsp tahini
- 3 tbsp cumin powder
- 2 tbsp Spanish paprika
- 3 tbsp lemon juice, freshly squeezed
- ¼ tsp salt
- 1 tbsp olive oil
- 1 tsp white sesame seeds, toasted
- ¼ cup fresh cilantro, chopped

Directions:

1. Place water, red beets and garlic clove into the Instant Pot Pressure Cooker. Lock the lid in place. Press the high pressure and cook for 1 minute.
2. When the beep sounds, choose the Quick Pressure Release. This will depressurize for 7 minutes. Remove the lid. Cool slightly before proceeding. Discard solids but keep 1 cup of the cooking liquid.
3. Transfer the beets to an immersion blender along with the cooking liquid. Season with tahini, cumin powder, Spanish paprika, lemon juice and salt. Process until smooth. Adjust the seasoning according to your preferred taste.
4. Pour beet hummus into a bowl. Garnish with sesame seeds, cilantro and olive oil. Serve with sliced cucumbers or crackers. Store leftovers in the fridge. Use as needed.

Nutrition: Low GL Calorie: 154; Fat: 12 g; Carbs: 1.9 g; Protein: 11 g; Fiber: 8 g; Sugar: 1 g; Cholesterol: 89 mg; Sodium: 248 mg; Potassium: 168 mg

154. Coconut Pudding with Tropical Fruit

Preparation Time: 15 minutes
Cooking Time: 45 minutes
Cooking Level: Moderate
Servings: 2
Ingredients:

- ¼ lb sticky rice balls
- 2 cups ripe plantains, sliced into thick disks
- 2 cans thick coconut cream, divided
- 1 cup taro, diced
- ½ cup tapioca pearls

- 1 cup sweet potato, diced
- 4 cups water
- 1 cup sugar
- Pinch salt

Directions:
1. Combine sticky rice balls, taro, ripe plantains, tapioca pearls, water, white sugar, sweet potato, 1 can of coconut cream and salt into the Instant Pot Pressure Cooker.
2. Lock the lid in place. Press the high pressure and cook for 10 minutes.
3. When the beep sounds, choose the Quick Pressure Release. This will depressurize for 7 minutes. Remove the lid.
4. Tip in the remaining can of coconut cream. Allow the residual heat to cook coconut cream.
5. To serve, ladle equal amounts into dessert bowls.

Nutrition: Low GL Calorie: 213; Fat: 11 g; Carbs: 2.7 g; Protein: 21 g; Fiber: 18 g; Sugar: 1 g; Cholesterol: 52 mg; Sodium: 212 mg; Potassium: 189 mg

155. Tofu with Salted Caramel Pearls

Preparation Time: 5 minutes
Cooking Time: 1 hour
Cooking Level: Difficult
Servings: 2
Ingredients:

- 1 cup tapioca pearls, no need to soak
- 2 packs 12 oz. soft silken tofu
- 5 cups water, divided
- 1 cup brown sugar
- 1/16 tsp salt

Directions:
1. Pour tapioca pearls and water into the Instant Pot Pressure Cooker crockpot. Lock the lid in place. Press the high pressure and cook for 10 minutes.
2. When the beep sounds, choose Natural Pressure Release. Depressurizing would take 20 minutes. Remove the lid. Reposition the lid and cook for another 5 minutes on high.
3. When the beep sounds, choose Natural Pressure Release. Depressurizing would take 20 minutes. Remove the lid. Pour out the contents of the pressure cooker over a colander to drain. Press the "sauté" button. Put back the tapioca pearls into the crockpot. Add silken tofu, brown sugar and salt.
4. Cook 10 minutes or until the caramel thickens. Turn off the machine. Meanwhile, scoop the silken tofu into heat-resistant cups. Pour tapioca pearls and caramel on top. Serve.

Nutrition: Low GL Calorie: 125; Fat: 18 g; Carbs: 1 g; Protein: 13 g; Fiber: 19 g; Sugar: 1 g; Cholesterol: 62 mg; Sodium: 375 mg; Potassium: 218 mg

156. Homemade Hummus

Preparation Time: 5 minutes
Cooking Time: 1 hour
Cooking Level: Difficult
Servings: 2
Ingredients:

- 3 cups water
- 1 cup dry chickpeas
- 2 fresh bay leaves
- 4 garlic cloves, peeled
- 5 pieces crackers per person as base
- 3 tbsp tahini
- ¼ tsp cumin powder
- ½ cup lemon juice, freshly squeezed
- ¼ tsp salt
- 1/16 tsp toasted black sesame seeds
- 1/16 tsp toasted white sesame seeds
- 1/16 tsp red pepper flakes
- 2 tbsp extra-virgin olive oil
- 1 sprig basil

Directions:
1. Place the chickpeas, bay leaves, garlic cloves and water into the Instant Pot Pressure Cooker. Lock the lid in place. Press the high pressure and cook for 20 minutes.
2. When the beep sounds, choose Natural Pressure Release. Depressurizing would take 20 minutes. Remove the lid. Reserve 1 cup of cooking liquid. Discard the rest.
3. Transfer the chickpeas to an immersion blender, along with the cooking liquid. Season with tahini, cumin powder, lemon juice and salt. Process until smooth. Adjust the seasoning according to your preferred taste.
4. Pour the chickpeas into a bowl. Garnish with toasted black and white sesame seeds, red pepper flakes, basil and olive oil. Serve with crackers. Store leftovers in the fridge. Use as needed.

Nutrition: Low GL Calorie: 122; Fat: 11 g; Carbs: 1.3 g; Protein: 13 g; Fiber: 21 g; Sugar: 1 g; Cholesterol: 89 mg; Sodium: 123 mg; Potassium: 318 mg

157. Parmesan and Pork Rind Green Beans

Preparation Time: 5 minutes
Cooking Time: 15 minutes
Cooking Level: Easy
Servings: 2
Ingredients:

- ½ pound fresh green beans
- 2 tbsp crushed pork rinds
- 2 tbsp olive oil
- 1 tbsp grated Parmesan cheese
- Salt and pepper, to taste

Directions:

1. Preheat the oven to 400°F.
2. Combine the green beans, pork rinds, olive oil and Parmesan cheese. Season and toss until the beans are thoroughly coated.
3. Spread the bean mixture on a baking sheet in a single layer, and roast for about 15 minutes. At the halfway point, give the pan a little shake to move the beans around or just give them a stir.
4. Divide the beans between two plates and serve.

Nutrition: Low GL Calories: 350; Total Fat: 30 g; Carbs: 1.6 g; Protein: 8 g; Fiber: 6 g; Sugar: 1 g; Cholesterol: 89 mg; Sodium: 397 mg; Potassium: 312 mg

158. Berry Jam with Chia Seeds

Preparation Time: 5 minutes
Cooking Time: 45 minutes
Cooking Level: Moderate
Servings: 2
Ingredients:

- 2 cups fresh blueberries, stemmed
- 1 ½ cups water
- 1 cup fresh raspberries, stemmed
- 1 cup sugar
- 1/16 tsp salt
- ½ cup chia seeds
- ¼ tbsp lemon juice, freshly squeezed

Directions:

1. Place raspberries, blueberries, water, sugar and salt into the Instant Pot Pressure Cooker. Stir.
2. Lock the lid in place. Press the high pressure and cook for 3 minutes.
3. When the beep sounds, choose the Quick Pressure Release. This will depressurize for 7 minutes. Remove the lid.
4. Add in the chia seeds and lemon juice. Process the jam into the desired consistency using a potato masher. You may choose to have your jam smooth or chunky. Allow cooling before storing the jam into an airtight container. Use as needed.

Nutrition: Low GL Calorie: 128; Fat: 11 g; Carbs: 4.8 g; Protein: 12 g; Fiber: 13 g; Sugar: 1 g; Cholesterol: 58 mg; Sodium: 348 mg; Potassium: 194 mg

159. Nectarines with Dried Cloves

Preparation Time: 5 minutes
Cooking Time: 50 minutes
Cooking Level: Moderate
Servings: 2
Ingredients:

- 4 dried cloves, whole
- 2 lb nectarine, cubed
- ¼ cup agave sugar, reserve for garnish
- 1/16 tsp cinnamon powder
- 2 cups water

Directions:

1. Combine dried cloves, nectarine, water, cinnamon powder and agave sugar into the Instant Pot Pressure Cooker.
2. Lock the lid in place. Press the high pressure and cook for 5 minutes.
3. When the beep sounds, choose the Quick Pressure Release. This will depressurize for 7 minutes. Remove the lid. Discard the dried cloves.
4. To serve, ladle just the right amount into dessert bowls. Sprinkle agave sugar.

Nutrition: Low GL Calorie: 267; Fat: 23 g; Carbs: 5 g; Protein: 21 g; Fiber: 19 g; Sugar: 1 g; Cholesterol: 89 mg; Sodium: 212 mg; Potassium: 212 mg

CHAPTER 9: SALADS AND SOUPS RECIPES

160. Roasted Portobello Salad

Preparation Time: 10 minutes
Cooking Time: 0 minutes
Cooking Level: Easy
Servings: 2
Ingredients:

- 1½ lb. Portobello mushrooms, stems trimmed
- 3 heads Belgian endive, sliced
- 1 small red onion, sliced
- 4 oz. blue cheese
- 8 oz. mixed salad greens

Dressing:

- 3 tbsp red wine vinegar
- 1 tbsp Dijon mustard
- ⅝ cup olive oil
- Salt and pepper, to taste

Directions:

1. Preheat the oven to 450°F.
2. Whisk mustard, vinegar, salt and pepper. Slowly add olive oil while whisking.
3. Arrange the mushroom on a baking sheet, coat with some dressing, and bake for 15 minutes.
4. Combine salad greens with endive, onion and cheese. Drizzle with the dressing. Add mushrooms

Nutrition: Low GL Calories: 501; Carbohydrates: 22.3 g; Protein: 14.9 g; Fiber: 2 g; Sugars: 2.1 g; Cholesterol: 89 mg; Sodium: 120 mg; Potassium: 312 mg

161. Drop Egg Soup

Preparation Time: 10 minutes
Cooking Time: 7 minutes
Cooking Level: Easy
Servings: 2
Ingredients:

- 4 cups chicken broth
- 4 tsp coconut aminos
- 8 medium mushrooms (thinly sliced)
- 4 medium green onions (thinly sliced)
- 1 tsp fresh ginger (grated)
- 1 tsp black pepper
- 4 large eggs
- Sea salt, as per taste

Directions:

1. Start by adding the chicken broth, mushrooms, coconut aminos, ginger, black pepper and onions into a medium-sized saucepan. Place pan on high and let it come to a boil. Reduce the flame and cook for a couple of minutes more.
2. Crack the eggs in a cup and whisk them well.
3. Slowly, pour the whisked eggs in a stream into the simmering soup. Keep stirring to get some smooth egg ribbons.
4. Stir salt as soon as you finish cooking the soup.

Nutrition: Fat: 6 g; Carbohydrates: 5 g; Protein: 10 g; Fiber: 12 g; Sugar: 4 g; Cholesterol: 57 mg; Sodium: 213 mg; Potassium: 282 mg

162. Shredded Chicken Salad

Preparation Time: 5 minutes
Cooking Time: 10 minutes
Cooking Level: Easy
Servings: 2
Ingredients:

- 2 chicken breasts, boneless, skinless
- 1 head iceberg lettuce, cut into strips
- 2 bell peppers, cut into strips
- 1 fresh cucumber, quartered, sliced
- 3 scallions, sliced
- 2 tbsp chopped peanuts
- 1 tbsp peanut vinaigrette
- Salt, to taste
- 1 cup water

Directions:

1. Simmer one cup of salted water.
2. Add the chicken, and cook for 5 minutes. Then remove the chicken and shred
3. Mix the vegetables with the cooled chicken, season, and sprinkle with vinaigrette and peanuts.

Nutrition: Low GL Calories: 117; Carbohydrates: 9 g; Protein: 11.6 g; Fiber: 8 g; Sugars: 4.2 g; Cholesterol: 81 mg; Sodium: 134.3 mg; Potassium: 310 mg

163. Cherry Tomato Salad

Preparation Time: 10 minutes
Cooking Time: 0 minutes
Cooking Level: Easy
Servings: 2
Ingredients:

- 40 cherry tomatoes, halved
- 1 cup mozzarella balls, halved
- 1 cup green olives, sliced
- 1 can (6 oz.) black olives, sliced
- 2 green onions, chopped
- 3 oz. roasted pine nuts

Dressing:

- ½ cup olive oil
- 2 tbsp red wine vinegar
- 1 tsp dried oregano
- Salt and pepper, to taste

Directions:

1. Combine olives, tomatoes and onions.
2. Combine red wine vinegar and olive oil, salt, pepper and oregano.

Nutrition: Low GL Calorie: 210; Carbohydrates: 10.7 g; Protein: 2.4 g; Fiber: 10 g; Sugars: 3.6 g; Cholesterol: 83 mg; Sodium: 217 g; Potassium: 212 mg

164. Asian Cucumber Salad

Preparation Time: 10 minutes
Cooking Time: 0 minutes
Cooking Level: Easy
Servings: 2
Ingredients:

- 1 lb. cucumbers, sliced
- 2 scallions, sliced
- 2 tbsp sliced pickled ginger, chopped
- ¼ cup cilantro
- ½ red jalapeño, chopped
- 3 tbsp rice wine vinegar
- 1 tbsp sesame oil
- 1 tbsp sesame seeds

Directions:

1. Combine all ingredients

Nutrition: Low GL Calories: 52; Carbohydrates: 5.7 g; Protein: 1 g; Fiber: 10 g; Total Sugars: 3.1 g; Cholesterol: 54 mg; Sodium: 211 g; Potassium: 276 mg

165. Sunflower Seeds and Arugula Garden Salad

Preparation Time: 5 minutes
Cooking Time: 10 minutes
Cooking Level: Easy
Servings: 2

Ingredients:

- ¼ tsp black pepper
- ¼ tsp salt
- 1 tsp fresh thyme, chopped
- 2 tbsp sunflower seeds, toasted
- 2 cups red grapes, halved
- 7 cups baby arugula, loosely packed
- 1 tbsp coconut oil
- 2 tsp honey
- 3 tbsp red wine vinegar
- ½ tsp stone-ground mustard

Directions:

1. Whisk together mustard, honey and vinegar. Slowly pour oil as you whisk.
2. In a large salad bowl, mix thyme, seeds, grapes and arugula.
3. Drizzle with the dressing and serve.

Nutrition: High GL Calories: 86.7 g; Fat: 3.1 g; Carbs: 13.1 g; Protein: 1.6 g; Fiber: 9 g; Sugar: 2 g; Cholesterol: 85 mg; Sodium: 258 mg; Potassium: 224 mg

166. Tabbouleh- Arabian Salad

Preparation Time: 5 minutes
Cooking Time: 10 minutes
Cooking Level: Easy
Servings: 2
Ingredients:

- ¼ cup chopped fresh mint
- 1 ⅝ cup boiling water
- 1 cucumber, peeled, seeded, and chopped
- 1 cup bulgur
- 1 cup chopped fresh parsley
- 1 cup chopped green onions
- 1 tsp salt
- ⅜ cup lemon juice
- ⅜ cup olive oil
- 3 tomatoes, chopped
- Ground black pepper, to taste

Directions:

1. Mix together boiling water and bulgur. Let it soak and set aside for an hour while covered.
2. After one hour, toss in cucumber, tomatoes, mint, parsley, onions, lemon juice and oil. Season with pepper and salt to taste. Toss well and refrigerate for another hour while covered before serving.

Nutrition: Low GL Calories: 185.5 g; Fat: 13.1 g; Carbs: 12.8 g; Protein: 4.1 g; Fiber: 7 g; Sugar: 2 g; Cholesterol: 89 mg; Sodium: 228 mg; Potassium: 312 mg

167. Cauliflower and Onion Salad

Preparation Time: 10 minutes
Cooking Time: 30 minutes
Cooking Level: Moderate
Servings: 2
Ingredients:

- 2 Cups Cauliflower Florets, Chopped Fine
- 3 Hard Boiled Eggs, Chopped
- 4 tbsp Heavy Cream
- 5 tbsp Sour Cream
- 2 tbsp Red Onion, Minced
- ½ Red Bell Pepper, Seeded and Chopped
- 2 tbsp Oregano, Fresh and Chopped
- 2 tbsp Chives, Fresh and Chopped
- Sea Salt and Black Pepper, to Taste

Directions:

1. **Take** out a large pot of water and bring the water to a boil. Cook your cauliflower florets for 5 minutes. They should be tender and then drain the water away. Run your florets over cold water to stop the cooking process, but drain well.
2. **Take** out a large bowl and whisk your heavy cream and sour cream, adding in your cauliflower next. Mix in your eggs, red onion, oregano, chive and bell pepper. Season with salt and pepper to taste before tossing until well combined.
3. Refrigerate for at least a half-hour before serving.

Nutrition: Low GL Calories: 215; Fat: 16 g; Protein: 9 g; Fiber: 4 g; Sugar: 3 g; Cholesterol: 83 mg; Sodium: 176 mg; Potassium: 189 mg

168. Corn Tortillas and Spinach Salad

Preparation Time: 3 minutes
Cooking Time: 5 minutes
Cooking Level: Easy
Servings:
Ingredients:

- 4 corn tortillas
- 2 cups baby spinach
- 2 tbsp red onion (chopped)
- 1 pepper
- 4 mini tomatoes (whole)
- 8 pitted small ripe olives
- 2 tsp balsamic vinegar
- ⅛ tsp salt
- ⅛ tsp pepper
- 1 tbsp extra-virgin olive oil

Directions:

1. Heat the tortillas according to the package instructions.
2. Mix the remaining ingredients in a salad bowl.
3. Serve tortillas and salad.
4. I often cook this dish for dinner, my children adore it

Nutrition: Low GL Calorie: 200; Fat: 3 g; Carbs: 35 g; Protein: 10 g; Fiber: 5.4 g; Sugar: 2 g; Cholesterol: 89 mg; Sodium: 281 mg; Potassium: 289 mg

169. Orange-Avocado Salad

Preparation Time: 10 minutes
Cooking Time: 0 minutes
Cooking Level: Easy
Servings:
Ingredients:

- 1 navel orange
- 1 avocado
- 1 tbsp fresh lime juice
- 1 tbsp extra-virgin olive oil
- ½ tsp arugula

Directions:

1. Mix lime juice, oil, and arugula
2. Add peeled and sectioned orange sections, tossing well.
3. Add diced avocado just before serving.

Nutrition: Low GL Calorie: 30; Fat: 2 g; Carbs 1 g; Protein: 2 g; Fiber: 2.4 g; Sugar: 2 g; Cholesterol: 81 mg; Sodium: 178.13 mg; Potassium: 222 mg

170. Israeli Salmon Salad

Preparation Time: 10 minutes
Cooking Time: 0 minutes
Cooking Level: Easy
Servings: 2
Ingredients:

- 1 cup flaked smoked salmon
- 1 tomato, chopped
- ½ small red onion, chopped
- 1 cucumber, chopped
- tbsp pitted green olives
- 1 avocado, chopped
- 2 tbsp avocado oil
- 2 tbsp almond oil
- 1 tbsp plain vinegar
- Salt and black pepper, to taste
- 1 cup crumbled feta cheese
- 1 cup grated cheddar cheese

Directions:

5. In a salad bowl, add salmon, tomatoes, red onion, cucumber, green olives and avocado. Mix well.
6. In a bowl, whisk the avocado oil, vinegar, salt and black pepper.
7. Drizzle the dressing over the salad and toss well.
8. Sprinkle some feta cheese and serve the salad immediately.

Nutrition: Low GL Calories: 415; Fat: 11.4 g; Carbohydrates: 3.8 g; Protein: 15.4 g; Fiber: 9.9 g; Sugar: 2 g; Cholesterol: 82 mg; Sodium: 233 mg; Potassium: 310 mg

171. Simple Lemon Farro and Steamed Broccoli

Preparation Time: 5 minutes
Cooking Time: 10 minutes
Cooking Level: Easy
Servings:
Ingredients:

- ⅜ cup pearled farro (substitute brown rice or quinoa, if desired)
- 1 (12-oz) pkg broccoli
- ½ tsp lemon rind
- 1,5 tsp lemon juice
- 1 tbsp extra-virgin olive oil
- ¼ tsp salt

Directions:

1. Cook the farro (you can find the directions on the package).
2. Mix farro, grated lemon rind, lemon juice, 1 tsp oil and ⅛ tsp salt.
3. Put broccoli in a steamer basket over boiling water. Steam 4 minutes.
4. Add 2 tsp oil and ⅛ tsp salt.

Nutrition: Low GL Calorie: 35; Fat: 1 g; Carbs: 7 g; Protein: 2 g; Fiber: 5 g; Sugar: 2 g; Cholesterol: 89 mg; Sodium: 328 mg; Potassium: 272 mg

172. Cauliflower and Spinach Salad

Preparation Time: 10 minutes
Cooking Time: 15 minutes
Cooking Level: Easy
Servings:
Ingredients:

- ½ (12-oz) pkg cauliflower florets
- 1 (5-oz) pkg spinach
- 1 (8.25-oz) can mandarin oranges (drained)
- ¼ cup almonds
- 1 tbsp extra-virgin olive oil
- 1 tbsp apple vinegar
- 2 tsp honey
- ⅛ tsp salt

Directions:

1. Cook cauliflower.
2. Mix vinegar, oil, honey and salt; add spinach and toss to combine.
3. Top the salad with oranges and almonds.
4. Serve alongside any meat dish.

Nutrition: High GL Calories: 27; Fat: 0 g; Carbs: 2 g; Protein: 3 g; Fiber: 3 g; Sugar: 2 g; Cholesterol: 89 mg; Sodium: 197 mg; Potassium: 311 mg

173. Slow Cooker Chicken Posole

Preparation Time: 10 minutes
Cooking Time: 6 hours 40 minutes
Cooking Level: Difficult
Servings: 2
Ingredients:

- 3 Skinless, boneless chicken breasts
- 4 cups chicken broth, low cholesterol 89 mg sodium
- 1 chopped white onion
- 2 chopped poblano peppers
- 1 tbsp cumin
- 2 cloves minced garlic
- 2 tsp chili powder
- 1 tbsp oregano
- 2 tsp kosher salt
- ½ tsp ground black pepper, fresh
- 15 oz drained hominy

For Garnish:

- ¾ cup Sliced green cabbage
- ½ cup Thinly sliced radish
- ¼ cup Fresh cilantro, chopped

Directions:

1. In a slow cooker, combine all the items, except the ingredients for the garnish and hominy. Cover and slow cook for 8 hours.
2. After cooking, take the chicken out of the slow cooker and shred it using a fork
3. Return to the slow cooker along with hominy. Cook it further 30 minutes.
4. Garnish it with cabbage, radish and cilantro before serving.

Nutrition: Low GL Calories: 105; Fat: 2.1 g; Carbohydrate: 16.6 g; Protein: 5.5 g; Dietary Fiber: 3.6 g; Sugars: 3.9 g; Cholesterol: 89 mg; Sodium: 0 mg; Potassium: 312 mg

174. Slow Cooker Lentil and Ham Soup

Preparation Time: 20 minutes
Cooking Time: 11 hours
Cooking Level: Difficult
Servings: 2
Ingredients:

- 1 cup Chopped celery
- 1 cup Dried lentils
- 1 cup Chopped onion
- 1 cup Chopped carrots
- 1½ cups Cooked ham, chopped
- 2 cloves Minced garlic
- ¼ tsp Dried thyme
- ½ tsp Dried basil
- 1 Bay leaf
- ½ tsp Dried oregano
- 32 oz Chicken broth
- ¼ tsp Black pepper
- 8 tsp Tomato sauce
- 1 cup Water

Directions:

1. Put celery, lentils, onion, carrots, ham and garlic in a 4-quart slow cooker, and combine thoroughly.
2. Season the ingredients with thyme, basil, bay leaf, oregano and pepper.
3. Pour chicken broth and stir well. Now, add tomato sauce and water into the slow cooker.
4. Close the lid and slow cook for 11 hours. Remove the bay leaf before serving.

Nutrition: Low GL Calories: 222; Fat: 6.1 g; Carbohydrate: 6.3 g; Protein: 15.1 g; Dietary Fiber: 11.4 g; Sugars: 4 g; Cholesterol: 87 mg; Sodium: 201 mg; Potassium: 594 mg

175. Beef Barley Vegetable Soup

Preparation Time: 20 minutes
Cooking Time: 5 Hours 30 minutes
Cooking Level: Difficult
Servings: 2
Ingredients:

- ½ cup Barley
- 3 pounds Beef chuck roast
- 2 tbsp Oil
- 1 Bay leaf
- 3 stalks Chopped celery
- 3 Chopped carrots
- 16 oz Mixed vegetables
- 1 Chopped onion
- 4 cubes Beef bouillon
- 4 cups Water
- ¼ tsp Ground black pepper
- 1 tbsp White sugar
- ¼ tsp Salt
- 28 oz Stewed tomatoes, diced

Directions:

1. Take a slow cooker and cook the chuck roast in the slow cooker at high heat for 5 until it becomes soft.
2. Add a bay leaf and barley into the slow cooker 1 hour before the end of cooking. Remove meat and chop it into small pieces.
3. Discard the bay leaf as well. Set the broth, beef and the barley aside. Pour oil into the cooking pot and bring it on medium heat. Sauté celery, onion, frozen mixed vegetables and carrots until they become soft.
4. Add beef bouillon cubes, water, pepper, sugar, beef or barley mixture and tomatoes. Boil the mix and reduce the heat; let it simmer for about 10 to 20 minutes. Season it with salt and pepper to taste before serving.

Nutrition: Low GL Calories: 321; Fat: 17.3 g; Carbohydrate: 12.4 g; Protein: 20 g; Dietary Fiber: 5.1 g; Sugars: 6 g; Cholesterol: 89 mg; Sodium: 62 mg; Potassium: 312 mg

176. Slow Cooker Corn Chowder

Preparation Time: 15 minutes
Cooking Time: 4 Hours
Cooking Level: Difficult
Servings: 2
Ingredients:

- 14 ¾ oz cream style corn
- 3 cups milk
- 4 oz chopped green chilies
- 10 ¾ oz condensed mushroom cream soup
- 2 cups hash brown potatoes, frozen and shredded
- 2 cups frozen corn
- 1 large chopped onion
- 2 cups cooked ham, cubed
- 2 tbsp hot sauce
- 2 tbsp butter
- 1 tsp chili powder
- 2 tsp dried parsley
- ¼ tsp salt
- ½ tsp ground black pepper

Directions:

1. Stir cream-style corn, milk, chopped green chilies, cream of mushroom soup, hash brown potatoes, frozen corn, ham, butter, onion, parsley, chili powder and hot sauce in a slow cooker.
2. Season the soup with pepper and salt as per your taste.
3. Cover the cooker and slow cook for 6 hours.
4. Serve hot.

Nutrition: Low GL Calories: 376; Fat: 18.7 g; Carbohydrate: 7.1 g; Protein: 14.9 g; Dietary Fiber: 3.6 g; Sugars: 12 g; Cholesterol: 89 mg; Sodium: 34 mg; Potassium: 312 mg

177. Potlikker Soup

Preparation Time: 15 minutes
Cooking Time: 20 minutes
Cooking Level: Easy
Servings: 2
Ingredients:

- 3 cups Chicken Broth (here) or store-bought low-Cholesterol: 89 mg; Sodium: chicken broth, divided
- 1 medium onion, chopped
- 3 garlic cloves, minced
- 1 bunch collard greens or mustard greens including stems, roughly chopped
- 1 fresh ham bone
- 5 carrots, peeled and cut into 1-inch rounds
- 2 fresh thyme sprigs
- 3 bay leaves
- Freshly ground black pepper, to taste

Directions:

1. Select the Sauté setting on an electric pressure cooker and combine ½ cup of chicken broth, the onion and garlic, and cook for 3 to 5 minutes, or until the onion and garlic are translucent.
2. Add collard greens, ham bone, carrots and the remaining 2½ cups of broth, thyme, and bay leaves.
3. Change to the Manual/Pressure Cook setting and cook for 15 minutes.
4. Once the cooking is complete, quick-release the pressure. Carefully remove the lid. Discard the bay leaves. Serve with Skillet Bivalves.

Substitution tip: To make this soup vegan, replace the ham bone with dried mushrooms and swap out the chicken broth for low-sodium vegetable broth.

Nutrition: Low GL Calories: 99; Fat: 4 g; Carbohydrates: 10 g; Protein: 6 g; Fiber: 3 g; Sugar: 4 g; Cholesterol: 81 mg; Sodium: 13 mg; Potassium: 302 mg

178. Burgoo

Preparation Time: 15 minutes
Cooking Time: 60 minutes
Cooking Level: Difficult
Servings: 2
Ingredients:

- 2 pounds pork butt, chopped into 1-inch pieces
- 2 pounds beef stew meat,
- 1 pound boneless, skinless chicken thighs, chopped into 1-inch pieces
- 1 tsp cayenne pepper
- 1 tsp Not Old Bay Seasoning
- 3 cups Chicken Broth (here) or store-bought low-Cholesterol: 89 mg; Sodium: chicken broth
- 2 pounds potatoes, cut into 1-inch cubes
- 3 onions, chopped
- 2 green bell peppers, chopped
- 4 carrots, peeled and chopped
- 2 cups frozen corn
- 1 pound okra, cut into 1-inch rounds
- 2 celery stalks, roughly chopped
- 1 cup frozen lima beans
- 2 large tomatoes, chopped

- 2 tbsp tomato paste
- ¼ large cabbage, roughly chopped

Directions:
1. In an electric pressure cooker, combine the pork, beef, chicken, cayenne and seasoning. Cover with the broth
2. Select the Manual/Pressure Cook setting, and cook for 20 minutes. Once the cooking is complete, allow the pressure to release naturally. Carefully remove the lid. Shred the meat
3. To the pressure cooker, add potatoes, onions, peppers, carrots, corn, okra, celery, lima beans, tomatoes, tomato paste and cabbage. Select the Manual/Pressure Cook setting, and cook for 10 minutes.
4. Once the cooking is complete, allow the pressure to release naturally. Carefully remove the lid. Return meat to the pressure cooker, change to the Sauté setting, and cook for 5 minutes, uncovered, or until the flavors meld.

Storage Tip: This dish can be stored in the refrigerator in an airtight container for up to 3 days.

Nutrition: Low GL Calories: 354; Fat: 12 g; Carbohydrates: 14 g; Protein: 36 g; Fiber: 5 g; Sugar: 6 g; Cholesterol: 89 mg; Sodium: 140 mg; Potassium: 312 mg

179. She-Crab Soup

Preparation Time: 15 minutes
Cooking Time: 25 minutes
Cooking Level: Easy
Servings: 2
Ingredients:

- 2 cups seafood broth (here)
- 1 shallot, chopped
- 2 celery stalks, chopped
- 1 garlic clove, minced
- 1 tsp Not Old Bay Seasoning
- 1 cup fat-free milk
- ½ cup half-and-half
- 1 tsp hot sauce
- 1 tsp Worcestershire sauce
- 1 ⅛ pound backfin lump crab meat
- 1 bunch chives, chopped
- Freshly ground black pepper, to taste
- Lemon wedges

Directions:
1. In a heavy-bottomed stockpot, bring the broth to a simmer.
2. Add shallot, celery, garlic and seasoning, and cook for 3 to 5 minutes, or until softened.
3. Reduce the heat to low and whisk in the milk, half-and-half, hot sauce and Worcestershire sauce. Simmer for 10 minutes.
4. Add the crab and cook for 5 to 7 minutes, or until the flavors come together. Serve with chives, pepper and lemon wedges.

Substitution Tip: If you don't have access to shallots, use half of a white onion.

Nutrition: Low GL Calories: 116; Fat: 4 g; Carbohydrates: 4 g; Protein: 16 g; Fiber: 1 g; Sugar: 3 g; Cholesterol: 59 mg; Sodium: 60 mg; Potassium: 312 mg

180. Spicy Chicken Stew

Preparation Time: 15 minutes
Cooking Time: 20 minutes
Cooking Level: Easy
Servings: 2
Ingredients:

- 3 cups Chicken Broth (here) or store-bought low-sodium chicken broth
- 6 boneless, skinless chicken breasts
- 1 tbsp Blackened Rub
- 2 carrots,
- 1 onion, roughly chopped
- 2 celery stalks, roughly chopped
- 1 medium sweet potato,
- 2 cups fresh peas
- 2 cups roughly chopped green beans
- 2 garlic cloves, minced
- 1 cup chopped tomatoes
- 1 tbsp tomato paste

Directions:
1. Select the Sauté setting on an electric pressure cooker and combine the broth, chicken and rub. Cook for 5 minutes, or until the exterior of the chicken is lightly browned.
2. Add carrots, onion, celery, sweet potato, peas, green beans, garlic, tomatoes and tomato paste.
3. Change to the Manual/Pressure Cook setting and cook for 15 minutes at high pressure.
4. Once cooking is complete, quick-release the pressure. Carefully remove the lid, and serve.

Nutrition: Low GL Calories: 145; Fat: 1 g; Carbohydrates: 12 g; Protein: 22 g; Fiber: 4 g; Sugar: 4 g; Cholesterol: 79 mg; Sodium: 109 mg; Potassium: 312 mg

181. Down South Corn Soup

Preparation Time: 10 minutes
Cooking Time: 35 minutes
Cooking Level: Moderate
Servings: 2
Ingredients:

- 1 tbsp extra-virgin olive oil
- ½ Vidalia onion, minced
- 2 garlic cloves, minced
- 3 cups chopped cabbage
- 1 small cauliflower, broken into florets or 1 (10-oz) bag frozen cauliflower
- 1 (10-oz) bag frozen corn
- 1 cup Vegetable Broth (here) or store-bought low-Cholesterol: 89 mg; Sodium: vegetable broth
- 1 tsp smoked paprika
- 1 tsp ground cumin
- 1 tsp dried dill
- ½ tsp Freshly ground black pepper to taste
- 1 cup plain unsweetened cashew milk

Directions:

1. Heat oil. Add onion and garlic, and sauté, stirring to prevent the garlic from scorching, for 3 to 5 minutes, or until translucent.
2. Add cabbage and a splash of water, cover, and cook for 5 minutes, or until tender.
3. Add cauliflower, corn, broth, paprika, cumin, dill and pepper. Cover and cook for 20 minutes, or until tender. Add cashew milk and stir well. Cover and cook for 5 minutes, letting the flavors come together.
4. Serve with a heaping plate of greens and seafood of your choice.

Substitution Tip: Use any unsweetened non-dairy milk alternative you like instead of cashew milk.

Nutrition: Low GL Calories: 120; Fat: 4 g; Carbohydrates: 18 g; Protein: 3 g; Fiber: 3 g; Sugar: 4 g; Cholesterol: 84 mg; Sodium: 0 mg; Potassium: 302 mg

182. Carrot Soup

Preparation Time: 15 minutes
Cooking Time: 25 minutes
Cooking Level: Easy
Servings: 2
Ingredients:

- 4 cups Vegetable Broth (here) or store-bought low-Cholesterol: 89 mg; Sodium: vegetable broth, divided
- 2 celery stalks, halved
- 1 small yellow onion, roughly chopped
- ½ fennel bulb, cored and roughly chopped
- 1 (1-inch) piece fresh ginger,
- 1 pound carrots, peeled and halved
- 2 tsp ground cumin
- 1 garlic clove, peeled
- 1 tbsp almond butter

Directions:

1. Select the Sauté setting on an electric pressure cooker and combine ½ cup of broth, celery, onion, fennel and ginger. Cook 5 minutes, or until vegetables are tender.
2. Add carrots, cumin, garlic, the remaining 3½ cups of broth and the almond butter.
3. Change to the Manual/Pressure Cook setting, and cook for 15 minutes.
4. Once the cooking is complete, quick-release the pressure. Carefully remove the lid and let cool for 5 minutes. Using a stand mixer or an immersion blender, carefully purée the soup. Serve with a heaping plate of greens.

Storage Tip: This soup can be stored for 3 to 5 days in an airtight container in the refrigerator.

Nutrition: Low GL Calories: 82; Fat: 2 g; Carbohydrates: 13 g; Protein: 3 g; Fiber: 3 g; Sugar: 5 g; Cholesterol: 59 mg; Sodium: 121 mg; Potassium: 212 mg

183. Four-Bean Field Stew

Preparation Time: 10 minutes
Cooking Time: 40 minutes
Cooking Level: Moderate
Servings: 2
Ingredients:

- 2 cups Vegetable Broth (here) or store-bought low-Cholesterol: 89 mg; Sodium: vegetable broth
- 1 cup dried lima beans
- 1 cup dried black beans
- 1 cup dried pinto beans
- 1 cup dried kidney beans
- 1 cup roughly chopped tomato
- 1 carrot, peeled and roughly chopped
- 1 zucchini, chopped
- ½ cup chopped white onion
- 1 celery stalk, roughly chopped
- 2 garlic cloves, minced
- 1 tsp dried oregano
- 1 tsp dried thyme
- ¼ tsp Freshly ground black pepper, to taste

Directions:

1. In an electric pressure cooker, combine the broth, lima beans, black beans, pinto beans, kidney beans, tomato, carrots, zucchini, onion, celery, garlic, oregano, thyme and pepper.
2. Select the Manual/Pressure Cook setting and cook for 40 minutes.
3. Once the cooking is complete, quick-release the pressure. Carefully remove the lid. Serve with Barbecue Chicken.

Substitution Tip: To reduce the cooking time by 20 minutes, use well-rinsed low-Cholesterol: 89 mg; Sodium: beans instead of dried beans.

Nutrition: Low GL Calories: 298; Fat: 1 g; Carbohydrates: 5 g; Protein: 19 g; Fiber: 13 g; Sugar: 4 g; Cholesterol: 89 mg; Sodium: 82 mg; Potassium: 312 mg

184. Pork Mushroom Stew

Preparation Time: 10 minutes
Cooking Time: 90 minutes
Cooking Level: Difficult
Servings: 2
Ingredients

- 1 (16-oz) can unsalted tomato sauce
- 2 cups carrots, sliced
- 1 medium green pepper, chopped
- ½ pound mushrooms, sliced
- 1 tsp dried basil
- ½ tsp dried rosemary, crushed
- 1 pound lean boneless pork,
- 1 cup onion, chopped
- ½ cup water
- ¼ tsp pepper

Directions:

1. Grease a large cooking pot or Dutch oven with some cooking oil and heat it over medium heat.
2. Add the pork and stir-cook to brown evenly. Add onion, seasonings, water and tomato sauce; stir.
3. Boil, cover, and simmer for 60 minutes until the pork is tender.
4. Add the other ingredients; combine and cook for 30 more minutes until the veggies are tender.

Nutrition: Low GL Calorie: 201; Fat: 7 g; Total carbs: 15 g; Protein: 18 g; Fiber: 5 g; Sugar: 0 g; Cholesterol: 89 mg; Sodium: 644 mg; Potassium: 225 mg

CHAPTER 10: VEGETARIAN RECIPES

185. Lentil Snack with Tomato Salsa

Preparation Time: 10 minutes
Cooking Time: 45 minutes
Cooking Level: Moderate
Servings: 2
Ingredients:

- ½ cup red lentils
- 1 small onion, red
- 1 cup wheat semolina
- 3 tbsp paprika tomato paste
- 2 tbsp mixed, chopped herbs (e.g. parsley, chervil, chives)
- ½ organic lemon
- Sea salt and black pepper
- 1 organic tomato
- ½ red chili pepper, small
- 1 spring onion
- Olive oil, as needed
- 1 tsp rice syrup or maple syrup

Directions:

1. Cook the lentils according to the package instructions. Peel the onion and cut it into small cubes. Mix the semolina with the finished lentils and leave to swell (about 3 minutes).
2. In the meantime, wash, dry and chop herbs. Add onion, paprika tomato paste (if you like), and herbs, stir and season with lemon juice, sea salt and pepper, then let cool.
3. For the tomato salsa, wash the tomatoes, remove the greens, and cut them into small cubes. Wash the chili peppers, cut lengthways, remove the seeds and partitions, wash again, and cut into very small pieces. Mix tomatoes, spring onions, chili peppers and a little paprika tomato paste, as well as olive oil and rice syrup, and season with sea salt and pepper.
4. Shape the lentil mixture into small rolls or balls and fry it brown all over or prepare it on the grill.

Nutrition: Low GL Calories: 394; Fat: 2.13 g; Carbohydrates: 76.77 g; Protein: 20.1 g; Fiber: 9 g; Sugar: 2 g; Cholesterol: 89 mg; Sodium: 165.28 mg; Potassium: 234 mg

186. Stuffed Eggplant

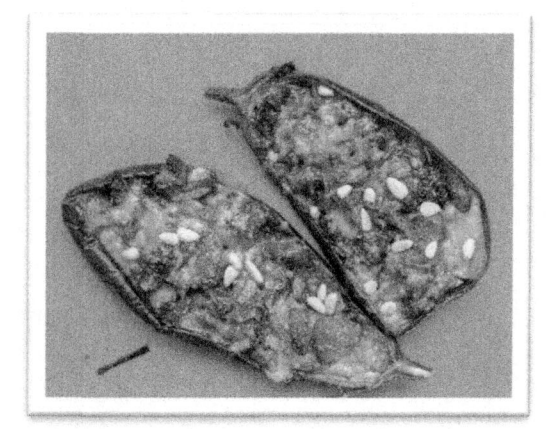

Preparation Time: 30 minutes
Cooking Time: 3 minutes
Cooking Level: Easy
Servings: 2
Ingredients:

- 2 small organic eggplants
- sea salt
- olive oil, as needed
- ½ small cauliflower
- 1 small onion, red
- 1 clove garlic
- ½ cup cream cheese, natural
- Sea salt and black pepper from the mill
- Rosemary and thyme, fresh
- ¼ cup cheese, grated e.g. Gouda

Directions:

1. Wash the eggplant, cut off the ends and cut in half lengthways. Cut out the pulp (except for a 1 cm wide edge) and cut into cubes. Heat oil in a pan, salt the eggplants and fry them for approx. 5–8 minutes (with the cut surface facing down), remove and dab off the excess oil with kitchen paper. Preheat the oven to 200°C.
2. Clean the cauliflower, cut it into florets, and wash thoroughly. Peel the onion and garlic, cut the onion into cubes, and chop the garlic very finely.
3. Heat a pan with a little oil, add diced eggplants, cauliflower, onion and garlic, and fry. Deglaze with a little water (approx. 50 ml), bring to a boil, cover with a lid, and simmer for approx. 5 minutes.
4. Wash and dry the rosemary and thyme, pluck off the leaves, and place in a bowl with the cream cheese, stir, and season with sea salt and pepper. Mix this mixture with the vegetables and fill the eggplant halves with it, sprinkle cheese on top, and bake for about 20 minutes.

Note: Eggplants are healthy and versatile. They are high in fiber, which is important for health. They also promote our feeling of satiety.

Nutrition: Low GL Calories: 199; Fat: 10.43 g; Carbohydrates: 22.67 g; Protein: 7.61 g; Fiber: 6.4 g; Sugar: 2 g; Cholesterol: 89 mg; Sodium: 312.28 mg; Potassium: 277 mg

187. Lentil Salad with Nuts and Feta

Preparation Time: 20 minutes
Cooking Time: 10 minutes
Cooking Level: Easy
Servings: 2
Ingredients:

- 200 ml orange juice, freshly squeezed
- ¼ cup lentils, red

- Lemon thyme, to taste
- ¾ cup small organic tomatoes
- ¼ cup feta (50% fat)
- ¼ cup organic rocket
- 5 tsp walnut kernels
- 2 tbsp organic apple cider vinegar
- ½ tsp mustard, sugar-free
- ½ tsp linden blossom honey
- 2 ½ tbsp olive oil
- 1 organic apple
- Sea salt and black pepper

Directions:
1. Halve the oranges and squeeze them, put them in a saucepan, and bring to a boil. Cook the lentils in the boiling orange juice according to the package instructions then cool for about 10 minutes.
2. In the meantime, wash and dry the thyme, and pluck the leaves off. Wash and clean the tomatoes (remove green), halve or quarter larger. Crumble the feta. Sort, wash, and dry the rocket. Roughly chop the walnuts and toast them in a pan without oil.
3. Mix vinegar, mustard, honey and oil well into a dressing. Wash and quarter the apple and core, cut into cubes, and place
4. Add lentils and dressing, and mix well, season with sea salt and pepper. Add walnuts and the other ingredients and stir gently.

Note: Lenses are good for diabetics. They contain a lot of fiber, and are high in iron, potassium, B1, and many vegetable proteins. These lower the glycemic index.

Nutrition: High GL Calories: 279; Fat: 21.32 g; Carbohydrates: 19 g; Protein: 6.82 g; Fiber: 6.7 g; Sugar: 2 g; Cholesterol: 89 mg; Sodium: 178.33 mg; Potassium: 267 mg

188. Vegetarian Chipotle Chili

Preparation Time: 5 minutes
Cooking Time: 6 Hours
Cooking Level: Difficult
Servings: 2
Ingredients:
- ¼ onion, diced
- 2 ¼ oz. corn, frozen
- ¾ carrots, diced
- Ground cumin
- 1 garlic clove, minced
- ½ medium sweet potatoes, diced
- ¼ tsp chipotle chili powder
- Ground black pepper
- 1 cup kidney beans, cooked from dried beans, or use rinsed canned beans
- ¼ tbsp salt
- 7 oz. tomatoes, diced, undrained
- ½ avocados, diced

Directions:
1. In a slow cooker, combine all the ingredients except the diced avocados.
2. Cook for 3 hours on high, and then cook for 3 hours on low until done. If desired, you can also cook for 4–5 hours on high or 7–8 hours on low until cooked through.
3. When done, serve with the diced avocado and enjoy!

Nutrition: Low GL Calories: 283; Fat: 8 g; Carbohydrates: 45 g; Protein: 11 g; Fiber: 4 g; Sugar: 2 g; Cholesterol: 59 mg; Sodium: 31 mg; Potassium: 273 mg

189. Smoky Carrot and Black Bean Stew

Preparation Time: 15 minutes
Cooking Time: 25 minutes
Cooking Level: Easy
Servings: 4
Ingredients:
- 1 (15-oz) can salt-free black beans
- 1 (14.5-oz) can salt-free diced tomatoes
- 1 cup carrots (chopped)
- 1 (14.5-oz) can vegetable broth
- 1 ½ tsp extra-virgin olive oil
- ¾ cup onion (chopped)
- 2 tsp smoked paprika
- 2 cloves garlic
- 1 avocado

Directions:
1. Heat extra-virgin olive oil in a large saucepan. Add carrots and onion; fry for 5 minutes.
2. Stir paprika and minced garlic; cook for 1 minute. Add broth, beans and diced tomatoes; bring to boil.
3. Reduce the heat; simmer until carrots are very tender.
4. Top each serving with chopped avocado.

Nutrition: Low GL Calorie: 100; Fat: 7 g; Carbs: 16 g; Protein: 15 g; Fiber: 7.4 g; Sugar: 2 g; Cholesterol: 89 mg; Sodium: 131.22 mg; Potassium: 276 mg

190. Hummus and Salad Pita Flats

Preparation Time: 15 minutes
Cooking Time: 0 minutes
Cooking Level: Easy
Servings: 2
Ingredients

- ¼ cup sweet roasted red pepper hummus
- 2-oz whole wheat pitas
- 8 pitted olives.
- 2 large eggs.
- 2 cups spring mix
- 2 tsp extra-virgin olive oil
- 1 tsp dried oregano

Directions:

1. Heat the pitas (you can find the directions on the package).
2. Spread hummus exactly over the pitas.
3. Top with chopped hard-cooked eggs, pitted olives and dried oregano.
4. Add the spring mix with extra-virgin olive oil, and arrange properly on each pita.

Nutrition: Low GL Calorie: 250; Fat: 2 g; Carbs: 50 g; Protein: 8 g; Fiber: 5 g; Sugar: 2 g; Cholesterol: 72 mg; Sodium: 122 mg; Potassium: 287 mg

191. Avocados with Walnut-Herb

Preparation Time: 7 minutes
Cooking Time: 4 minutes
Cooking Level: Easy
Servings: 4
Ingredients:

- ¼ cup walnuts
- 1 avocado
- 1 tbsp fresh basil
- 1/5 tsp lemon juice (fresh)
- ½ tsp extra-virgin olive oil
- ⅛ tsp salt
- ¼ tsp pepper

Directions:

1. Fry the chopped nuts for 3 to 4 minutes.
2. Mix nuts, chopped basil, oil, lemon juice, salt and pepper.
3. Cut the avocado in half lengthwise.
4. Top the avocado halves with the nut mixture.

Nutrition: Low GL Calorie: 200; Fat: 17 g; Carbs: 7 g; Protein: 2 g; Fiber: 6.4 g; Sugar: 2 g; Cholesterol: 89 mg; Sodium: 312.28 mg; Potassium: 278 mg

192. Beans with Mustard Sauce and Spicy Cucumbers

Preparation Time: 5 minutes
Cooking Time: 7 minutes
Cooking Level: Easy
Servings: 2
Ingredients:

- ⅜ cups beans
- 1 cucumber
- 2 tbsp mayonnaise (reduced-fat)
- 1 tbsp Greek yogurt (fat-free)
- ½ tsp mustard
- ⅛ tsp salt
- ⅛ tsp pepper
- 1 tbsp fresh lemon juice
- 1 tsp hot sauce

Directions:

1. Cook the beans.
2. Mix reduced-fat mayonnaise, fat-free yogurt, mustard, pepper and salt.
3. Toss the beans with the mayonnaise mixture.
4. Add lemon juice and hot sauce over the peeled and sliced cucumbers.
5. You can serve beans and cucumbers alongside any fish dish.
6. Bon Appetit!

Nutrition: Low GL Calorie: 60; Fat: 1 g; Carbs: 8 g; Protein: 7 g; Fiber: 27 g; Sugar: 1 g; Cholesterol: 56 mg; Sodium: 242.15 mg; Potassium: 238 mg

193. Mashed Butternut Squash

Preparation Time: 5 minutes
Cooking Time: 25 minutes
Cooking Level: Easy
Servings: 2
Ingredients:

- 3 pounds whole butternut squash (about 2 medium)
- 2 tbsp olive oil
- Salt and pepper, to taste

Directions:
1. Preheat the oven to 400°F and line a baking sheet with parchment.
2. Cut the squash in half and remove the seeds. Cut the squash into cubes and toss with oil, then spread on the baking sheet.
3. Roast for 25 minutes until tender, then place in a food processor.
4. Blend smooth, then season with salt and pepper to taste.

Nutrition: Low GL Calorie: 90; Total Fat: 4.8 g; Carbs: 10.2 g; Protein: 1.1 g; Fiber: 2.1 g; Sugar: 2.3 g; Cholesterol: 82 mg; Sodium: 4 mg; Potassium: 302 mg

194. Cilantro Lime Quinoa

Preparation Time: 5 minutes
Cooking Time: 25 minutes
Cooking Level: Easy
Servings: 2
Ingredients:

- 1 cup uncooked quinoa
- 1 tbsp olive oil
- 1 medium yellow onion, diced
- 2 cloves minced garlic
- 1 (4-oz) can diced green chiles, drained
- 1 ½ cups fat-free chicken broth
- ¾ cup fresh chopped cilantro
- ½ cup sliced green onion
- 2 tbsp lime juice
- Salt and pepper, to taste

Directions:
1. Rinse the quinoa thoroughly in cool water using a fine-mesh sieve. Heat oil in a large saucepan over medium heat.
2. Add onion and sauté for 2 minutes, then stir chile and garlic. Cook for 1 minute, then stir quinoa and chicken broth.
3. Bring to a boil, then reduce heat and simmer, covered, until the quinoa absorbs the liquid; about 20 to 25 minutes.
4. Remove from the heat. Stir cilantro, green onions and lime juice. Season with salt and pepper to taste and serve hot.

Nutrition: Low GL Calorie: 150; Total Fat: 4.1 g; Carbs: 9.8 g; Protein: 6 g; Fiber: 2.7 g; Sugar: 1.7 g; Cholesterol: 88 mg; Sodium: 179 mg; Potassium: 252 mg

195. Oven-Roasted Veggies

Preparation Time: 5 minutes
Cooking Time: 25 minutes
Cooking Level: Easy
Servings: 2
Ingredients:

- 1 pound cauliflower florets
- ½ pound broccoli florets
- 1 large yellow onion, cut into chunks
- 1 large red pepper, cored and chopped
- 2 medium carrots, peeled and sliced
- 2 tbsp olive oil
- 2 tbsp apple cider vinegar
- Salt and pepper, to taste

Directions:
1. Preheat the oven to 425°F, and line a baking sheet with parchment.
2. Spread the veggies on the baking sheet and drizzle with oil and vinegar. Toss well and season
3. Spread the veggies in a single layer, then roast for 20 to 25 minutes, stirring every 10 minutes, until tender.
4. Adjust the seasoning to taste and serve hot.

Nutrition: Low GL Calorie: 100; Total Fat: 5 g; Carbs: 8.2 g; Protein: 3.2 g; Fiber: 4.2 g; Sugar: 5.5 g; Cholesterol: 53 mg; Sodium: 51 mg; Potassium: 198 mg

196. Garlic Sautéed Spinach

Preparation Time: 5 minutes
Cooking Time: 10 minutes
Cooking Level: Easy
Servings: 2
Ingredients:

- 1 ½ tbsp olive oil
- 4 cloves minced garlic
- 6 cups fresh baby spinach
- Salt and pepper, to taste

Directions:
1. Heat oil in a large skillet over medium-high heat.
2. Add garlic and cook for 1 minute.
3. Stir spinach and season with salt and pepper.
4. Sauté for 1 to 2 minutes until just wilted. Serve hot.

Nutrition: Low GL Calorie: 60; Total Fat: 5.5 g; Carbs: 1.5 g; Protein: 1.5 g; Fiber: 1.1 g; Sugar: 0.2 g; Cholesterol: 85 mg; Sodium: 36 mg; Potassium: 289 mg

197. Creamed Spinach

Preparation Time: 10 minutes
Cooking Time: 15 minutes
Cooking Level: Easy
Servings: 2
Ingredients:

- 2 tbsp unsalted butter
- 1 small yellow onion, chopped
- 1 cup cream cheese, softened
- 2 (10-oz) packages frozen spinach,
- 2–3 tbsp water
- Salt and ground black pepper, as required
- 1 tsp fresh lemon juice

Directions:

1. Melt some butter and sauté the onion for about 6–8 minutes.
2. Add cream cheese and cook for about 2 minutes or until melted completely.
3. Stir water and spinach, and cook for about 4–5 minutes.
4. Stir salt, black pepper and lemon juice, and remove from heat. Serve immediately.

Nutrition: Low GL Calories: 214; Fat: 9.5 g; Carbohydrates: 2.1 g; Protein: 4.2 g; Fiber: 2.3 g; Sugar: 1 g; Cholesterol: 79 mg; Sodium: 233 mg; Potassium: 179 mg

198. Beet Salad with Basil Dressing

Preparation Time: 10 minutes
Cooking Time: 0 minutes
Cooking Level: Easy
Servings: 2
Ingredients:

Ingredients for the Dressing:

- ¼ cup blackberries
- ¼ cup extra-virgin olive oil
- Juice 1 lemon
- 2 tbsp minced fresh basil
- 1 tsp poppy seeds
- A pinch sea salt

For the Salad:

- 2 celery stalks, chopped
- 4 cooked beets, peeled and chopped
- 1 cup blackberries
- 4 cups spring mix

Directions:

1. To make the dressing, mash the blackberries
2. Whisk in the oil, lemon juice, basil, poppy seeds and sea salt.
3. To make the salad: Add celery, beets, blackberries and spring mix to the bowl with the dressing.
4. Combine and serve.

Nutrition: Low GL Calories: 192; Fat: 15 g; Carbohydrates: 15 g; Protein: 2 g; Fiber: 8 g; Sugar: 6 g; Cholesterol: 77 mg; Sodium: 120 mg; Potassium: 218 mg

CHAPTER 11: VEGAN RECIPES

199. Tomato, Avocado, and Cucumber Salad

Preparation Time: 5 minutes
Cooking Time: 5 minutes
Cooking Level: Easy
Servings: 2
Ingredients:

- ½ cup grape tomatoes, halved
- 4 small Persian cucumbers or 1 English cucumber, peeled and finely chopped
- 1 avocado, finely chopped
- ¼ cup crumbled tofu
- 1 tbsp vinaigrette salad dressing (I use Primal Kitchen Greek Vinaigrette)
- Pink Himalayan salt, to taste
- Pepper, to taste

Directions:

1. Combine the tomatoes, cucumbers, avocado and tofu.
2. Add vinaigrette and season with Pink Himalayan salt to taste and pepper. Toss to thoroughly combine.
3. Divide salad between two plates and serve.

Nutrition: Low GL Calories: 516; Total Fat: 45 g; Carbs: 2.3 g; Protein: 10 g; Fiber: 12 g; Sugar: 11 g; Cholesterol: 61 mg; Sodium: 327 mg; Potassium: 219 mg

200. Cauliflower "Potato" Salad

Preparation Time: 5 minutes
Cooking Time: 45 minutes
Cooking Level: Moderate
Servings: 2
Ingredients:

- ½ head cauliflower
- 1 tbsp olive oil
- Pink Himalayan salt, to taste
- Pepper, to taste
- ⅜ cup vegan mayonnaise
- 1 tbsp mustard
- ¼ cup diced dill pickles
- 1 tsp paprika

Directions:

1. Preheat the oven to 400°F. Line a baking sheet with aluminum foil or a silicone baking mat. Cut the cauliflower into 1-inch pieces.
2. Put the cauliflower
3. Add olive oil, season with the Pink Himalayan salt to taste and pepper, and toss to combine.
4. Spread cauliflower on the baking sheet and bake for 25 minutes, or just until the cauliflower begins to brown.
5. Mix cauliflower together with the vegan mayonnaise, mustard and pickles. Sprinkle the paprika on top and chill in the refrigerator for 3 hours before serving.

Nutrition: Low GL Calories: 772; Total Fat: 74 g; Carbs: 2.6 g; Protein: 10 g; Fiber: 10 g; Sugar: 1 g; Cholesterol: 89 mg; Sodium: 237 mg; Potassium: 54 mg

201. Loaded Cauliflower Mashed "Potatoes"

Preparation Time: 10 minutes
Cooking Time: 10 minutes
Cooking Level: Easy
Servings: 2
Ingredients:

- 1 head fresh cauliflower, cut into cubes
- 2 garlic cloves, minced
- 6 tbsp olive oil
- ½ tbsp soi yogurt
- Pink Himalayan salt, to taste
- Freshly ground black pepper, to taste
- 1 cup shredded vegan cheese

Directions:

1. Boil a pot of water over high heat. Add cauliflower. Simmer for 8 to 10 minutes,
2. Drain the cauliflower in a colander and turn it out onto a paper towel-lined plate to soak up the water. Wipe to remove any remaining water from the cauliflower pieces. This step is important; you want to get out as much water as possible so the mash won't be runny.
3. Add cauliflower to the food processor (or blender) with the garlic, butter, soia yogurt, and season. Mix for about 1 minute, stopping to scrape down the sides of the bowl every 30 seconds.
4. Divide cauliflower mix evenly among four small serving dishes and top each with the vegan cheese.

Nutrition: Low GL Calories: 131; Total Fat: 132 g; Carbs: 3.4 g; Protein: 58 g; Fiber: 12 g; Sugar: 1 g; Cholesterol: 78 mg; Sodium: 267 mg; Potassium: 293 mg

202. Keto Bread

Preparation Time: 5 minutes
Cooking Time: 25 minutes
Cooking Level: Easy
Servings: 2
Ingredients:

- 5 tbsp olive oil
- 1 ½ cups almond flour
- 3 tsp baking powder
- Pinch Pink Himalayan salt, to taste

Directions:

1. Preheat the oven to 390°F. Coat a 9-by-5-inch loaf pan with 1 tbsp of olive oil.

2. Use a hand mixer to mix, almond flour, remaining 4 tbsp of olive oil, baking powder, and Pink Himalayan salt to taste until thoroughly blended. Pour into the prepared pan.
3. Bake for 25 minutes
4. Slice and serve.

Nutrition: Low GL Calories: 165; Total Fat: 178 g; Carbs: 4.6 g; Protein: 74 g; Fiber: 19 g; Sugar: 2 g; Cholesterol: 89 mg; Sodium: 327 mg; Potassium: 187 mg

203. Vegan Stuffed Mushrooms

Preparation Time: 10 minutes
Cooking Time: 15 minutes
Cooking Level: Easy
Servings: 2

Ingredients:

- 2 large mushrooms, clean, remove stems, and chop stems finely
- 1 ½ tbsp fresh parsley, chopped
- 4 garlic cloves, minced
- ½ cup tofu, grated
- 3 oz cream vegan cheese
- 1 tbsp olive oil

Directions:

1. Preheat the oven to 375° F. Toss the mushrooms with vegetable oil and place them onto a baking tray.
2. In a bowl, combine vegan cheese, chopped mushrooms stems, parsley, garlic, parmesan cheese, tofu and salt.
3. Stuff the vegan cheese mixture into the mushroom caps and arrange the mushrooms on the baking tray.
4. Bake in a preheated oven for 10–15 minutes. Serve and luxuriate.

Nutrition: Low GL Calorie: 79; Fat: 6.3 g; Carbohydrates: 1.5 g; Protein: 4 g; Fiber: 9 g; Sugar: 0.5 g; Cholesterol: 57 mg; Sodium: 16 mg; Potassium: 310 mg

204. Perfect Cucumber Salsa

Preparation Time: 5 minutes
Cooking Time: 5 minutes
Cooking Level: Easy
Servings: 10

Ingredients:

- 2 ½ cups cucumbers, peeled, seeded, and chopped
- 2 tsp fresh cilantro, chopped
- 2 tsp fresh parsley, chopped
- 1 ½ tbsp fresh lemon juice
- 1 garlic clove, minced
- 1 small onion, chopped
- 2 large jalapeno peppers, chopped
- 1 ½ cups tomatoes, chopped
- ½ tsp salt

Directions:

1. Add all the ingredients into a massive bowl and blend until well combined.
2. Serve and luxuriate.

Nutrition: Low GL Calorie: 14; Fat: 0.2 g; Carbohydrates: 3 g; Protein: 0.6 g; Fiber: 6 g; Sugar: 1.6 g; Cholesterol: 62 mg; Sodium: 0 mg; Potassium: 309 mg

205. Soia Yogurt and Avocado Dip

Preparation Time: 5 minutes
Cooking Time: 5 minutes
Cooking Level: Easy
Servings: 2

Ingredients:

- 2 avocados
- 1 lime juice
- 3 garlic cloves, minced
- ½ cup Soia yogurt
- Pepper and salt, to taste

Directions:

1. Scoop out the avocado flesh using the spoon and place it in a bowl.
2. Mash avocado flesh using the fork.
3. Add the remaining ingredients and stir to mix.
4. Serve and luxuriate.

Nutrition: Low GL Calorie: 139; Fat: 11 g; Carbohydrates: 9 g; Protein: 4 g; Fiber: 9 g; Sugar: 2 g; Cholesterol: 64 mg; Sodium: 15 mg; Potassium: 189 mg

206. Keto Macadamia Hummus

Preparation Time: 10 minutes
Cooking Time: 5 minutes
Cooking Level: Easy
Servings: 2

Ingredients:

- 1 cup macadamia nuts,
- 1 ½ tbsp tahini
- 2 tbsp water
- 2 tbsp fresh lime juice
- 2 garlic cloves
- ⅛ tsp cayenne pepper
- Pepper and salt, to taste

Directions:

1. Blend the ingredients in a food processor until smooth.
2. Serve and enjoy.

Nutrition: Low GL Calorie: 138; Fat: 14.2 g; Carbohydrates: 3.2 g; Protein: 1.9 g; Fiber: 9 g; Sugar: 1.9 g; Cholesterol: 67 mg; Sodium: 0 mg; Potassium: 309 mg

207. Eggplant Chips

Preparation Time: 10 minutes
Cooking Time: 20 minutes
Cooking Level: Easy

Servings: 2

Ingredients:

- 1 large eggplant, thinly sliced
- ¼ cup vegan cheese, grated
- 1 tsp dried oregano
- ¼ tsp dried basil
- ½ tsp garlic powder
- ¼ cup olive oil
- ¼ tsp pepper
- ½ tsp salt

Directions:

1. Preheat the oven to 325°F. Using a small bowl, mix oil and dried spices.
2. Coat the eggplant with oil and the spice mixture, and arrange the eggplant slices on a baking tray.
3. Bake for 20 minutes. Turn halfway through.
4. Remove from oven and sprinkle with vegan cheese. Serve and luxuriate.

Nutrition: Low GL Calorie: 77; Fat: 5.8 g; Carbohydrates: 2 g; Protein: 3.5 g; Fiber: 7 g; Sugar: 0.9 g; Cholesterol: 89 mg; Sodium: 8 mg; Potassium: 312 mg

208. Creamy Mushrooms with Garlic and Thyme

Preparation Time: 5 minutes
Cooking Time: 15 minutes
Cooking Level: Easy
Servings: 2

Ingredients:

- 4 tbsp olive oil
- ½ cup onion, chopped
- 1-pound button mushrooms
- 2 tsp garlic, diced
- 1 tbsp fresh thyme
- 1 tbsp parsley, chopped
- ½ tsp salt
- ¼ tsp black pepper

Directions:

1. Put olive oil in a pan. Place the mushrooms into the pan. Add salt and pepper. Cook the mushroom mix for about 5 minutes until they're browned on each side.
2. Add garlic and thyme. Additionally, sauté the mushrooms for 1–2 minutes. Top them with parsley.

Nutrition: Low GL Calorie: 99; Carbohydrates: 45 g; Fat: 8 g; Protein: 3 g; Fiber: 9 g; Sugar: 0.2 g; Cholesterol: 79 mg; Sodium: 294 mg; Potassium: 322 mg

209. Veggie Fajitas

Preparation Time: 10 minutes
Cooking Time: 3 Hours and 30 minutes
Cooking Level: Difficult
Servings: 2

Ingredients:

- 1 Onion, chopped
- 8 oz Cherry Tomatoes, halved
- 3 Peppers, cut into strips
- 1 tsp Paprika
- 1 tsp Chili Powder
- 1 tbsp Olive Oil
- 6 Mini Tortillas

Directions:

1. Place onion, peppers, olive oil, chili powder and paprika inside your Slow Cooker.
2. Put the lid on and cook for 90 minutes on high.
3. Open the lid and stir the tomatoes.
4. Put the lid back on and cook for 2 more hours. Serve inside the flour tortillas.

Nutrition: Low GL Calorie: 250; Fats: 6 g; Carbs: 16 g; Protein: 5 g; Fiber: 2.4 g; Sugar: 2 g; Cholesterol: 77 mg; Sodium: 147 mg; Potassium: 189 mg

210. Air Fryer Soft Pretzels

Preparation Time: 10 minutes
Cooking Time: 6 minutes
Cooking Level: Easy

Servings: 2

Ingredients
- 1 ½ cup warm (110 to 115 degrees F) water
- 2 tsp kosher salt
- 1 tbsp sugar
- 1 package active dry yeast
- 4 tbsp olive oil
- 4 ½ cups all-purpose flour
- ⅝ cup baking soda
- 10 cups water
- ½ cup Soia yogurt
- Pretzel salt

Directions:
1. In a bowl of your stand mixer fitted with a dough hook, mix water, salt and sugar together. Sprinkle on top with yeast and let sit for 5 minutes. Pour flour into the bowl and add olive oil; combine the mixture together on low speed.
2. Increase speed and knead the dough for 5 minutes until smooth. Transfer the dough to a greased bowl; cover with plastic wrap. Let dough sit for 50 to 60 minutes at a warm temperature until the size has doubled. Spray with oil two baking sheets with parchment paper lining
3. Heat the fryer to 400°F. Meanwhile, combine in a large roasting pan or stock pot the baking soda and 10 cups of water; bring to a boil. Lay the pretzel dough on a greased work surface and equally divide it into 12 pieces. Roll each dough piece into an 18" rope and then twist to form a pretzel shape. Working on each piece of pretzel, place in the boiling water for thirty seconds and quickly remove from water. Transfer the pretzels to a baking sheet.
4. Beat the soia yogurt in 1 tbsp of water and brush over the pretzels. Sprinkle the pretzels with pretzel salt and load about 3 to 4 pieces into the air fryer basket. Cook for 6 minutes at 400°F; turn over and cook for additional 6 minutes or until dark golden brown.

Nutrition: Low GL Calorie: 79; Fat: 6.3 g; Carbohydrates: 1.5 g; Protein: 4 g; Fiber: 9 g; Sugar: 0.5 g; Cholesterol: 84 mg; Sodium: 16 mg; Potassium: 272 mg

CHAPTER 12: DESSERTS RECIPES

211. Chocolate Raspberry Parfait

Preparation Time: 5 minutes
Cooking Time: 50 minutes
Cooking Level: Moderate
Servings: 2
Ingredients:

Raspberry Chia Seeds:
- 3 tbsp chia seeds
- ½ cup almond milk, unsweetened
- ¼ tsp sugar
- 1 cup frozen raspberries, reserve some for garnish
- ⅛ tsp lemon juice, freshly squeezed

Chocolate Tapioca:
- ½ tbsp Dutch cocoa powder
- ⅛ cup seed tapioca, picked over
- 1 cup almond milk, unsweetened
- 1 cup water
- 4 squares dark chocolate, chopped, reserve some for garnish

Directions:
1. For the raspberry chia seeds, combine chia seeds, almond milk, sugar, raspberries and lemon juice
2. Mix well. Mash the berries. Seal with saran wrap. Refrigerate until ready to use.
3. For the chocolate tapioca, put together cocoa powder, tapioca, almond milk, water and dark chocolate into the crockpot. Stir.
4. Lock the lid in place. Press the high pressure and cook for 8 minutes. When the beep sounds, choose Natural Pressure Release. Depressurizing would take 20 minutes. Remove the lid.
5. To serve, spoon in half portions of chocolate tapioca in a heat-proof glass. Put just the right amount of raspberry-chia mixture on top. Garnish with whole raspberries and chopped chocolate.

Nutrition: Low GL Calorie: 321; Fat: 22 g; Carbs: 4 g; Protein: 26 g; Fiber: 11 g; Sugar: 1 g; Cholesterol: 81 mg; Sodium: 248 mg; Potassium: 274 mg

212. Mango Cashew Cake

Preparation Time: 15 minutes
Cooking Time: 1 hour
Cooking Level: Difficult
Servings: 2
Ingredients:

- ¼ tsp coconut oil, for greasing
- 1 tsp baking powder
- ½ tsp baking soda
- ¼ cup coconut butter
- 1 tbsp flour
- ½ cup all-purpose flour
- ¼ cup mango jam
- ½ cup cashew milk
- ¼ cup ground cashew nuts
- 1 tsp vanilla essence
- ½ cup powdered sugar
- 2 ½ cups water

Directions:

1. Lightly grease the Instant Pot Pressure Cooker with coconut oil. Dust with flour. Set aside.
2. Meanwhile, combine all-purpose flour, coconut butter, baking powder, cashew milk, baking soda, vanilla essence, mango jam and cashew. Stir until all the ingredients come together. Pour the batter on a Bundt pan.
3. Place trivet on the pressure cooker. Pour 2 ½ cups of water. Lock the lid in place. Press the high pressure and cook for 35 minutes. When the beep sounds, choose Natural Pressure Release. Depressurizing would take 20 minutes. Remove the lid.
4. Take out the Bundt cake. Transfer to a cake rack. Let it cool. Turn the cake over on a serving dish. Sprinkle powdered sugar. Slice and serve.

Nutrition: Low GL Calorie: 213; Fat: 21; Fiber: 5; Carbs: 1.9 g; Protein: 21 g; Sugar: 1 g; Cholesterol: 89 mg; Sodium: 226 mg; Potassium: 178 mg

213. Keto Waffles

Preparation Time: 20 minutes
Cooking Time: 30 minutes
Cooking Level: Moderate
Servings: 2
Ingredients:

For the Ketogenic waffles:

- 8 oz cream cheese
- 5 large pastured eggs
- ⅜ cup coconut flour
- ½ tsp xanthan gum
- 1 pinch salt
- ½ tsp vanilla extract
- 2 tbsp swerve
- ¼ tsp baking soda
- ⅜ cup almond milk

Optional ingredients:

- ½ tsp cinnamon pie spice
- ¼ tsp almond extract

To prepare the low-carb Maple Syrup:

- 1 cup water
- 1 tbsp maple flavor
- ¾ cup powdered Swerve
- 1 tbsp almond butter
- ½ tsp Xanthan gum

Directions:

For the waffles:

1. Make sure all your ingredients are exactly at room temperature. Place all your ingredients for the waffles, from cream cheese to pastured eggs, coconut flour, Xanthan gum, salt, vanilla extract, the Swerve, the baking soda and almond milk except for the almond milk with the help of a processor.
2. Blend your ingredients until it becomes smooth and creamy; then transfer the batter to a bowl. Add almond milk and mix your ingredients with a spatula.
3. Heat a waffle maker to a high temperature. Spray the waffle maker with oil and add about ¼ of the batter in it evenly with a spatula into your waffle iron.
4. Close your waffle and cook until you get the color you want. Carefully remove the waffles to a platter.

For the Ketogenic Maple Syrup:

1. Place 1 and ¼ cups of water, the swerve and the maple in a small pan, let it boil over low heat; then let simmer for about 10 minutes.
2. Add coconut oil.

3. Sprinkle the gum over the top of the waffle and use an immersion blender to blend smoothly.
4. Serve and enjoy your delicious waffles!

Nutrition: Low GL Calories: 316; Fat: 26 g; Carbohydrates: 7 g; Fiber: 3 g; Protein: 11 g; Sugar: 0.2 g; Cholesterol: 89 mg; Sodium: 294 mg; Potassium: 312 mg

214. Coconut Brown Rice Cake

Preparation Time: 5 minutes
Cooking Time: 55 minutes
Cooking Level: Moderate
Servings: 2
Ingredients:

- 1 cup brown rice
- ½ cup coconut flakes, for garnish
- ¼ cup raisins
- 2 cans thick coconut cream, reserve 3 tsp for garnish
- ⅛ tsp coconut oil, for greasing
- ½ cup water
- ¼ cup brown sugar

Directions:

1. Pour the coconut flakes into the Instant Pot Pressure Cooker. Press the "sauté" button. Toast flakes until lightly brown. Set aside.
2. Meanwhile, lightly grease the sides and bottom of the pressure cooker. Add in brown rice, 1 can of coconut cream, water, brown sugar and raisins.
3. Lock the lid in place. Press the high pressure and cook for 30 minutes. When the beep sounds, choose Natural Pressure Release. Depressurizing would take 20 minutes. Remove the lid.
4. To serve, place just the right amount of rice cake on a dessert plate. Put coconut flakes on top. Spoon coconut cream.

Nutrition: Moderate GL Calorie: 216 Fat: 32 Fiber: 11 Carbs 4.9 Potassium: 282 mg; Protein: 26 Sugar: 1 g; Cholesterol: 59 mg; Sodium: 329 mg

215. Peanut Butter and Berry Oatmeal

Preparation Time: 5 minutes
Cooking Time: 5 minutes
Cooking Level: Easy
Servings: 2
Ingredients:

- 1 ½ cups unsweetened vanilla almond milk
- ¾ cup rolled oats
- 1 tbsp chia seeds
- 2 tbsp natural peanut butter
- ¼ cup fresh berries, divided (optional)

Directions:

1. Add almond milk, oats and chia seeds to a small saucepan, and bring to a boil.
2. Cover and continue cooking, stirring often, or until the oats have absorbed the milk.
3. Add peanut butter and keep stirring until the oats are thick and creamy.
4. Divide the oatmeal into two serving bowls. Serve topped with the berries.

Nutrition: Low GL Calories: 260; Fat: 13.9 g; Protein: 10.1 g; Carbs: 26.9 g; Fiber: 7.1 g; Sugar: 1.0 g; Cholesterol: 82 mg; Sodium: 130 mg; Potassium: 302 mg

216. Paleo Almond Banana Pancakes

Preparation Time: 10 minutes
Cooking Time: 10 minutes
Cooking Level: Easy
Servings: 2
Ingredients:

- ¼ cup almond flour
- ½ tsp ground cinnamon
- 3 eggs
- 1 banana, mashed
- 1 tbsp almond butter
- 1 tsp vanilla extract
- 1 tsp olive oil
- Sliced banana, to serve

Directions:

1. Whisk the eggs in a mixing bowl until they become fluffy. In another bowl, mash the banana using a fork and add to the egg mixture.
2. Add vanilla, almond butter, cinnamon and almond flour. Mix into a smooth batter. Heat olive oil in a skillet.
3. Add one spoonful of the batter and fry them on both sides.
4. Keep doing these steps until you are done with all the batter. Add some sliced banana on top before serving.

Nutrition: Low GL Calorie Per Serving: 306 Protein: 14.4 g; Carbs: 3.6 g Fat: 26.0 g; Fiber: 1 g, Sugar: 0.2 g, Cholesterol: 49 mg; Sodium: 212 mg; Potassium: 188 mg

217. Cherry, Chocolate, and Almond Shake

Preparation Time: 5 minutes
Cooking Time: 0 minutes
Cooking Level: Easy
Servings: 2
Ingredients

- 10 oz frozen cherries
- 2 tbsp cocoa powder
- 2 tbsp almond butter
- 2 tbsp hemp seeds
- 8 oz unsweetened almond milk

Directions:

1. Combine the cherries, cocoa, almond butter, hemp seeds and almond milk in a blender, and blend on high speed until smooth. Serve immediately.

Nutrition: Low GL Calorie: 28; Fat: 16 g, Carbohydrates: 32 g, Fiber: 7 g, Protein: 10 g, Cholesterol: 89 mg, Sodium: 308 mg, Potassium: 312 mg, Sugar: 2 g

218. Greek Yogurt Sundae

Preparation Time: 5 minutes
Cooking Time: 0 minutes
Cooking Level: Easy
Servings: 2
Ingredients:

- ¾ cup plain nonfat Greek yogurt
- ¼ cup mixed berries (blueberries, strawberries, blackberries)
- 2 tbsp cashew, walnut, or almond pieces
- 1 tbsp ground flaxseed
- 2 fresh mint leaves, shredded

Directions:

1. Spoon the yogurt into a small bowl. Top with the berries, nuts and flaxseed.
2. Garnish with the mint and serve.

Substitution tip: Use fresh or frozen berries in this sundae, as available. If using frozen, take the berries out of the freezer about 10 or 15 minutes before you make the sundae so they can thaw.

Nutrition: Low GL Calories: 237; Fat: 11 g; Protein: 21 g; Carbohydrates: 16 g; Sugars: 9 g; Fiber: 4 g; Cholesterol: 56 mg; Sodium: 176 g Potassium: 277 mg

219. Almond Berry Smoothie

Preparation Time: 5 minutes
Cooking Time: 0 minutes
Cooking Level: Easy
Servings: 2
Ingredients:

- 2 cups frozen berries of choice
- 1 cup plain low-fat Greek yogurt
- 1 cup unsweetened vanilla almond milk
- ½ cup natural almond butter

Directions:

1. In a blender, add berries, almond milk, yogurt and almond butter. Process until fully mixed and creamy. Pour into four smoothie glasses.
2. Serve chilled or at room temperature.

Nutrition: Low GL Calories: 279; Fat: 18.2 g; Protein: 13.4 g; Carbs: 19.1 g; Fiber: 6.1 g; Sugar: 11.1 g; Cholesterol: 89 mg; Sodium: 138 mg; Potassium: 312 mg

220. Gluten-Free Carrot and Oat Pancakes

Preparation Time: 10 minutes
Cooking Time: 20 minutes
Cooking Level: Easy
Servings: 2
Ingredients:

- 1 cup rolled oats
- 1 cup shredded carrots

- 1 cup low-fat cottage cheese
- 2 eggs
- ½ cup unsweetened plain almond milk
- 1 tsp baking powder
- ½ tsp ground cinnamon
- 2 tbsp ground flaxseed
- ¼ cup plain non-fat Greek yogurt
- 1 tbsp pure maple syrup
- 2 tsp canola oil, divided

Directions:
1. In a blender jar, process the oats until they resemble flour. Add carrots, cottage cheese, eggs, almond milk, baking powder, cinnamon and flaxseed to the jar. Process until smooth.
2. Stir the maple syrup and yogurt. Set aside.
3. In a large skillet, heat 1 tsp of oil over medium heat. Using a measuring cup, add ¼ cup of batter per pancake to the skillet. Cook until the pancakes are browned and cooked through. Repeat with the remaining 1 tsp of oil and the remaining batter.
4. Serve warm topped with maple yogurt.

Ingredient tip: While oats are naturally gluten-free, many brands are processed in facilities that also process grains with gluten, making cross-contamination risk high.

Nutrition: Low GL Calories: 226; Fat: 8 g; Protein: 15 g; Carbohydrates: 24 g; Fiber: 4 g; Sugars: 7 g; Cholesterol: 89 mg; Sodium: 403 mg; Potassium: 187 mg

221. Peaches and Cream Oatmeal Smoothie

Preparation Time: 10 minutes
Cooking Time: 5 minutes
Cooking Level: Easy
Servings: 2
Ingredients:
- 1 cup frozen peach slices
- 1 cup Greek yogurt
- ¼ cup oatmeal
- ¼ tsp vanilla extract
- 1 cup almond milk

Directions:
1. Blend everything until smooth.

Nutrition: Low GL Calorie: 331; Fat: 4 g, Carb: 4.6 g, Protein: 29 g, Sugars: 7 g, Cholesterol: 89 mg, Sodium: 403 mg, Potassium: 312 mg, Fiber: 7 g

222. Kiwi-apple Smoothies

Preparation Time: 10 minutes
Cooking Time: 0 minutes
Cooking Level: Easy
Servings: 2
Ingredients:
- 2 medium ripe kiwis, peeled and chopped
- 1 small Granny Smith apple
- 1 cup ice cubes
- ⅜ cup unsweetened apple juice
- 2 tsp honey

Directions:
1. Blend all the ingredients until smooth, about 2 minutes.

Nutrition: High GL Calories 014 g; Carb 5.6 g Fat: 0 mg; Sugar: L 1 g; Fiber: 1 g; Protein: 2 mg; Potassium: 302 mg; Cholesterol: 79 mg;

223. Raspberry Frozen Yogurt

Preparation Time: 10 minutes
Cooking Time: 0 minutes
Cooking Level: Easy
Servings: 2
Ingredients:
- 1½ cup fresh raspberries
- 2 cup Greek yogurt
- ½ cup sweetener

Directions:
1. Purée half of the raspberries in a food processor.
2. Mix in the yogurt and sweetener, and pour into a container. After 1 hour, gently fold in the remaining raspberries.
3. Freeze again for 30 minutes, mix with a fork, and freeze for a final 30 minutes or until solid.
4. Remove from the freezer before serving.

Nutrition: Low GL Calories: 79 Carbs 7 g, Fat: 4 g, Protein: 3 g, Cholesterol: 84 mg; Sodium: 40 mg; Potassium: 272 mg; Sugar: 0 g; Fiber: 10 g

224. Figs with Honey and Yogurt

Preparation Time: 5 minutes
Cooking Time: 10 minutes
Cooking Level: Easy
Servings: 2
Ingredients:

- ½ tsp vanilla
- 8 oz. non-fat yogurt
- 2 figs, sliced
- 1 tbsp walnuts, chopped and toasted
- 2 tsp honey

Directions:
1. Stir vanilla into yogurt.
2. Mix well.
3. Top with the figs and sprinkle with walnuts.
4. Drizzle with honey and serve.

Nutrition: High GL Calories: 316; Fat: 23.3 g; Protein: 22.3 g; Carbs: 6.2 g; Fiber: 1.1 g; Sugar: 2.2 g; Cholesterol: 74 mg; Sodium: 475 mg; Potassium: 282 mg

225. Rice Dumplings in Coconut Sauce

Preparation Time: 5 minutes
Cooking Time: 45 minutes
Cooking Level: Moderate
Servings: 2
Ingredients:

- ½ cup glutinous rice flour
- ¼ cup water
- 2 tbsp heaping tapioca pearls, uncooked, picked over
- 2 15-oz. cans each thick coconut cream, divided
- ¼ cup sugar
- 1/16 tsp salt
- 2 cups water
- ½ cup fresh ripe jackfruits, shredded, reserved half for garnish

Directions:
1. For the dumplings, put together glutinous rice flour and water
2. Knead until dough forms into a soft ball. Seal the bowl with saran wrap. Let the dough rest for 5 minutes. Roll dough. Place on a baking sheet lined with parchment paper.
3. For the coconut sauce, pour tapioca pearls, 1 can of coconut cream, sugar, salt, water and ripe jackfruit into the Instant Pot Pressure Cooker Lock the lid in place. Press the high pressure and cook for 7 minutes.
4. When the beep sounds, choose the Quick Pressure Release. This will depressurize for 7 minutes. Remove the lid. Press the "Sauté" button once again. Bring the coconut sauce to a boil.
5. Drop the dumplings or until they rise to the top of the cooking liquid. Do not stir. Turn off the machine. Stir the remaining can of coconut cream. Adjust the seasoning according to your preferred taste. To serve, ladle equal amounts into dessert bowls. Garnish with shredded jackfruits.

Nutrition: Low GL Calorie: 149 Fat: 33 Fiber: 13 Carbs 3.9 Potassium: 182 mg; Protein: 23 Sugar: 1 g; Cholesterol: 89 mg; Sodium: 377 mg

226. Tropical Yogurt Kiwi Bowl

Preparation Time: 5 minutes
Cooking Time: 0 minutes
Cooking Level: Easy
Servings: 4
Ingredients:

- 1½ cups plain low-fat Greek yogurt
- 2 kiwis, peeled and sliced
- 2 tbsp shredded unsweetened coconut flakes
- 2 tbsp halved walnuts
- 1 tbsp chia seeds

Directions:
1. Divide the yogurt between two small bowls.
2. Top each serving of yogurt with half of the kiwi slices, coconut flakes, walnuts and chia seeds.

Nutrition: Low GL Calories: 261; Fat: 9.1 g; Protein: 21.1 g; Carbs: 23.1 g; Fiber: 6.1 g; Sugar: 14.1 g; Cholesterol: 89 mg; Sodium: 84 mg; Potassium: 312 mg

CHAPTER 13: BONUS RECIPES

227. Pork Loin, Carrot, and Gold Tomato Roast

Preparation Time: 5 minutes
Cooking Time: 40 minutes
Cooking Level: Moderate
Servings: 2
Ingredients:

- 1 pound (454 g) pork loin
- 2 tsp honey
- ½ tsp dried rosemary
- ¼ tsp Pepper, to taste
- 1 tbsp extra-virgin olive oil, divided
- 4 (6-inch) carrots, chopped into ½-inch rounds
- 2 small gold potatoes, chopped into 2-inch cubes

Directions:

1. Preheat the oven to 350ºF (180ºC).
2. On a clean work surface, rub pork with honey, rosemary, black pepper and ½ tbsp of olive oil. Brush the carrots and gold potatoes with the remaining olive oil.
3. Place the pork, carrots and potatoes in s single layer on a baking sheet.
4. Roast in the preheated oven for 40 minutes or until the pork is lightly browned and the vegetables are soft. Remove them from the oven. Allow cooling for 10 minutes before serving.

Nutrition: High GL Calories: 346; Fat: 9.9 g; Protein: 26.1 g; Carbs: 25.9 g; Fiber: 4.1 g; Sugar: 5.9 g; Cholesterol: 85 mg; Sodium: 107 mg; Potassium: 277 mg

228. Spicy Grilled Portlets

Preparation Time: 20 minutes
Cooking Time: 15 minutes
Cooking Level: Easy
Servings: 2
Ingredients:

- Sliced mango or chili peppers
- ¼ cup lime juice
- 1 tbsp olive oil
- ¼ tsp salt
- 2 cloves garlic, minced
- 1 tsp ground cinnamon
- 1 tbsp chili powder
- 2 tsp ground cumin
- ½ tsp hot pepper sauce
- 4 pork rib chops, cut ¾ inch thick

Directions:

1. Place the chops in a plastic bag. To make the marinade, add chili powder, lime juice, cumin, oil, cinnamon, garlic, hot pepper and salt.
2. Pour over the chops and seal the bag. Turn the bag to coat chops well. Place the chops in the fridge for 24 hours.
3. Make sure to turn the bag to even out the marinade. Drain the chops and discard the marinade.
4. Grill the chops until pork juices run clear. Turn once. Garnish with mango or chili peppers. Serve.

Nutrition: Low GL Calorie: 196 Fat: 9 g; Carbohydrates 3 g; Protein: 25 g; Cholesterol: 89 mg; Sodium: 159 mg; Potassium: 312 mg; Fiber: 3 g; Sugar: 2 g

229. Bacon and Feta Skewers

Preparation Time: 15 minutes
Cooking Time: 10 minutes
Cooking Level: Easy
Servings: 2
Ingredients:

- 2 lb. feta cheese, cut into 8 cubes
- 8 bacon slices
- 4 bamboo skewers, soaked
- 1 zucchini, cut into 8 bite-size cubes
- Salt and black pepper, to taste
- 3 tbsp almond oil for brushing

Directions:

1. Wrap each feta cube with a bacon slice.
2. Thread one wrapped feta on a skewer; add a zucchini cube, then another wrapped feta, and another zucchini.
3. Repeat the threading process with the remaining skewers.
4. Preheat a grill pan to medium heat, generously brush with the avocado oil, and grill the skewer on both sides for 3 to 4 minutes per side or until the set is golden brown and the bacon is cooked. Serve afterward with the tomato salsa.

Nutrition: Low GL Calories: 290; Fat: 15.1 g; Fiber: 4.2 g; Carbohydrates: 4.1 g; Protein: 11.8 g; Sugar: 2 g; Cholesterol: 59 mg; Sodium: 197 mg; Potassium: 282 mg

230. Avocado and Prosciutto Deviled Eggs

Preparation Time: 20 minutes
Cooking Time: 10 minutes
Cooking Level: Easy
Servings: 2
Ingredients:

- 4 eggs
- Ice bath
- 4 prosciutto slices, chopped
- 1 avocado, pitted and peeled
- 1 tbsp mustard
- 1 tsp plain vinegar
- 1 tbsp heavy cream
- 1 tbsp chopped fresh cilantro
- Salt and black pepper, to taste
- ½ cup (113 g) mayonnaise
- 1 tbsp coconut cream
- ¼ tsp cayenne pepper
- 1 tbsp avocado oil
- 1 tbsp chopped fresh parsley

Directions:

1. Boil the eggs for 8 minutes. Remove the eggs into the ice bath, sit for 3 minutes, and then peel the eggs. Slice the eggs lengthwise into halves and empty the egg yolks into a bowl.
2. Arrange the egg whites on a plate with the hole side facing upwards. While the eggs are cooked, heat a non-stick skillet over medium heat and cook prosciutto for 5 to 8 minutes. Remove the prosciutto onto a paper towel-lined plate to drain grease.
3. Put the avocado slices into the egg yolks and mash both ingredients with a fork until smooth. Mix in the mustard,

vinegar, heavy cream, cilantro, salt and black pepper until well-blended. Spoon the mixture into a piping bag and press the mixture into the egg holes until well-filled.
4. In a bowl, whisk the mayonnaise, coconut cream, cayenne pepper and avocado oil. On serving plates, spoon some of the mayonnaise sauce and slightly smear it in a circular movement. Top with the deviled eggs, scatter the prosciutto on top and garnish with the parsley.

Nutrition: Low GL Calories: 265; Fat: 11.7 g; Fiber: 4.1 g; Carbohydrates: 3.1 g; Protein: 7.9 g; Sugar: 2 g; Cholesterol: 89 mg; Sodium: 283 mg; Potassium: 222 mg

231. Sloppy Joes

Preparation Time: 10 minutes
Cooking Time: 15 minutes
Cooking Level: Easy
Servings: 2
Ingredients:

- 1 tbsp extra-virgin olive oil
- 1 pound (454 g) 93% lean ground beef
- 1 medium red bell pepper, chopped
- ½ medium yellow onion, chopped
- 2 tbsp low-Cholesterol: 89 mg; Sodium: Worcestershire sauce
- 1 (15-oz / 425-g) can low-Cholesterol: 89 mg; Sodium: tomato sauce
- 2 tbsp low-Cholesterol: 89 mg; Sodium, sugar-free ketchup
- 4 whole-wheat sandwich thins, cut in half
- 1 cup cabbage, shredded

Directions:

1. Heat olive oil
2. Add beef, bell pepper and onion to the skillet and sauté for 8 minutes
3. Pour Worcestershire sauce, tomato sauce and ketchup into the skillet. Simmer for 5 minutes.
4. Assemble the sandwich thin halves with the beef mixture and cabbage to make the sloppy Joes, then serve warm.

Nutrition: Low GL Calories: 329; Fat: 8.9 g; Protein: 31.2 g; Carbs: 3.9 g; Fiber: 7.9 g; Sugar: 10.9 g; Cholesterol: 79 mg; Sodium: 271 mg; Potassium: 302 mg

232. Steak Sandwich

Preparation Time: 10 minutes
Cooking Time: 10 minutes
Cooking Level: Easy
Servings: 2
Ingredients:

- 2 tbsp balsamic vinegar
- 2 tsp freshly squeezed lemon juice
- 1 tsp fresh parsley, chopped
- 2 tsp fresh oregano, chopped
- 2 tsp garlic, minced
- 2 tbsp olive oil
- 1 pound (454 g) flank steak, trimmed of fat
- 4 whole-wheat pitas
- 1 tomato, chopped
- 1 oz (28 g) low-Cholesterol: 89 mg; Sodium: feta cheese
- 2 cups lettuce, shredded
- 1 red onion, thinly sliced

Directions:

1. Combine the balsamic vinegar, lemon juice, parsley, oregano, garlic and olive oil
2. Dip the steak in the bowl to coat well, then wrap the bowl in plastic and refrigerate for at least 1 hour.
3. Preheat the oven to 450°F (235°C). Remove the bowl from the refrigerator. Discard the marinade and arrange the steak on a baking sheet lined with aluminum foil.
4. Broil in the preheated oven for 10 minutes for medium. Flip the steak halfway through the cooking time. Remove the steak from the oven and allow it to cool for 10 minutes. Slice the steak into strips.
5. Assemble the pitas with steak, tomato, feta cheese, lettuce and onion to make the sandwich, and serve warm.

Nutrition: Low GL Calories: 345; Fat: 15.8 g; Protein: 28.1 g; Carbs: 21.9 g; Fiber: 3.1 g; Carbs: 18.8 g; Cholesterol: 89 mg; Sodium: 295 mg; Potassium: 312 mg

233. Shrimp and Pork Rind Stuffed Zucchini

Preparation Time: 15 minutes
Cooking Time: 25 minutes
Cooking Level: Easy
Servings: 2
Ingredients:

- 4 medium zucchinis
- 1 pound (454 g) small shrimp, peeled, deveined
- 1 tbsp minced onion
- 2 tsp butter
- ¼ cup chopped tomatoes
- Salt and black pepper, to taste
- 1 cup pork rinds, crushed
- 1 tbsp chopped basil leaves
- 2 tbsp melted butter

Directions:

1. Preheat the oven to 350°F (180°C) and trim off the top and bottom ends of the zucchinis. Lay the shrimp flat on a chopping board, and cut a ¼-inch off the top to create a boat for the stuffing. Scoop seeds with a spoon and set the zucchinis aside.
2. Melt butter in a small skillet and sauté the onion and tomato for 6 minutes. Transfer the mixture to a bowl and add the shrimp, half of the pork rinds, basil leaves, salt and black pepper.
3. Combine the ingredients and stuff the zucchini boats with the mixture. Sprinkle the top of the boats with the remaining pork rinds and drizzle the melted butter over them.
4. Bake for 15 to 20 minutes. The shrimp should no longer be pink by this time. Remove the zucchinis after and serve with a tomato and Mozzarella salad.

Nutrition: Low GL Calories: 136; Fat: 14.2 g; Carbs: 3.4 g; Protein: 24.4 g; Fiber: 0.3 g; Sugar: 3.1 g; Cholesterol: 75 mg; Sodium: 167 mg; Potassium: 189 mg

234. Easy and Perfect Meatballs

Preparation Time: 10 minutes
Cooking Time: 20 minutes
Cooking Level: Easy
Servings: 2
Ingredients:

- 1 egg, lightly beaten
- 3 garlic cloves, minced
- ½ cup mozzarella cheese, shredded

- ½ cup parmesan cheese, grated
- 1 lb. ground beef
- Pepper and salt, to taste

Directions:
1. Preheat the oven to 400°F. Line a baking tray with parchment paper and put it aside.
2. Add all the ingredients into the blending bowl and blend until well combined.
3. Make small balls from the meat mixture and place them on a prepared baking tray.
4. Bake for 20 minutes. Serve and luxuriate.

Nutrition: Low GL Calorie: 157 Fat: 6.7 g; Carbohydrates 0.5 g; Protein: 21.5 g; Sugar: 0.1 g; Cholesterol: 89 mg; Sodium: 280 mg; Potassium: 312 mg; Fiber: 2 g

235. Roasted Cauliflower with Prosciutto, Capers, and Almonds

Preparation Time: 5 minutes
Cooking Time: 23 minutes
Cooking Level: Easy
Servings: 2
Ingredients:

- 12 oz cauliflower florets (I get precut florets at Trader Joe's)
- 2 tbsp leftover bacon grease, or olive oil
- Salt and pepper, to taste
- 2 oz sliced prosciutto, torn into small pieces
- ¼ cup slivered almonds
- 2 tbsp capers
- 2 tbsp grated Parmesan cheese

Directions:
1. Preheat the oven to 400°F. Line a baking pan with a baking mat or parchment paper.
2. Put the cauliflower florets in the prepared baking pan with the bacon grease and season with Pink Himalayan salt to taste and pepper. Or if you are using olive oil instead, drizzle the cauliflower with olive oil and season
3. Roast the cauliflower for 15 minutes. Stir the cauliflower so all sides are coated with the bacon grease.
4. Distribute the prosciutto pieces in the pan. Then, add slivered almonds and capers. Stir to combine. Sprinkle the Parmesan cheese on top and roast for 10 minutes more. Divide between two plates, using a slotted spoon so you don't get excess grease in the plates, and serve.

Nutrition: Low GL Calories: 576; Total Fat: 48 g; Carbs: 1.4 g; Fiber: 6 g; Protein: 28 g; Sugar: 1 g; Cholesterol: 77 mg; Sodium: 277 mg; Potassium: 232 mg

A Gift for You!!

Hello and thank you for purchasing the book!
I have prepared a **NICE SURPRISE FOR YOU**.
Scan the qr-code **NOW**
and find our how what it´s all about!

Free eBook

A Special Request

Your brief amazon review could help us.

You know, this is very easy to do, go to the **ORDERS** section
of your Amazon account and click on the
"Write a review for the product" button.
It will automatically take you to the review section.

CHAPTER 14: 28-DAY MEAL PLAN

28-DAY MEAL PLAN

DAY 1
1. PUMPKIN PIE FRENCH TOAST
2. SPINACH, ARTICHOKE, AND GOAT CHEESE BAKE
3. SPICY CHICKEN STEW

DAY 2
1. BREAKFAST CHEESE BREAD CUPS
2. ISRAELI SALMON SALAD
3. CROCK PORK TENDERLOIN

DAY 3
1. BREAKFAST COD NUGGETS
2. SHRIMP ALFREDO
3. DOWN SOUTH CORN SOUP

DAY 4
1. VEGETABLE EGG PANCAKE
2. HAM IN CIDER
3. FETA BRUSSELS SPROUTS AND SCRAMBLED EGGS

DAY 5
1. ORIENTAL OMELET
2. BRUSSELS SPROUT HASH AND EGGS
3. FOUR-BEAN FIELD STEW

DAY 6
1. CRISPY BREAKFAST AVOCADO FRIES
2. GRILLED GREEK CHICKEN
3. BEEF VEGETABLE RAGOUT

DAY 7
1. CHEESE AND EGG BREAKFAST SANDWICH
2. SLOW COOKER CHICKEN POSOLE
3. DROP EGG SOUP

DAY 8
1. BAKED MINI QUICHE
2. TOMATO-HERB OMELET
3. CRAB PATTIES

DAY 9
1. PEANUT BUTTER AND BANANA BREAKFAST SANDWICH
2. GREEK TURKEY BURGERS
3. LEMONY SEA BASS FILLET

DAY 10
1. EGGS AND COCOTTE ON TOAST
2. ROASTED LEG LAMB
3. CURRIED FISH WITH SUPER GREENS

DAY 11
1. CRUNCHY FRIED FRENCH TOAST STICKS
2. LAMB CHOPS CURRY
3. ROASTED BROCCOLI WITH SESAME SEEDS

DAY 12
1. PUMPKIN OATMEAL WITH RAISINS
2. PORK CUTLETS IN CUCUMBER SAUCE
3. GARLIC-LEMON MAHI MAHI

DAY 13
1. MUSHROOM AND BLACK BEAN BURRITO
2. GRILLED LAMB CHOPS
3. FLAVOR CIOPPINO

DAY 14
1. YOGURT RASPBERRY CAKE
2. SCALLOPS IN CREAMY GARLIC SAUCE
3. CORN ON THE COB WITH HERB BUTTER

DAY 15
1. SPINACH AND TOMATO EGG CUP
2. SHRIMP AND ARTICHOKE SKILLET
3. IRISH PORK LOAF

DAY 16
1. EGG MUFFINS WITH BELL PEPPER
2. SARDINES WITH ZOODLES
3. STEAK SANDWICH

DAY 17
1. EGG-IN-A-HOLE
2. CHIMICHURRI GRILLED SHRIMP
3. BEEFY PIE

DAY 18
1. EGG AND CHEESE POCKETS
2. SALMON AND CUCUMBER PANZANELLA
3. APPLESAUCE MEATLOAF

DAY 19
1. HUEVOS RANCHEROS
2. BLACKENED TILAPIA TACOS
3. RAINBOW VEGETABLE FRITTERS

DAY 20
1. JALAPEÑO POTATO HASH
2. RICE DUMPLINGS IN COCONUT SAUCE
3. ROASTED PORK LOIN

DAY 21
1. SHRIMP RICE FRITTATA
2. SHRIMP AND PORK RIND STUFFED ZUCCHINI
3. SLOPPY JOES

DAY 22
1. VEGETABLE FRITTATA
2. SLOW COOKER LENTIL & HAM SOUP
3. GREEK TUNA SALAD

DAY 23
1. GINGER BLACKBERRY BLISS SMOOTHIE BOWL
2. BEEF BARLEY VEGETABLE SOUP
3. GLAZED CARROTS AND CAULIFLOWER

DAY 24
1. HEART-HEALTHY YOGURT PARFAITS
2. SLOW COOKER CORN CHOWDER
3. BROTH-BRAISED CABBAGE

DAY 25
1. TOADS IN HOLES
2. SLOW COOKER CHICKEN POSOLE
3. BAKED FETA WITH DELICIOUS VEGETABLES

DAY 26
1. CANADIAN BACON AND EGG MUFFIN CUPS
2. POTLIKKER SOUP
3. CAULIFLOWER AVOCADO MASH WITH CHICKEN BREAST

DAY 27
1. SAUSAGE AND PEPPER BREAKFAST BURRITO
2. BURGOO
3. SLOW "ROASTED" TOMATOES

DAY 28
1. PUMPKIN WALNUT SMOOTHIE BOWL
2. GRILLED GREEK CHICKEN
3. CONVENTIONAL BEEF POT ROAST

1 = BREAKFAST   2 = LUNCH   3 = DINNER

AMANDARAY

APPENDIX 1: CONVERSION TABLES OF THE VARIOUS UNITS OF MEASUREMENT

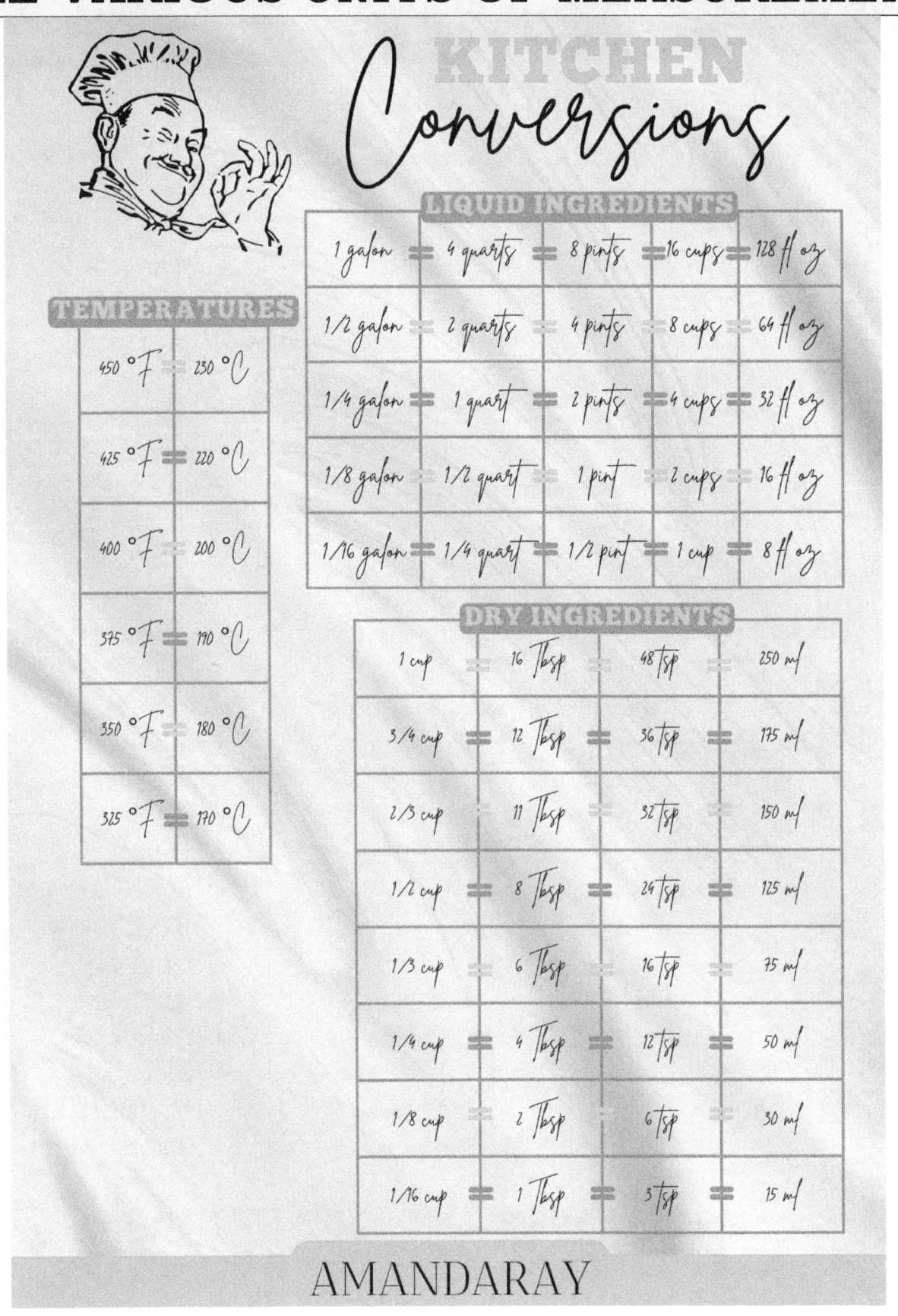

KITCHEN Conversions

LIQUID INGREDIENTS

1 galon	= 4 quarts	= 8 pints	= 16 cups	= 128 fl oz
1/2 galon	= 2 quarts	= 4 pints	= 8 cups	= 64 fl oz
1/4 galon	= 1 quart	= 2 pints	= 4 cups	= 32 fl oz
1/8 galon	= 1/2 quart	= 1 pint	= 2 cups	= 16 fl oz
1/16 galon	= 1/4 quart	= 1/2 pint	= 1 cup	= 8 fl oz

TEMPERATURES

450 °F	= 230 °C
425 °F	= 220 °C
400 °F	= 200 °C
375 °F	= 190 °C
350 °F	= 180 °C
325 °F	= 170 °C

DRY INGREDIENTS

1 cup	= 16 Tbsp	= 48 tsp	= 250 ml
3/4 cup	= 12 Tbsp	= 36 tsp	= 175 ml
2/3 cup	= 11 Tbsp	= 32 tsp	= 150 ml
1/2 cup	= 8 Tbsp	= 24 tsp	= 125 ml
1/3 cup	= 6 Tbsp	= 16 tsp	= 75 ml
1/4 cup	= 4 Tbsp	= 12 tsp	= 50 ml
1/8 cup	= 2 Tbsp	= 6 tsp	= 30 ml
1/16 cup	= 1 Tbsp	= 3 tsp	= 15 ml

AMANDARAY

APPENDIX 2: SHOPPING LIST

A grocery list will usually vary from week to week, based on needs and wants.

- Grapefruit
- Green Beans
- Honey
- Hot Sauces
- Kidney Beans
- Legume Pasta
- Lentils
- Low-Fat: Greek Yogurt
- Low-Fat: Milk
- Millet
- Mustard
- Oatmeal
- Olive Oil
- Onions
- Oranges
- Parmesan, Ricotta, Or Cottage Cheese
- Peaches
- Pears
- Pinto Beans
- Plain Yogurt
- Plums
- Quinoa
- Red, Green, Orange, Or Yellow Peppers
- Romaine Lettuce

- Salsa
- Salt
- Sardines
- Skimmed Milk
- Squash
- Strawberries
- Sweet Potatoes
- Tempeh
- Tofu
- Tomatoes
- Tuna
- Turkey Breast
- Vinegar
- Walnuts Or Other Raw Nuts
- White Beans
- White Fish Fillets
- Whole-Grain
- Whole-Grain Bread
- Whole-Wheat
- Whole-Wheat Flour
- Wild Rice
- Fresh Vegetables
- Frozen Vegetables
- Salad Greens
- Salmon
- Eggs

- All Berries
- Almond Milk
- Amaranth
- Any Spice Or Herb
- Any Variety Of Extracts
- Apples
- Apricots
- Asparagus
- Barley
- Black Beans
- Black Pepper
- Broccoli
- Brussel Sprouts
- Cauliflower
- Cherries
- Chicken Breasts
- Chickpeas
- Coffee
- Corn
- Cornmeal
- Cucumber
- Fat-Free Greek
- Flax Milk
- Fresh Basil
- Fresh Mozzarella Cheese

AMANDARAY

APPENDIX 3: THE DIRTY DOZEN AND THE CLEAN FIFTEEN

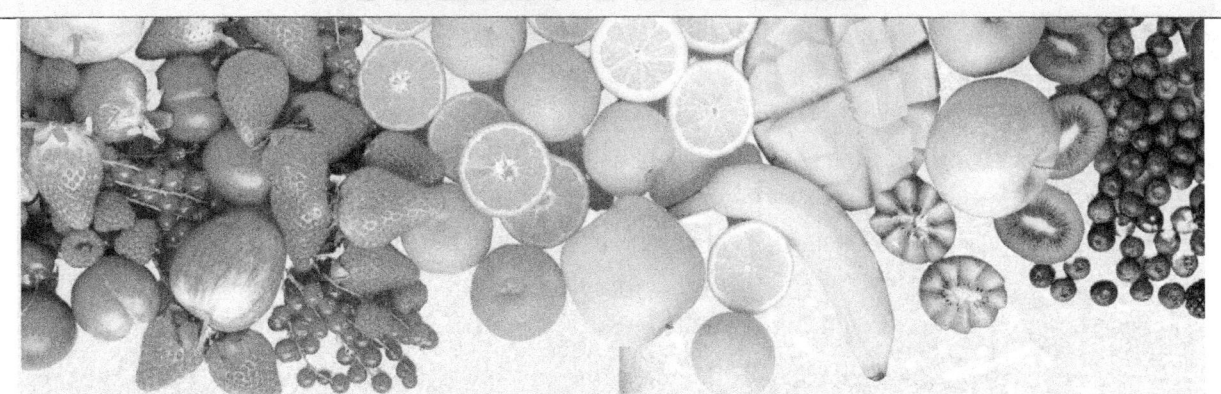

Clean 15

1. Avocados
2. Sweat corn
3. Pineapple
4. Onions
5. Papaya
6. Sweat peas (frozen)
7. Asparagus
8. Honeydew melon
9. Kiwi
10. Cabbage
11. Mushrooms
12. Cantaloupe
13. Mangoes
14. Watermelon
15. Sweet potatoes

Dirty 12

1. Strawberries
2. Spinach
3. Kale, collard & mustard greens
4. Nectarines
5. Apples
6. Grapes
7. Bell & hot peppers
8. Cherries
9. Peaches
10. Pears
11. Celery
12. Tomatoes

UPTATED 2022

AMANDARAY

CONCLUSION

Diabetes is a life-threatening disease caused by a lack of insulin. Insulin is a hormone that is required for the body's healthy functioning. The cells in a person's body do not respond to insulin effectively when they acquire diabetes. As a result, the cells do not get the energy and nutrients they require, and they begin to die.

Being diagnosed with diabetes will bring some major changes in your lifestyle. From the time you are diagnosed with it, it would always be a constant battle with food. You need to be much more mindful of your food choices and the amount you consume. Every meal will feel like a major effort. You will be planning every day for the whole week well in advance. Depending upon the type of food you ate, you have to keep checking your blood sugar levels. You may get used to taking long breaks between meals and staying away from snacks between dinner and breakfast.

Food would be treated as a bomb like it can go off at any time. According to an old saying, "When the body gets too hot, then your body heads straight to the kitchen."

Managing diabetes can be a very, very stressful ordeal. There will be many times that you will mark your glucose levels down on a piece of paper like you are plotting graph lines or something. You will mix your insulin shots up and then stress about whether or not you are giving yourself the right dosage. You will always be over-cautious because it involves a LOT of math and a really fine margin of error. But now, those days are gone!

With the help of technology and books, you can stock your kitchen with the right foods, like meal plans, diabetic-friendly dishes, etc. You can also get an app that will even do the work for you. You can also people-watch on the internet and find the know-how to cook and eat right; you will always be a few meals away from certain disasters, like a plummeting blood sugar level. Always carry some sugar in your pocket. You won't have to experience the pangs of hunger but if you are unlucky, you will have to ration your food and bring along some simple low-calorie snacks with you.

This is the future of diabetes. As you've reached the end of this book, you have gained complete control of your diabetes and this is where your expedition towards a better, healthier life starts. I hope I was able to inculcate some knowledge into you and make this adventure a little bit less of a struggle.

I would like to remind you that you're not alone in having to manage this disease and that nearly 85% of the new cases are 20 years old or younger.

Regardless of the length or seriousness of your diabetes, it can be managed! Take the information presented here and start with it!

Preparation is key to having a healthier and happier life.

It's helpful to remember that every tool at your disposal can help in some way.

Type-2 diabetes is a chronic condition that occurs when there is too much sugar in the blood. There are two ways for people to develop type-2 diabetes: either their body becomes resistant to the effects of insulin or they do not produce enough insulin. Untreated, type-2 diabetes can lead to serious health problems, including heart disease and blindness. Fortunately, by following a balanced diet and engaging in regular physical activity, it's possible to manage this condition successfully.

In conclusion, i want to remind you about the signs and symptoms of diabetes. Talk to your doctor if you think you might be diabetic — it can save your life!

Printed in Great Britain
by Amazon